WITHDRAWN

BACKPACKER'S
Digest
(Second Edition)

By C.R. Learn And Mike O'Neal

DBI BOOKS, INCORPORATED, NORTHFIELD, ILLINOIS
(FORMERLY DIGEST BOOKS, INCORPORATED)

Produced By

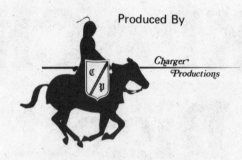

Charger
Productions

EDITORIAL DIRECTOR
Jack Lewis

PRODUCTION EDITOR
Bob Springer

COPY EDITORS
Deborah Payne
Rusty Springer

STAFF ARTISTS
Janet Crawford
Lorie Disney

PRODUCTION COORDINATOR
Wendy Lee Wisehart

PRODUCTION ASSISTANT
Jo Anna Simpson

ASSOCIATE PUBLISHER
Sheldon L. Factor

ISBN 0-695-80645-9

Library of Congress Catalog Card Number 72-97509

CONTENTS

The Authors:

C. R. "BOB" LEARN was born and raised in the Rocky Mountains of Colorado. He spent his summers in the high country and the remainder of his early years in the valley, attending school.

He served eight years in the U.S. Navy as an aerial photographer, being attached to a mapping squadron for four of those years.

After being discharged, Learn settled in Southern California, earned a journalism degree at San Diego State College, then worked five years as a newspaper photographer.

The years in school and working for the paper afforded little opportunity for enjoying the outdoor activities that he regarded as a primary interest, so he turned to freelance writing, using his photo skills to illustrate the articles he produced. With the bulk of his output slanted for the outdoor magazines, he was able to combine business with pleasure to a gratifying extent.

"I got into backpacking so as to be able to work into areas where the hunters did not outnumber the game by so heavy a margin," Learn remembers. "Thanks to experienced advice from friends such as Andy Drollinger, I was able to bypass many of the problems and pitfalls that lurk in wait for the beginning backpacker and I've incorporated these lumps of lore into the book at hand."

Presently, Learn augments his livelihood as a writer/photographer by teaching advanced press photography in the journalism department of his alma mater, since redesignated as Cal State/San Diego.

Looking back, from the vantage of hindsight, Learn's sole regret in regard to backpacking is that he did not become involved with it sooner.

MIKE O'NEAL was born in Washington, D.C., and lived in seven different states during a series of family moves that taught him the rudiments of efficient packing from the age of 5.

Ten years later he had seen nearly forty of the forty-eight continental states and had developed a taste for outdoor living through such experiences as family camping expeditions into the high altitudes of the New Mexico mountains, weekend trips into the San Bernardino ranges of California and hunting and hiking around his family's 137-acre farm in Baldwin County, Georgia.

His taste for moving around took him from east coast to west and to various Southern California communities before enlisting in the U.S. Marine Corps. After completing the Basic Journalism course at the Defense Information School, Ft. Benjamin Harrison, Indiana, O'Neal spent the next four years as a military newspaper reporter, photographer and editor, including a one-year tour of duty on the Japanese island of Okinawa, where much of his work was published in civilian publications ranging from a weekly community entertainment magazine to the Japanese language daily newspaper, Asahi Shinbun.

On release from active duty, O'Neal joined the editorial staff of Charger Productions and Gallant Publishing as the assistant managing editor of GUN WORLD Magazine, one of several publications published by Gallant/Charger for outdoor enthusiasts. A graduate of Grant High School, Van Nuys, California, he is currently continuing his studies at a Southern California college in the field of Administration of Justice.

THE MYSTIQUE OF BACKPACKING

An Indefinable Sense Of Being, Rather Than Simply Belonging, Draws Many Into New Trails

CHAPTER 1

Backpacking is a must for the more serious-minded fisherman.

BACKPACKING, A ONE-TIME NECESSITY OF life dating as far back as when man first inhabited this earth, today, has skyrocketed to the forefront of the new back-to-nature sports that have captured the fancy of the more sports-minded Americans.

Since prehistoric time, man has endeavored to find a better means, other than his own muscle power, to move both himself and any necessary life commodities from one location to another. Although strapping it on one's back and setting off on one's own two feet at that time certainly was not considered too demeaning, it could be more strenuous than what was desired.

Consequently, being of an inventive nature, man soon learned to domesticate the four-legged creatures that inhabited his world. The dog, horse, oxen and whatever other animal man could corral soon, literally, became the beast of burden and man had made his first step toward the age of high speed carriers and the likes of the Bekin moving man.

Little did he know that one day his ancestors would willingly return to the old way of strapping one's belongings on one's back and setting off for distant horizons.

Today, this is exactly what thousands of Americans are

doing and the sport of backpacking continues to gain in popularity each day.

To understand the recent popularity of backpacking, it is of interest to look into the history of backpacking in America.

Disregarding the American Indian, who learned early to domesticate the dog and, later, the horse, the earliest ancestor of the modern backpacker was the mountain man who roamed the hills looking for fur-bearing animals during this country's formative years.

This early hunter, however, was not backpacking for the sport of it, but rather out of necessity. He had to carry whatever he needed for a several-day trip into the hills and, in order to reach the high country where pelt animals normally dwell, he had to hike once he ran out of navigable waterways. This is when he took to backpacking.

The first backpacks were crude affairs and did not allow the hunter to carry a great deal; however, they did seem to serve the purpose. Normally they were made at the point where the hunter left the river and discarded when he reached his destination. Crude, uncomfortable and prone to cause aching muscles, these makeshift packs were the fore-

*Summer, spring, winter or fall;
backpacking has no seasons, but
can be enjoyed the year around.*

*Whatever the year group, backpacking
has its supporters. Here a young girl
contemplates the wonders of nature.*

runners of the modern, lightweight, comfortable packs utilized by today's backpacker. Chances are that, if modern packers used the old hunter's pack, they would never reach their destination or, at least, not with all the gear originally packed!

Another early backpacker was the prospector of past times, who packed enormous loads over mountains and across deserts in search of that one strike that would change his life to one of fame and fortune.

Additionally, backpacking always has — and still does — play an important role in the exploration of unknown territories. Many areas still are inaccessible by any mode

other than by foot; examples being the Antarctic and the Alaskan Klondike. In early explorations of these areas, before the advent of the helicopter and snowmobile, explorers had to pack in and out, carrying all their supplies with them, sometimes enough for several months. This was backpacking at its very toughest and would appeal to only a small minority of today's backpacking enthusiasts.

What is it about backpacking that is so appealing to today's generation? The answers are many and rarely does one find two sport backpackers who will give the same reason for taking up the sport. It is truly an individualistic sport and, as such, each individual's motivation for be-

*With your pack on your back
the world is your home; whether
it's the forest, or wherever you stop.*

*Terrain can be as rough or as easy
as the backpacker wants it. Here
the hiker has selected the roughest.*

coming a backpacking enthusiast is unique unto himself.

Perhaps the leading factor in the recent popularity of backpacking is the desire to escape from the maddening pace of modern technological society.

Pollution, population explosion, high speed freeways, smog-infested cities, increasing crime rates...all are beginning to drive modern man, literally, up the proverbial wall. He is seeking an escape — an escape back to something that is only a distant memory.

Backpacking offers this escape. The smell of clear air intermixed with pine, not excessive portions of carbon dioxide...the sight of the Milky Way almost within one's reach on a clear night...the distant chirping of a bird or soft melody of a running creek...all are but hazy memories.

What better way is there to recapture these memories than by packing what few necessities one needs and setting off into the forest or up over the hill, away from the destruction that man is inflicting upon himself and his environment in his frantic scramble for technological advancement?

By being willing to hike in, forsaking the self-contained

Bird-watching is only one of the many hobbies practiced by backpacking nature lovers.

camper with its many comforts, one can find areas where nature is still as it was intended to be. No cars, no high-rise apartments, no freeways, by one's self and nature. This is what motivates many who are taking up backpacking.

Others take to backpacking because of the emphasis it places on physical fitness. Few doctors will disagree that walking is one of the best overall exercises; and there is no denying that walking through the splendors of nature certainly is more enjoyable than four laps around the block after dinner. The beginning backpacker may experience sore muscles at first, but by conditioning himself and using the proper equipment, these soon disappear and all that remains is the joy of "being away from it all."

For nature lovers — be they bird watchers, wildlife photographers, or rock collectors — there is no sport in existence that is equal to backpacking for the enjoyment of these pastimes.

Backpacking is a family affair; one of the few recreations that builds family unity.

packing...by being there away from the convenience of motel, camper or cabin.

"Americans have an unequaled opportunity to visit some of the finest remote outdoor areas of the world, from the woodland trails of the Appalachians, through the dry, rocky canyons of our central deserts, to the ever majestic alpine crags of the High Sierra. The Forest Service lends a hand by establishing and maintaining a criss-cross network of foot trails and attractive campsites, marking all on easily read maps. When you carry your home on your back, you have more area you can visit, a great variety of terrain spread out over a wider part of our nation than does any other type of outdoor enthusiast!

"What better way is there to undergo a complete change of pace...the name of the game in taking a vacation, anyway. If nothing else, the pure air found amid the tall mountain peaks gives us maybe our only opportunity in this modern day and age to draw a deep breath without gagging. Isn't that something? As a city dweller, we can spend our whole life and not know the taste of fresh water or the smell of fresh air!

"There's something to be said for shouldering your pack

Peering off into the distance, the backpacker on the left calculates how many miles he has left to go.

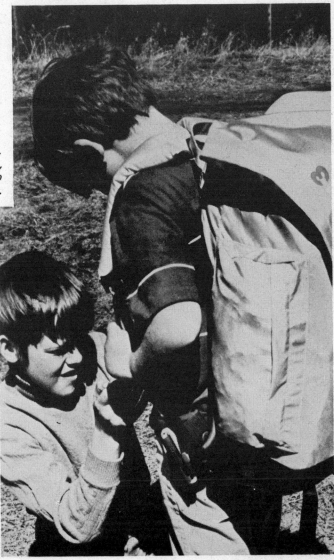

Backpacking is a sport for all ages. Buckling the last pack strap, two young hikers prepare to set off on their journey.

To many, backpacking is a challenge...a measure of endurance. To them, hiking through an area never before explored by them, or setting their own hiking endurance record, offers the same thrill...the same challenge, as a never-before-scaled mountain does to a mountain climber.

The ardent fisherman or hunter should not overlook the sport of backpacking. Here is a sport that allows the fisherman to get to that lake or stream, unaccessible by motorized conveyance, where the fish practically jump into the net. For the hunter, here is a means to reach that hunting area where trophy size quarry are abundant and have not long ago been driven off by other-enthusiastic hunters. To a hunter or fisherman who takes his hunting or fishing seriously, the ability to backpack is almost a necessity.

To appreciate the appeal that backpacking has for many people, it is often best to hear what a truly dedicated backpacker has to say about a sport that he not only loves, but spends many hours enjoying. Doug Kittredge of Mammoth, California — a reknowned backpacker and author of several books about backpacking — has enjoyed the sport with his family for over twenty-five years. He has this to say about the joys of backpacking:

"The out-of-doors can be as dramatic as a thunder clap...as peaceful as a dew sparkling meadow at dawn...as sudden as a spill off a slippery rock...and, there is no beauty to match late evening twilight mirrored on an alpine lake. You become a part of these experiences by back-

and walking away from the road, away from the telephones and TVs and, perhaps, even away from a house full of screaming young'uns, into a world of dusty trails and peaceful meadows, where clock-time is replaced by sun-time. You soon find the frantic city-bred need to be always doing something is replaced by a feeling of 'if not today, then perhaps tomorrow.'

"The man with the pack is not restrained. He goes when he wants; he stops when he wants. It affords the fisherman a chance to visit lakes and streams far beyond the reach of those who depend upon motorized means. It lets him be there where and when the action is, in the early morning or late evening. The hunter, too, finds the pack on his back a form of independence that lets him find the game late in the day and far from his base camp, then to just set up a small camp and be there on the spot in the early morning.

"To backpack is to get to know yourself. As with skiing, mountain climbing or car racing, what you do, you do yourself...no one can do it for you. As you slowly struggle step by step up the steep mountain pass, you learn that you can't quit, even if your breath comes in husky puffs and your legs are rubbery tired. For where in this world of granite would you camp and where would you find water amongst this dry boulder pile? No, you learn how to disci-

For the hunter who wants to go where quarry is abundant, backpacking is more than a pleasant outing.

pline yourself. How to set a goal and achieve it. How to put a little effort in and then to put in a little more. You learn both what you can do and what you cannot do.

"This is a recreation where you can truly include the entire family as a team with the common interest involved with starting at one place and, through collective efforts, going to another where a camp is established for the benefit of the entire group because everyone pitches in and gets the job done. There is something about an outdoor camp in the back country that provides the glue to really bond a family together. I remember a trip with my number one son, arriving at a high lake, right on the timberline, late in the afternoon with huge thunderheads about ready to cut loose and give us an instant drenching. My boy immediately became a tower of strength and bustled hither and yon gathering wood, setting up a small tent, getting our gear under cover...each a task that would have yielded at least a half-hour session of gripes and moans if it had been attempted at home! It's amazing how working together on the same trail and undergoing common difficulties instills in each member of the group a desire to work together and to do their share.

"Backpacking can develop a hidden pioneer spirit. You

Backpacking develops hidden pioneer spirit. You can go where no man has set foot.

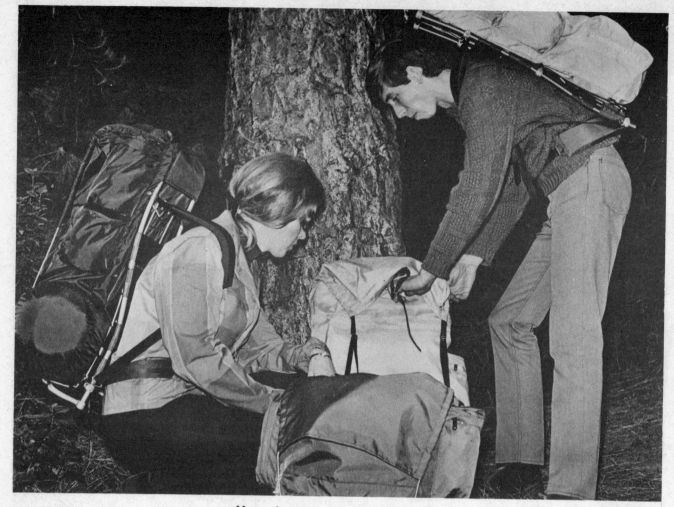

Many of today's ecology-minded young
are taking up the sport of backpacking.

know you are roughing it; doing something others often look upon as too much work; but a pride of accomplishment swells within you everytime you finally make it to the top of that pass, or look for the first time into the crystal clear depths of that lake where fish seem as long as your arm. Like the early mountain man, you go where you want and when you want. You can look on country seen only by he who walks on foot. You develop a feel for the woods, mountains and streams different from that known by your fellow man.

"Long ago I stood at the road's end, shivering a bit in the early morning cold while silently watching the sun's rays just touching the very tips of the errie, gray granite peaks rising through the half-light, so high around me that my head struck the top of my pack as I looked up. There was a deeply felt feeling of being in the unknown, of strangeness, of loneliness. I was held there for a moment, unable to move, for this was a totally new and different country. Then the spell was broken and boots clanked along the trail. One more experience was locked up with a thousand others that couldn't have been reproduced by any activity other than backpacking. This is the joy of backpacking."

The foregoing narrative is, of course, the opinion of only one man, but one who has enjoyed and participated in the sport of backpacking for many years. The points brought out, however, make it easily understandable why the sport

of backpacking is the up and coming back-to-nature sport that is capturing the devotion of thousands of Americans.

Naturally, like any other sport, backpacking is not for everyone, but it should not be passed up because of age, sex or, to some extent, physical condition. Unfortunately, far too often it is considered a sport for only the most rugged outdoor man. Nothing could be further from the truth. Backpacking is a sport that can be enjoyed by almost anyone who is in normal physical condition — be they male or female — young or over thirty.

Backpacking can be, but is not necessarily a test of great endurance or physical stamina, for a pack trip does not have to be over rough terrain, nor need it be for a long distance. All the distance required is just enough to get away from the road or a few miles up a secluded beach. Some of the most pleasurable pack trips are less than two miles long.

If you never have the desire to tackle the long treks over rough terrain, you still can become a devoted backpacker. Or if, on the other hand, you are seeking a sport that will test your endurance, your physical stamina...then it is a sport for you as well.

Whatever your motivation is for taking up backpacking, or whether you are a beginner or seasoned packer, it is hoped that the following sections will add to your enjoyment of one of America's truly great pastimes...the sport of backpacking.

THE NAME OF THE GAME in backpacking is walking, and once you leave the end of the road you're on your own. It's your own two feet that are going to get you there and back again — no other mode of transportation is available. Consequently, the proper care of these two appendages cannot be overemphasized.

The most important consideration in caring for one's feet is the wearing of proper footwear. Trying to economize on equipment, especially hiking boots, is truly false economy! A pair of cheap boots may save a few dollars on the initial investment, but when you pull the sole loose as you stumble over a sharp outcropping many miles from

BOOT VERSUS LOOT

With little choice in the terrain, the combat Marine knows the importance of a good, durable, hiking boot.

CHAPTER 2

You Get What You Pay For, So To Avoid Sore Feet And Bad Temper, Choose The Right Type At The Value Price!

nowhere, the consequences can prove extreme.

Additionally, a backpacker with blistered, aching feet caused by an improperly fitted pair of boots is certainly not going to enjoy his chosen sport. It is extremely difficult to appreciate the wonders of nature or "just being away from it all," when every step one takes is painful.

Your feet absorb all the roughness of the terrain — rocks, water, dirt and any other hazard in your path. The least you can do for your feet is ensure that they are properly booted.

SELECTION OF BOOTS

Boots are one of the three most important items in backpacking equipment, and it is one item that it pays not to economize on when purchasing. A good hiking boot will cost anywhere from $25 to $55, depending upon the size, make and type. Notice that a "hiking" boot is specified. A Western boot or other popular boot styles are not meant for the serious backpacker and should not be used.

Many beginning backpackers will try hiking in tennis

Boot on the left may be ideal for a cyclist, but for a backpacker, it's verboten. A better boot is on the right.

shoes or other type of soft-soled canvas shoe. This type of footwear is suitable for short distances over easy terrain. However, for longer distances over rough terrain, the average individual will find that he soon develops foot problems from wearing this type of shoe.

Hunters often will wear high top laced shoes with a

Vibram sole for moving in the back country. Without a pack this type of shoe is normally more than adequate. However, add twenty or more pounds on your back and the situation rapidly changes.

There are a few makes of high top slip-on boots that some hikers have found suitable for backpacking. These

From the right to left: a street shoe; lightweight, medium and heavy duty hiking boots. The choice is yours.

BODY WEIGHT		TRAIL WALKING NO PACK	WITH 35 LB PACK	CROSS COUNTRY WITH 45 LB PACK
	To 140	Light Trail Shoe	Light Trail Shoe (women)	Medium
	140 To 185	Light Trail Shoe	Medium	To Upper Medium
	185 To 210	Light Trail Shoe	Upper Medium	Upper Medium To Heavy
	210 Up	Light Trail Shoe	Heavy	Heavy

though, like any other type of shoe, have their own peculiar problems when adapted to backpacking. One factor to consider is that, with a backpack, you are adding poundage to your overall physical weight and this extra weight will definitely affect your feet over a period of miles.

If you merely plan to pack a lunch and a few items to a small lake or stream only one or two miles off the road, almost any type of footwear is appropriate. However, if you plan to hike into the back country or make a cross-country trip, you should become very critical in the selection of your footwear. Hobbling home one time with blistered, tender feet normally will cure any doubter who feels that the selection of a good hiking boot is of little importance.

There are several manufacturers of hiking boots who have their products available at most sporting goods stores or at the many specialty backpacking stores springing up all over the country. This chapter will discuss the various types of hiking boots available; what to look for in a good boot, and what some of the problems are that you will encounter in purchasing hiking footwear.

As mentioned, one of the most important factors to consider in a boot is whether it is strong enough to support both your own weight and the weight of the pack you will be carrying. If you refer to the weight chart included in this chapter, you can determine the type of boot you will need if you are taking up backpacking seriously.

The chart shows that the more weight you place on your feet, the more rigid a shoe you need to support that weight. A rule of thumb is that: if, with your pack on your back, you can feel the rocks through the soles as you move over the terrain, the shoe is not suitable for your weight. In this case, you can do one of two things: buy a heavier shoe or reduce your load. Quite often this lighter shoe might be adequate on marked trails over even terrain, but if you decide to move into rocky, rough country, you will find that you are a bit light in the foot department.

In purchasing your first pair of hiking boots, you should make certain that you examine all the types of footwear available. With some, you will be able to tell immediately that they are too light for your size.

The first thing you should check on a boot is the sole. You definitely want the Vibram-lugged sole for any serious backpacking. This type of sole will take you over the easiest trails or the roughest, with good support, and it will wear for many years.

Look for a layer of leather just above the sole. If there is just the rubber sole attached, usually by bonding to the upper vamp, beware — it may be too soft a boot. The weight of the boot can be determined easily by checking the inner or support sole. If there is only one layer of leather above the sole, this boot will fall into the category of a lightweight boot that is excellent for the ladies, but is not normally suited for a man.

PROPER LACING FOR 3-LOOP LACE LOCK WITH CORRECT UPPER LACE HOOKING

1 Lace boot up through main large eyelet.

2 Twist 3-loop lace lock and <u>feed lace back through main large eyelet.</u>

3 Pull lace lock tight and continue lacing around hooks <u>exactly</u> as shown.

Over top and under up to bow

Through loop up and over

4 Final lacing view indicating lacing gap and lace lock for sure fit and comfort.

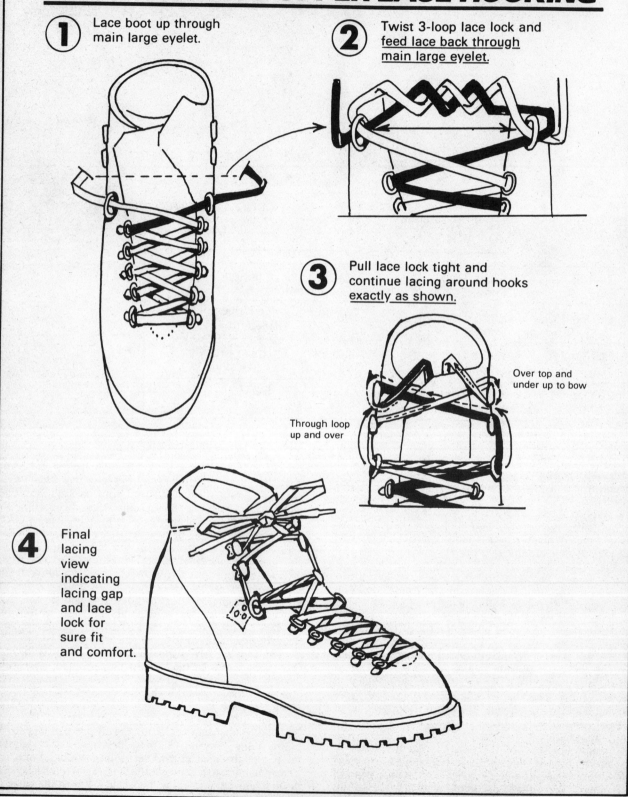

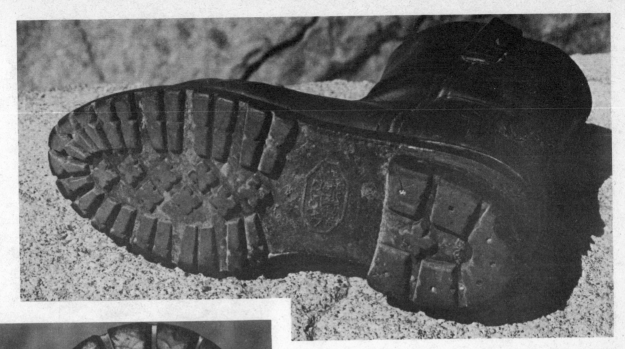

Many street boots (above) have the Vibram sole, but do not have the extra feature of screws through the heel and the shank as does the heavyweight boot below.

For a man, who is normally heavier and carries more weight in his pack, a boot should have at least two layers of leather support between the sole and the upper section. If you are a heavy person or plan eventually to carry heavy loads, you should select the biggest and heaviest boot on the rack. It will have several layers of leather laminated together, then sewn as well as glued to the Vibram sole on the bottom. This is the normal method of attaching the Vibram type lugged sole to better hiking boots. Many of the light weight and medium weight boots will show nothing but the leather support and the glued Vibram. In the maximum boot, the heel, midsection and toe of the Vibram sole is sewn into the support leather for added strength. This is the ultimate in the backpacker boot.

There are many other types of boots which appear similar to the above boot, but are, in fact, specialty boots. One example would be that worn by the rock climber. This boot has a rubber flange coming halfway up the side of the leather upper and is extremely stiff. This boot has a steel shank running the entire length to give the rock climber the maximum support he needs from toe to heel. It appears to be a lightweight boot; however, it is not and is uncomfortable for backpacking, since it will not bend at all.

Using this sole checking technique is your first step in selecting a backpacking boot. Another factor to consider is the lacing method of the boot. Many have the standard eyelet into the leather upper and this method is adequate in lighter boots. As you move up to the heavier styles, they will usually have a D ring lacing method with rivets attaching the D ring to the leather upper. Some also incorporate a speed lacing of two or three hooks on the upper section. These are quite adequate for the heavier style.

The upper section of the boot is also important. This is the section of the boot that covers the foot, aids in supporting the ankle and takes the bangs from the rocks, limbs and other trail hazards. You should insist that the uppers be made of full-grain cowhide. These are made of one piece in the better boots, with no seams except at the heel.

If you find a bargain boot in split cowhide, you might

The lightweight boot has no screws or sewing to attach the Vibram sole to the upper of the boot as does the heavier boot.

consider it, but the problem with the split cowhide boot is that the leather will stretch with use and before long the laces will be meeting over the foot and you have no more adjustment. They do cost less, but are not as strong or as durable as those with one-piece cowhide uppers.

In selecting your hiking boots, be certain the rivets that hold the D rings on the lacing system do not have the bare rivet against the sock or open on the inside of the boot. This will become a wearing point and a hiking irritant in time.

A good boot will have a gusset of light leather that comes up about halfway on the foot for a dust and dirt barrier. This feature also helps keep out water when fording streams. The tongue will be padded and extend above the top of the boot. Many of the boots on the market today have what is called a ski flap that crosses over each side and closes the top of the boot to dirt and dust.

Around the ankle, the boot should have what is called a stretch scree guard. This is a section of foam rubber covered with soft leather, such as goatskin, that prevents scree (small rocks), dust and dirt from getting on the ankles and into the boot. This padding also protects the Achilles tendon at the back of the foot from rock abrasion.

The ideal hiking boot for the serious backpacking

The medium weight boot is a better boot, but it also does not have screws attaching the sole to the body of the boot.

Many medium weight boots have an overlapping flap to prevent small rocks and dirt from getting into the boot and irritating the hiker. Not as good as a scree guard, but it is better than no protection.

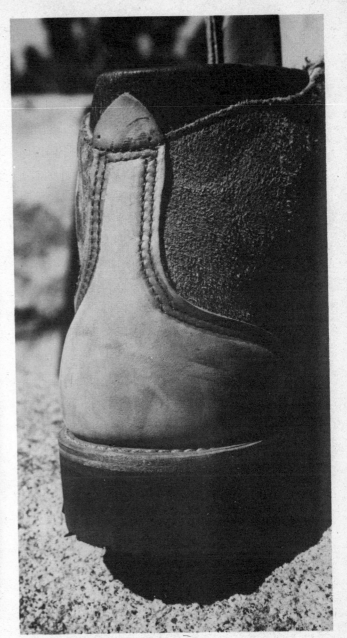

Above is the heel conformation of a better medium heel. This type of heel gives extra durability to a medium boot.

enthusiast should include all of the above features. The number of leather laminates in the sole depends on the weight of boot that you desire. One final item that should be considered is that the boot should have woven nylon laces, since leather laces stretch, rot and can provide problems on the trail.

Once you have found the boots that you feel are suitable, you should try them on. In trying them on, wear a pair of light socks — usually regular weight cotton — and a second pair of heavy socks. This second pair may be all wool or a mixture of wool and nylon or other synthetic material.

Always wear two pair of socks when trying on a pair of boots, since when you are in the field, you will be wearing at least two pair. The first pair cushions the foot, while the heavier pair over them absorbs some of the moisture of the foot and the feet remain dry even in damp weather. Another reason for wearing two pair of socks is that the

foot can move between the two pair; the lighter pair staying with the foot while the heavier pair moves with the boot, allowing the socks to absorb any sliding that might occur. Needless to say, if the foot slides in the boot, it can cause rather painful blisters.

Hiking boots are similar to other shoes in that they are made over what is called a last. This last will vary from company to company, but perhaps the biggest difference is between European and American-made boots. European boots are measured in centimeters and the lasts are different; consequently, if possible, it is best to select an American-made boot, since it will normally fit better.

It goes without saying that the most important feature in the selection of a boot is proper fit. If you normally wear a size 9D shoe, that is the place to start. When the boot is placed on the foot, with the two pair of socks, it should not be the least bit tight. The best method to check the fit is to bang the toe of the boot up against something solid

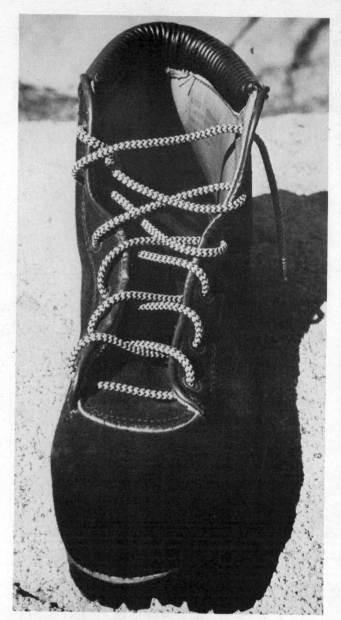

The standard method of lacing for a better heavy weight boot is the lace to toe D-ring method. This allows for maximum adjustment in lacing the boot.

Most light weight hiking boots do not have D-rings, but use the standard eyelet style of lacing. This allows little adjustment.

(preferably not the shinbone of the salesman), then attempt to place a finger down the back of the boot. If you cannot place your index finger down the back of the boot between the heel and the boot back, the boot is too small. You may find that you have to move up to a size 9½EE to obtain the proper fit.

Once you have found a boot that allows you to place a finger behind the heel, bang the heel on the floor, sliding the heel to the back of the boot. Now, take up the slack in the lacing, starting at the toe, allowing the salesman to take some slack and hand you the laces for you to retain the tension as he pulls them even tighter. Once properly laced, wear them around the store for five minutes or more. Naturally they will be stiff and cold at first, but will warm up from your body warmth. Once they have loosened up, you will be able to adjust the lacing more if you desire.

At this point, you should be able to move the foot around in the boot without too much looseness. The toe shouldn't come in contact with the boxed tip of the boot

and the heel should be firm in the boot. Better boots will have a padded leather-covered section around the ankle to protect the ankle, as well as provide a better fit. When you are properly fitted the boot will be snug on the foot without being tight.

Your new boots may look awkward, clumsy and feel very heavy at first; however, you will soon become accustomed to walking in them. The weight will not be noticed after awhile; you will begin to walk with a somewhat rolling gait, because soles of hiking boots do not bend as readily as normal street shoes do. In selecting boots, remember that you are not buying a modish shoe for street wear, but a rugged back country style that will take you into easy, medium and rough terrain and bring you back home — without sore feet. A good hiking boot should absorb most of the shock of the trail, leaving you free to concentrate on the enjoyment of the trip.

After purchasing your hiking boots, you should break them in by wearing them around the house for awhile be-

A lightweight boot (above) is fine for ladies and easy terrain, but if inclined towards rock climbing, the rock climbing boot below is better.

fore taking off on a back country trip. Often the scree guard will cause a soreness around the ankle before the boot is broken in, especially with individuals inexperienced in wearing a boot this heavy.

There are two methods of alleviating this soreness. The easiest is to lace the boot up to the last two holes and tie it there, leaving these last two lace holes free. This allows the foot more freedom as you break in the new boot.

A second method of curing the scree rubbing is to place a section of moleskin, a soft adhesive-type material available at most stores and drug stores, on the ankle at the chafed area. This is only a temporary cure, but will work until the leather of the boot has softened and works to your foot.

Never take a new pair of boots on a long trail hike. It has been done, but it normally results in some mighty sore feet

before the trip is done. These boots should always be broken in gradually around the house before striking out for the wilderness.

If you haven't yet decided how involved you want to become in the sport of backpacking, you might try a few short easy trips with another type of footwear. There are

Above shows the scree guard of a lightweight boot. Below shows the riveted conformation of a better heavyweight hiking boot.

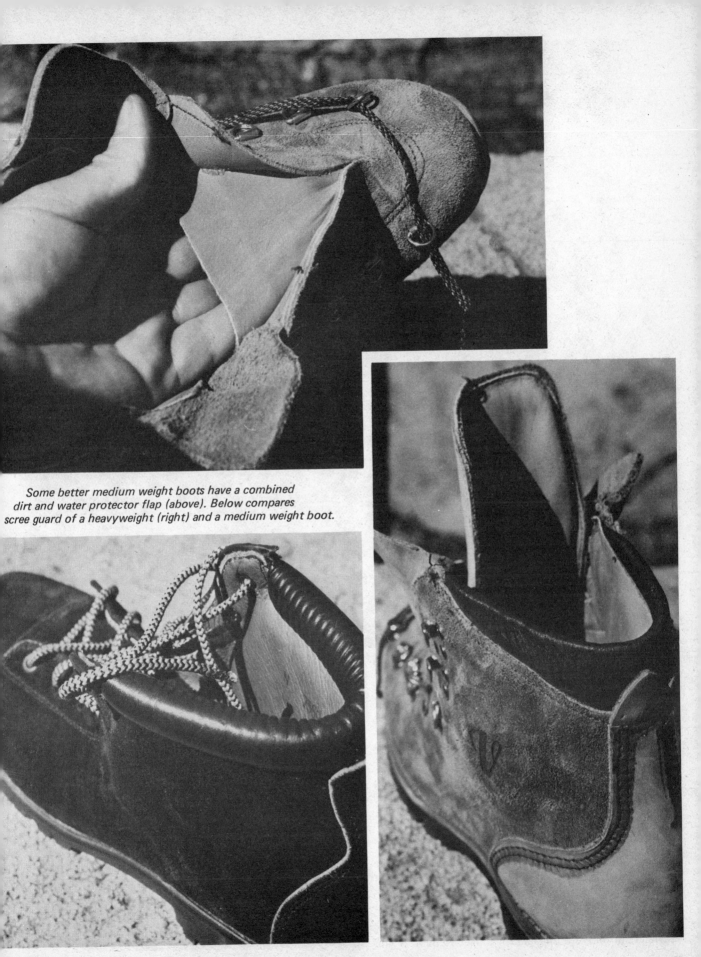

Some better medium weight boots have a combined dirt and water protector flap (above). Below compares scree guard of a heavyweight (right) and a medium weight boot.

For durability heavy boots have stitching as well as glue to attach the sole to the boot. Below is a close up of the layers of leather between the vibram sole and the upper.

many moderately level, easy hiking trails, especially in the East, and many hikers will experiment on these trails wearing a low oxford-style shoe. These still should have the Vibram sole, but need not have the six-inch height and scree guard to keep out the dirt and rocks.

To be certain about your footgear, begin with short jaunts, then lengthen the time and distance until you feel certain you are capable of going longer distances. You cannot always change your mind once you are mid-point in your hike, so begin with the shorter distances and work up to the longer journeys.

There are some stores that allow an individual to take boots home and break them in (on a carpet to prevent marring the leather and soles). If you can find such a store, take advantage of this opportunity and, then if they don't fit properly, return them for another pair that does.

Certain stores feature a type of footwear that is fine for easier terrain, but is unsuitable for rougher terrain. If you

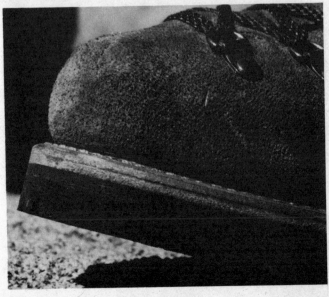

Better medium boots also have stitching, but do have fewer leather inlays between the sole of the boot and the upper.

buy a good, rugged pair to begin with, you will be prepared not only for the easy hikes, but the roughest as well, with perhaps the exception of rock climbing, which will be covered later in this book.

There are other styles of boots that do not lace to the toe. These are still the proper type of shoe for backpacking, the only difference being that these do not allow the amount of adjustment that the lace-to-toe style does. The advantage of the lace-to-toe style is that you can adjust the tension in the lacing and prevent the foot from sliding, even a minute amount, toward the toe of the boot in downhill hiking. Then, once you have reached the bottom of the grade, you can relace them for level or uphill walking. The lace-to-toe style also allows for the adjustment needed when wearing heavy socks for cold weather hiking. In general, if you don't plan to tackle the more arduous trails or cross-country trips, the normal lace type will be adequate.

The metal shank — steel in the top grade boots — men-

Without proper care after use, even the best in hiking boots will deteriorate long before they should. Every boot should be waterproof upon purchase.

tioned previously will be found in better hiking boots, as well as rock climbing boots. This shank is placed under the arch to prevent the boot from sagging at this weak point and is built into the boot between the leather laminates and the Vibram sole.

If you remember to carefully check all the points that have been brought out when buying a hiking boot, you should end up with a good, rugged boot that will take you over any type of terrain that you desire to explore. In the long run, by careful selection and willingness to spend a few extra dollars in initial outlay, you will find that you will not regret either the time or the money.

BOOT CARE

The care and time spent selecting a good hiking boot is lost, if once having bought the boots, you neglect to care for them properly after use.

One of the first things you should do to a new pair of boots is to treat them with a leather conditioner or water-proofing material. There are many types of leather conditioners on the market and you can use a brand that is familar or ask the salesman who sold you the boot what

type is best for that particular leather.

If the boot has a smooth leather surface, a standard conditioner such as boot oil or a waterproofing conditioner like Snow Seal can be used. If the boot has a rough leather outer surface, it should be brushed with a soft wire brush to remove dirt and dust, then treated with a silicone dressing. The conditioner should be worked into the seams and around the welt of the boot, but should not be applied to the composition sole. If oil is used, it helps to warm the boot before applying the oil. After applying the oil, allow it to dry overnight, then wipe off the excess.

There are many well intended methods for treating boots that have gotten wet. However, there are some that should never be used. Never dry a boot over a hot fire, radiator or other high heat source. This type of heat will dry out and shrink the leather in the uppers and in the leather welt, shortening the life of the boot. Continued use of this method of drying will cause the leather to become brittle and crack beyond repairable use.

The recommended method of drying wet boots is to place them in a well circulated area, away from excessive heat with the top of the boot hanging down. This allows

*A good, durable boot will take
you over every type of terrain,
whether it's rough or fairly level.*

the warm air, not heat, to enter the boot and, since warm air rises, it will move to the toe of the boot, drying all parts gradually. After the boots have been in the inverted position for some time — until almost dry — set them upright to finish drying. When they are completely dried, leather conditioner should be applied to prevent cracking.

There are many tales as to the best method to stretch a boot that is too tight. One of the most popular is to soak them thoroughly, then walk them dry while they are still on the feet. Perhaps this will make them fit better, but the boot will not last, since no leather should be soaked in this manner — it shortens the life of the leather and the boot.

Another method used in the past to stretch a tight boot was to take it to the barn, fill it with wheat or corn and pour water over it to swell the grain and stretch the boot. This again is not recommended. The only recommended method to stretch a boot, if it cannot be returned for a larger size, is to take it to a qualified cobbler and have him stretch it, which is more likely to be successful, without ruining the boot.

If you do any backpacking at all, there is going to come a time when your boots are going to get wet, whether it's fording a stream or a sudden summer storm. If they have been properly treated with a leather conditioning and

weatherproofing compound, chances are they are not going to be damaged. If they are taken care of immediately and dried properly, even if they have been thoroughly soaked, they are not going to be harmed. Common sense, and not listening to old wives tales, will prevent them from deteriorating from careless and quick drying methods.

A hint that is not thought of often is placing boots inside your shelter or at the bottom of your sleeping bag when camping out at night. This keeps them out of the damp night air-warm and dry for use the next day.

A good, well cared for pair of hiking boots will last for many years and will bring you many miles of enjoyment. However, considerable care should be taken in the initial selection of the type of boot, as well as time and effort expended in upkeep of the boot.

It takes only one long hike that turns into a painful nightmare because of unsuitable or improperly cared for boots, to make one realize that the boot does make a difference in backpacking.

Boots are one of the most important pieces of equipment that a backpacker will buy. A little extra money and effort in selection always pays off — on the trail where it counts.

Chapter 3

REQUIEM FOR A HORSE BLANKET

John Muir and His Mountaineer Buddies Never Had It So Good

Sleeping bags designed to zip together can help the novice backpacker get into the spirit of the trail buddy system.

THE DYING YELLOW and orange flames of the evening's cookfire dance across the small pine needle carpeted clearing, throwing fading shadows against the roughly oblong bundles resting on either side of the small circle of scorched rocks that keep the blaze from spreading to nearby overhanging branches.

At one end of each bundle, a drawstring crimps dacron material tightly against the lined and weary faces of two outdoor worshipers who have done their twelve trail miles, cooked and eaten a nourishing meal and are now settled in to rest up for tomorrow's return to civilization.

The chilling mountain wind moving in with the darkness to stir the campfire coals to their final moments of life and to ruffle the outer shells of the sleepers' bags does not penetrate to pull life-sustaining heat from the campers' bodies; does not chill their stockinged toes in their special boots. These are experienced campers, who have dealt with the elements of cold and dampness before; who know their killing powers and how to keep them at bay.

They were not always so knowledgeable. Both could tell several goose-bumping tales of lying awake, sleeping only in miserable fits through the night and taking turns replenishing a fire to reduce at least a little of the violence of their shivering attacks. It was the price they paid for the so-called bargain sleeping bags and the weight they saved by not including a ground cloth and some kind of sleeping pad in their list of necessities.

Experience taught both that, while it was not necessary to finance the cost of a good sleeping bag, a well-constructed bag, designed to meet the weather conditions of their favorite camping region, was worth many times its cost in terms of healthy sleeping comfort.

Top-line manufacturers such as North Face are now making and distributing sleeping bags lined with polyester fill.

Most beginning backpackers start their outdoor sleeping experiences in a dacron-filled, rectangular summer bag.

The days when such hardy mountain conquerors as John Muir rolled up an old horse blanket and headed for the high country are long gone. Modern campers have advantages these early explorers never knew, and properly equipped backpackers do not suffer the cold-related diseases that hindered their efforts to open the wilderness.

When the subject of sleeping outdoors comes up in mild conversation around the hunting lodge hearth, today's enjoyers of the wilderness talk of polyester fill versus goose down in terms of loft and their respective insulating qualities; compare the pros of channel block to the drawbacks of square box construction and point up the best aspects of zipper baffle and foot construction.

The backpacker's sleeping bag will rate right next to his boots and his pack in terms of how a good one can help make a trip and a bad one kill a newcomer's appetite for further outdoor experiences. A well-made sleeping bag will mean a warmer, more comfortable bed in which to rest trail-weary bones, while a poorly made bag can keep the tired hiker up all night and even leave him open to such maladies as pneumonia or hypothermia.

Shopping for a sleeping bag is pretty much the same as buying anything else. The shopper wants the best-quality item he can find at the lowest price he can arrange to pay

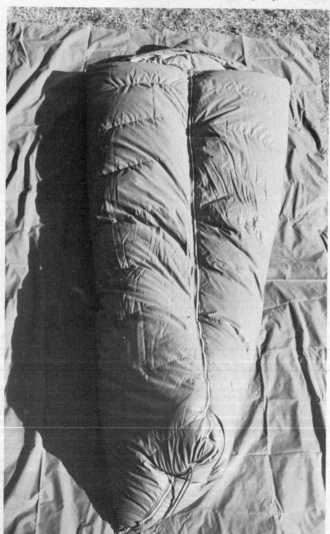

This mid-priced down bag is designed in a modified mummy shape. Thick loft and a suitable baffle system hold heat.

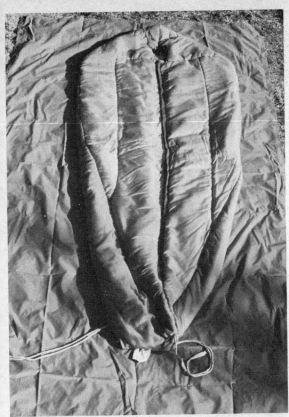

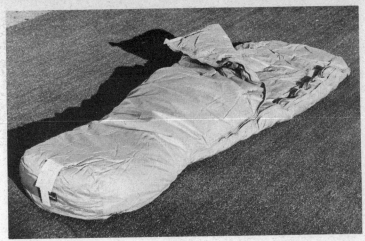

With over eight inches of loft, this winter weight down bag will keep the tired trail hound warm in below-zero cold.

This inexpensive dacron mummy bag is light and can be packed tightly rolled, but won't protect in weather below 40 degrees.

The half-bag, or bivouac bag, lacks a zipper, is used to encase a climber's legs and waist in cramped situations.

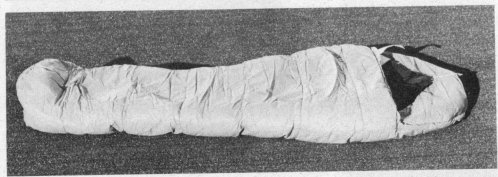

and still get an item that will fulfill his need. Since the amount of weight any backpacker can carry is going to be limited — twenty-five percent of body weight is the general guide — the difference between, for instance, a 1½-pound bag — one using 1½ pounds of fill — and a three-pound bag will be felt in the areas of weight and cost.

A synthetic-fill bag, one using a man-made fill such as Dac II, Polargard or Fiberfill, will weigh more but cost less than a down-fill bag. A down-fill bag — usually filled with goose or duck down — will be lightweight, warm and more expensive. The backpacker must find out what the prevailing temperatures will be in the region he wants to camp out in, and balance the thickness of his wallet with the type and thickness of his chosen fill.

Down is rated by filling power. A bag labeled "550 fill, Prime Northern Goose Down" is one which requires one pound of that type of down to fill a space of 550 cubic inches. One fireside argument often heard is whether goose down is better than duck down for insulating against cold weather. The new sleeping bag buyer might be interested to learn that both types have the same chill rating, but goose down costs more. The synthetic fills are less costly, but also less effective as insulation. Their advantage over down is that, if wet, they are easy to dry and retain more of their

The three items above — the two sleeping bags and tent — must be purchased separately. The backpacker would have to provide his own means of pre-warming the cold bag.

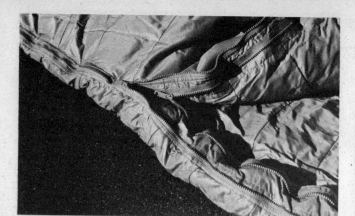

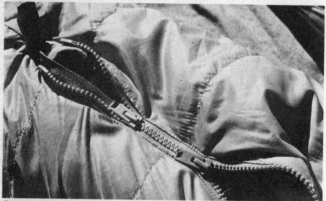

Better quality sleeping bags can be zipped open and closed at both ends. This gives the tired backpacker a way to ventilate both his head and his feet.

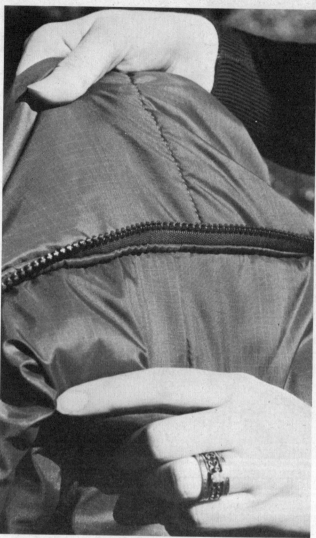

A tube or section of insulation sewn behind the zipper provides better protection against stray breezes that might otherwise get through to the tired trailhound.

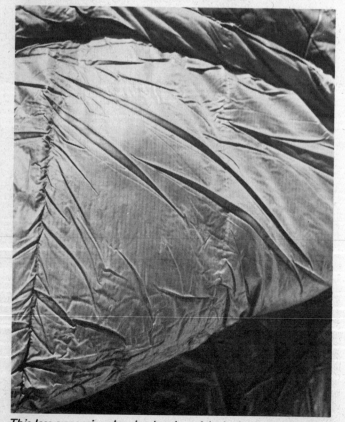

This less expensive sleeping bag has eight inches between each baffle. This type of arrangement allows the down fill to shift, causing cold spots in the bottom of the bag.

original loft. A wet down bag is useless on the trail and quite a chore to dry out at home.

Loft indicates the thickness of the insulating material that is packed in between the inner case and outer shell of a sleeping bag. The method of stitching these two shells together is another indication of whether a bag will hold in warmth or allow cold air to carry off body heat. Obviously, the thicker the fill, the more cold-resistant the bag, but this, too, must be balanced against weight and cost. A bag with 1½ pounds of goose down may be certified suitable for weather as cold as zero degrees centigrade. One with 3½ pounds of fill may be certified as low as minus thirty-five degrees centigrade. If planning a trip onto the frozen slopes of a mountain winter, the down bag may be worth the extra investment. If a humid climate with more temperate temperatures is anticipated, synthetic fill, with its reduced cost, may be the right choice.

Once the determination of down versus synthetic fill has

A separate covering wrapped around the sleeper would give added comfort on a bitter winter night. Several types of commercial wraps are currently available.

been made, other considerations become important in getting the best bag for the backpacker's needs. Is the zipper heavy duty and double pull, with an opening and closing tab both inside and outside? Is it nylon or metal and is there a baffle between it and the sleeper? Are the stress points bar tacked and the bag double stitched where extra-strong seams are needed? Check closely for good workmanship. Two sleeping bags of similar materials and chill rating may differ in price by twenty or thirty percent, depending on how well they are put together. Avoid a bag whose seams are sewn through to the inner shell. Look instead for one with baffles between inner and outer layers that block cold air.

There is little point to buying more sleeping bag than is needed. A summer camper who makes the larger investment in a down winter bag is wasting money that might be better spent on extra food or such a luxury as a two-way radio. A too heavy bag can defeat its purpose in warmer weather by

Compartmented stitching provides better insulation than types with stitches sewn through inner and outer layers.

Sleeping pad can be tied in roll, packed in stuff sack, and tied to top of pack for easy loading, carrying.

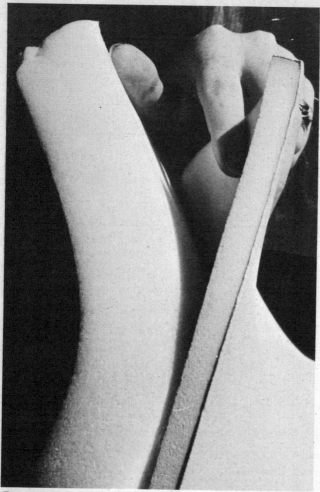

Foam padding (left) provides thicker insulation than the Insolite Pad (at right). Pad, though, is easier to pack.

With practice, getting bulky pad into small stuff sack becomes an easy chore, accomplished in seconds on trail.

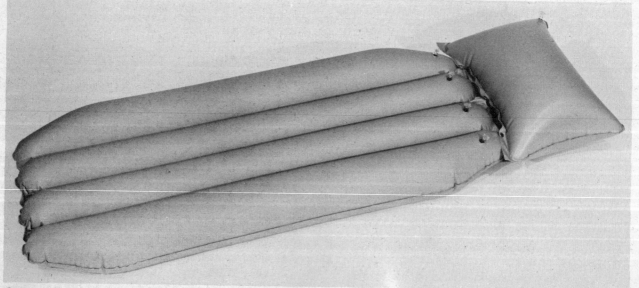

One answer to need for sleeping pad is air mattress like those used in swimming pool. A problem is that cold air moving through the tubes can conduct away vital body heat and puncture can leave sleeper flat on his back.

Insolite pad can make the rockiest trail bed as soft as a feather and will keep sleeping backpacker's body heat from being conducted away through cold, rock or snow-covered ground. A soft bed is preferable.

being so warm the camper has to sleep with it open or roast, leaving himself open to the elements as if he had no sleeping bag.

Even with a high-quality down bag, the camper must protect himself from allowing his body heat to be conducted away by the cold, perhaps dew-dampened ground on which he lies. Down compresses to a negligible thickness under a person's weight, requiring some additional insulation to be laid out under the bag, especially under hips, shoulders, knees and the back of the head. Most experienced campers use either a foam pad or an air mattress like those used by swimmers to handle this problem. Those who use the foam pads find that, though they are more bulky than an air mattress, they are lighter to carry and more efficient insulators as cold air moving in the tubes of an inflated mattress will conduct away body heat.

How a backpacker eats before bedding down will affect his sleeping comfort, especially in cold weather. A high-energy snack, such as a candy bar or a handful of dried fruit, will provide the camper's body with heat-producing sugar that will fuel his inner body furnace through the night.

Other factors that may have an adverse effect on comfortable sleep might include the camper's general physical condition, his level of fatigue when he rolls into his sleeping bag at day's end and his normal metabolic rate. A person who is normally sensitive to cold or wind should make the extra investment of a more heavily insulated bag to sleep as warmly as his thicker-hided trail buddy.

Caring for this expensive piece of gear will help it to give the buyer many years of effective use. A sleeping bag will absorb body oils through constant use and should be cleaned at least once a season. Storing a dirty bag will only compound the problem. Sending it to a professional cleaner with experience in cleaning such gear or washing it at home, carefully following the manufacturer's directions, will keep a considerable investment from going down the drain.

When not using the bag, store it in a clean, dry place. Hang it on an oversized coat hanger with a piece of plastic cover to keep out bugs and moisture. Fluff the bag before storing and hang it in a closet — not out in the garage, where dampness or dry rot can eat holes in the fabric.

Start by pushing one end all the way into the sack until it is pressed against the bottom, then push in more bag.

Packing that bulky sleeping bag into its small stuff sack takes practice and patience. Eventually, it fits.

Continue to force the bag material into the sack, tamping in each handful. Keep pushing until material feels solid.

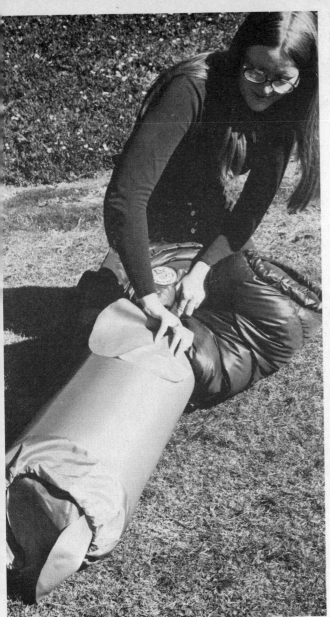

Some stuff sacks are open at both ends, which may make stuffing in the bulky bag that much easier. Be sure the bag isn't just coming out the other end.

Finally, the entire bag has been forced into its stuff sack and makes an unbelievably compact bundle which will hang from the bottom of the pack, secured by thongs.

Never store a sleeping bag in its stuff sack. The stuff sack is used to keep the outer shell of a sleeping bag from being ripped out on the trail. At home, a bag needs to be aired out and stored in a protected place.

On the trail, protecting that expensive bag is a simple matter of making the additional small investment in a heavy-gauge nylon stuff sack. A fall against tree bark could mean an accidental puncture. The extra covering of the multi-purpose stuff sack will help prevent this. If planning a hike in rainy country, plan to make room in the living pack for the sleeping bag. Other items can then hang at the bottom of the pack in that stuff sack.

As with any piece of expensive gear, the buyer wants to get value and long use for his money. A little judicious shopping and a few simple precautions will keep that sleeping bag serviceable, affording the backpacker many comfortable nights on the trail.

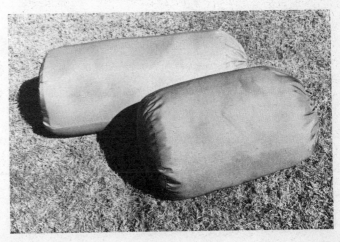

CHAPTER 4
WHAT MAKES A BACKPACKER

The Right Pack Can Make Or Break The Beginner

The taller a backpacker is and the more he weighs, the more equipment he can comfortably carry on his back. The recommended limit is 25% of body weight.

COMES FRIDAY AFTERNOON and the neatly dressed company executive walks through the front door of his apartment and, with a snort of disgust, pitches into the closest closet that hated symbol of his week-long bondage, his briefcase. He takes long, lanky strides over shaggy plushness to his bedroom, shrugging off his suitcoat and clawing loose his tie enroute; steps inside and firmly shuts the door.

From behind the bedroom door comes an off-key bellow, heard even over the static roar of needle spray. Then the water stops and the bellow is replaced by a soft humming that grows louder as, after a spate of rustling noises, the bedroom door is opened and out trots a changed man. Gone are the knit slacks, the wide-collar shirt and the highly polished loafers. They are replaced by a newly purchased checked wool hunting shirt, dungarees and heavy brogans.

Moving quickly now, with frequent anxious glances at his watch, the converted country boy jams head and shoulders into the same closet into which he banished his briefcase and emerges with a triumphant grin, gripping tightly a battered relic from his military days — a ragged duffle bag of faded green. Heading for the kitchen, he rummages in whirlwind fashion through cupboards and cabinets, dropping in dehydrated vegetables, soups, meat and fruits. Back in the bedroom he tops off the load with

an extra shirt and pants, and stuffs into the last space at the top of his bag a musty surplus sleeping bag that was probably retired before the era when Super Teddy was teaching the boys how to charge uphill.

Snapping the shoulder strap, the intrepid adventurer jogs out the front door and down the stairs to where his VW waits patiently with engine idling. Tossing the bulging duffle into the back seat, effectively blocking his rear window, the transformed executive slides behind the wheel, revs the little washing machine engine and pops the clutch to go weaving out into six o'clock demolition derby.

After an hour and a half of dodging sleepy truckdrivers, mothers distracted by fighting children and other happy commuters, the weekend warrior makes a relieved exit from the turmoil of the freeway and begins to wind his way up a steadily steeper mountain road. Another hour of driving gets him to the entrance gate of Escapeland National Park and in fifteen minutes he skids to a stop in the gravel parking lot of the ranger station where he is to meet the rest of his hiking group. The master plan is to spend the night in a nearby lodge and get an early start in the morning.

Pushing open the rustic wooden door, he drags his duffle bag into the middle of a scene from Bedlam; a kaleidoscope of greens and browns, swirls of cigarette smoke and the

In preparing for a back country outing of a week or more, these men have turned to the largest type of pack in which to fit their survival gear.

decibel level of seventeen simultaneous conversations over which the bellowed instructions of the harried group leader can barely be heard.

Standing uncertainly at the edge of the milling group, the novice woodsman is startled to feel a grip on his shoulder and to be spun around face-to-belt buckle with a 6½-foot tall and a 1½-yard-wide's worth of living-in-the-wilds experience in the form of the party's guide. The sun-wrinkled, wind-seared features of said guide are twisted in a grimace of distaste and one banana-fingered hand is braced heavily on the novice's shoulder. The other hand is pointing roughly in the direction of the battered duffle.

In a gravelly voice tinged with suspicious disbelief, the giant of the north woods inquires, "What is that?"

After an abortive attempt to turn out from under that heavy hand, the novice cranes his head over one shoulder at his beloved duffle, turns back to face his interrogator with a weak grin and replies, "That's my pack sack."

This is an internal frame pack, which is suitable for the ski-touring en-thusiast or mountain climber who will need a lighter load and more mobility.

The oversized guide, his suspicions confirmed, rolls his eyes toward the ceiling, then brings them to bear once more on the now-trembling weekender.

"Not in my forest, you don't," he rumbles, confusing his new charge cross-eyed. Patiently, he reaches down and raps the novice sharply on the forehead with two-inch-wide knuckles to bring his eyes back into focus and says, "Look, goofy. You want to be a backpacker, right? So where's your backpack?"

A skier might be a Head-man, a K2-man, a Kneissl-man or a Rossignal-man, but if he doesn't have skis, he is not a skier. The backpacker may be a Kelty-man, a Mountain Equipment-man, a North Face-man or a Jansport-man, but he will have to have some kind of pack to be a backpacker. He should know before starting out to shop what kind of pack will best suit his kind of trip and how to distinguish a good store from a bad one so as to get the best pack for his money. A good pack can make the trip and a bad one can

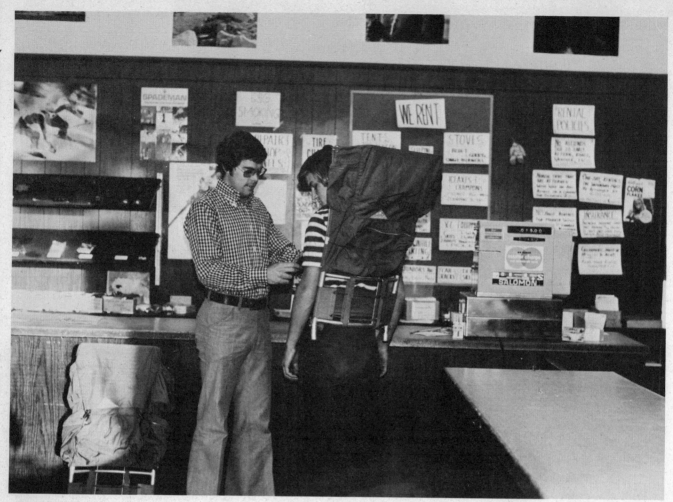

When buying a pack, the backpacker should make certain that the pack he decides on fits properly.

spoil it completely as perhaps no other piece of gear can.

Those with military service in their background may well remember the eighty-pound backbreaker that every infantryman has carried on a training deployment or into an actual battle where the rifleman stayed on the move and had to carry all the necessities of daily existence with him. They are not — though they would like to think so — the only ones who have faced the problems of trying to live off the land. Many civilian backpackers, who took up the sport as a means of recreation — try to explain that one to a tired and grubby dogface at the end of a three-day forced march — and as a way to get out ahead of the glittering clots of campers and canvas tents that started to spring up in national parks in the late Fifties and early Sixties, will remember the Trapper Nelson variety of wooden pack frame from the even earlier Forties. Others will recall the sunny days of youth in the woods living out of a Boy Scout rucksack.

In most such cases — always with the G.I. back-buster — the old methods of carrying a load on the back were downright uncomfortable. Weight was poorly distributed, the straps dug into shoulders and the weight of the old canvas pack was excessive before any survival gear was even loaded into it.

In the early Fifties, Dick Kelty set out to change all that. He devised an aluminum frame, incorporating a mesh backband, padded shoulder and waist straps, and a lightweight, synthetic fabric to put together the forerunner of today's modern pack assemblies. The Kelty Company led the state of the art in the Fifties, but since then, many backpack manufacturers have added their contributions to advancing backpack design. Hip-load frames, waterproof and abrasion-resistant fabrics, self-healing nylon zippers and synthetic-core, cotton-sheath threads all combine to make the modern backpack. Other technical innovations present the buyer of a new backpack with a wide variety of styles and sizes to fit his many on-the-trail needs.

As the art continues to advance, packs have become specialized in form and function. Internal frame, external frame, bike packs, haul sacks, ski-touring packs, climbing packs and other types are now available, running the gamut of prices. There are over fifteen major domestic manufacturers of frame packs, some offering hip-load models, such as the A-16; some offering shoulder-load models, such as Sierra Designs; and some offering both types, such as Mountain Equipment, Incorporated. Besides the manufacturers' brand names, many retailers offer models made by others under their company name, such as E.M.S. Numerous importers bring packs in from the Orient under all sorts of labels.

The first thing the backpacker must decide is how much he wants to spend. Imported packs can retail for as low as $11 or $12, while Ambercrombie and Fitch offers a special

Padded shoulder straps and waist belt, optional side pouches and external tie-downs for special gear are part of climbing pack.

Lightweight day packs usually have one main compartment, may include an extra external pouch.

model at $160. The best way to judge is to decide how often the pack will be used. A $12 pack frame that breaks after three days' use will cost $4 per day for its use, while one purchased for $60 that gives good service two weeks a year for four years without breaking would mean a $1 outlay per day reduced by the extra time it can still be used. The $60 variety is probably also more comfortable than the cheapie.

A mild controversy that pops up whenever two or more experienced backpackers meet at roadhead or trail junction is whether hip-load frames are better than the shoulder-suspension types, or if the internal-frame models are even better yet. Some backpackers swear by the hip loaders and others just can't use them, preferring the shoulder type. The choice of a suitable type frame is based on how a given type will fit an individual's body structure, general bulk and muscular type. It is generally accepted that a tubular-frame pack is better for long-distance travel with a heavier load.

Internal-frame types are a rather recent innovation, with the aluminum or plexiglass strips that give the pack its rigidity sewn into the inside of the pack material. The guide here is that the more mobility required, such as in climbing or ski touring, and the less weight and bulk to be carried, the more the backpacker might look to an internal-frame model.

A rather specialized type of pack is the Chinard Ultima Thule model. It is an internal-frame type without frame components. The load provides its own suspension and it must be packed very carefully to carry well. When stuffed, the sleeping bag hip compartment makes a semirigid hip belt, while the rest of the pack is load rigid.

Day packs and light rucksacks are used for short hikes of one day or less. If planning a longer trip, more weight will have to be carried as more equipment becomes needed, so a larger, more sturdily constructed pack will be necessary.

When setting out to buy a pack, the most important

By carrying along the basic necessities for survival as well as comfort items for the day, these youngsters are fully prepared to meet any trail emergency that might delay their return to camp or cause injuries.

consideration is fit. Every body is different; different shoulder-to-hip distance, different bone structure, different front-to-back dimensions, different posture and center of gravity. All of these factors must be considered when fitting a new pack. Not only must the backpacker select the right size pack but, since sizes vary from manufacturer to manufacturer, he must exercise great care in selecting the pack that fits his dimensions. The more adjustments available on the pack, the more likely it is that the buyer can get a good fit. Insist on fitting the pack — with a load, perhaps — before buying it. Some store clerks may resist the idea but if the opportunity to at least try on the chosen pack is denied, go to another store.

When a pack fits well and seems to carry well, carefully inspect it inside and out before buying. Check all seams for workmanship flaws and all grommets to insure they are locked properly. Put the pack on the floor on its corner and balance full weight on it. If it gives, apologize and leave quickly. Such embarrassment is probably less than the backpacker would suffer if the pack should break twenty miles upcountry. Check all adjustments to find out if they will give under stress. Work all the zippers to insure problem-free operation. See if the pack material has been coated for waterproofing. Nothing will spoil a beautiful day on the trail quicker than soggy food and a wet sleeping bag from that quickie rain shower or a surprise fall in a creek.

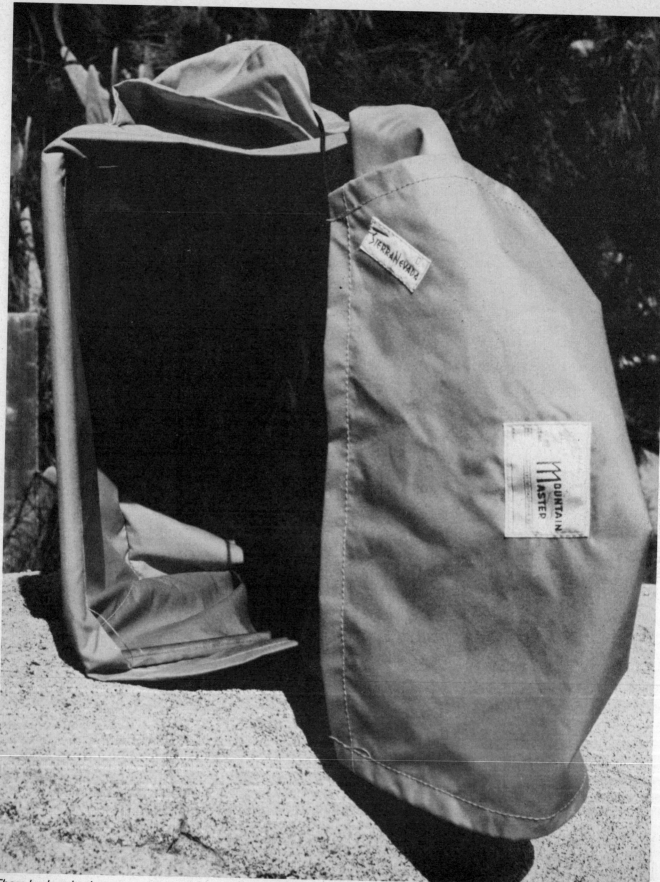

Those backpacks that are equipped with a hold-open bar around the mouth make loading easier.

This day pack is equipped with well-padded shoulder straps and a light waist belt to prevent the load from digging into shoulders, bouncing as hiker walks.

A well-made backpack is a sound investment and should give many years of good service if cared for as the major investment it is.

The first place to care for the backpack is in packing it for the trail. Try to pack sharp objects so they won't touch the fabric. A knife blade or the square corner of a metal mess kit can quickly punch a hole in the toughest material when bounced up and down a rocky path. When taking the pack off, don't drop it; set it down gently no matter how much the shoulder bones ache. The force of forty pounds coming to a sudden stop from a height of two or three feet can do unbelievable damage to stitches and zippers. At night, hang the pack from a tree. A hungry bear rummaging

Fanny pack holds emergency gear, leaves both hands free.

This external frame pack has tie-down flap that can be extended to fit in more gear, zippers protected by concealing flaps, adjustable hip belt, frame contoured to human back, padded shoulder straps.

Bowhunters, who must stalk to within close ranges of skittish game, are taking up backpacking to get into areas that most hunters don't get into.

through a pack left on the ground could easily result in the backpacker returning home with his remaining equipment piled in his arms. Pack all food and liquid in airtight containers to avoid spillage or damage to other gear in the pack.

Care between trips is a simple matter of hosing off the inside and outside of the pack and letting it dry thoroughly before storing it in a dry place where temperatures do not fluctuate above one hundred degrees or below thirty-two degrees. A garage is not a good storage place for anything made of synthetic material. Put such gear in the hall closet instead.

With the hold-open bar keeping the mouth of his pack open, this backpacker can more easily arrange his equipment, packing it in reverse order of use.

Contoured internal frame pack
is divided down the center.

Sewn-in nylon dividers can aid the backpacker in arranging and balancing the myraid items of food, clothing, medical supplies, etc., in handiest way.

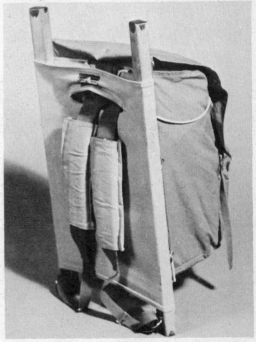

Older backpackers will recall dubious pleasure of getting away from it all with Trapper Nelson kit.

Once the newcomer to the backpacking fraternity has selected his basic gear, he must then turn to planning what he will take on his trip and how to pack it. The average person cannot carry more than one third of his body weight with any comfort for more than short distances. A good rule of thumb is to carry no more than one quarter of normal body weight.

In preparing for a two-man, one-week trip, the trailhound will have to make allowance for the 4½-pound average weight of his pack, three pounds for his sleeping bag, two pounds of personal clothing for a summer trip, about two pounds for a small cooking stove and extra fuel cells, about three pounds for first-aid kit, rope and flashlight, perhaps two pounds of mess gear, about 1½ pounds of food per man per day for a total of 10½ pounds for seven days. With Insolite sleeping pad and a plastic ground cloth, this load comes to approximately twenty-six pounds — a full pack for a person weighing 105 pounds. A 175-pound backpacker still has another eighteen pounds available before he reaches his comfort limit. This — in

Frequent training exercises got troops used to the military back-buster, but few ever came to enjoy the 80-lb. albatross.

addition to the novice's inexperience — is another strong argument for the buddy system of backpacking, where one lends his knowledge — and perhaps part of his extra packing room — to a less able trail companion so that both may survive to enjoy the trip.

With the severe weight limitations of backpacking, the packer's first consideration is to be selective in what he chooses to take along. A jug of wine might add a lovely glow to the evening fire, but its weight would limit the amount of a more vital liquid — water — that the backpacker could carry. A portable radio might be a nice touch of civilization in the wilds, but a two-way Citizens Band transceiver could be a source of similar entertainment and a useful item of survival gear if trouble should rear its ugly head on the trail.

Once he has completed his list of essentials, the backpacker must then figure out how all this stuff is going to fit into one backpack. If he thought about this while shopping for his pack, the backpacker probably selected one with several separate pockets to make easier the job of organizing and balancing his load.

When organizing supplies in a pack of this type, most

The padded front, padded shoulder straps and contoured hip belt of this internal frame pack make load ride well.

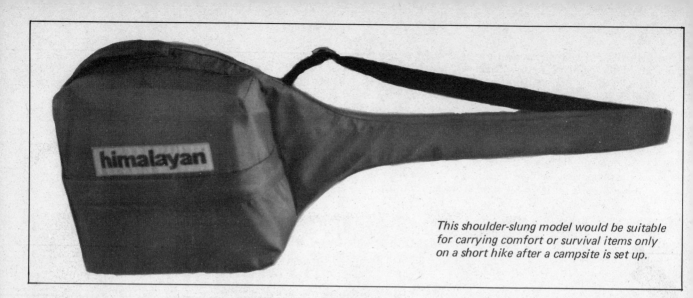

This shoulder-slung model would be suitable for carrying comfort or survival items only on a short hike after a campsite is set up.

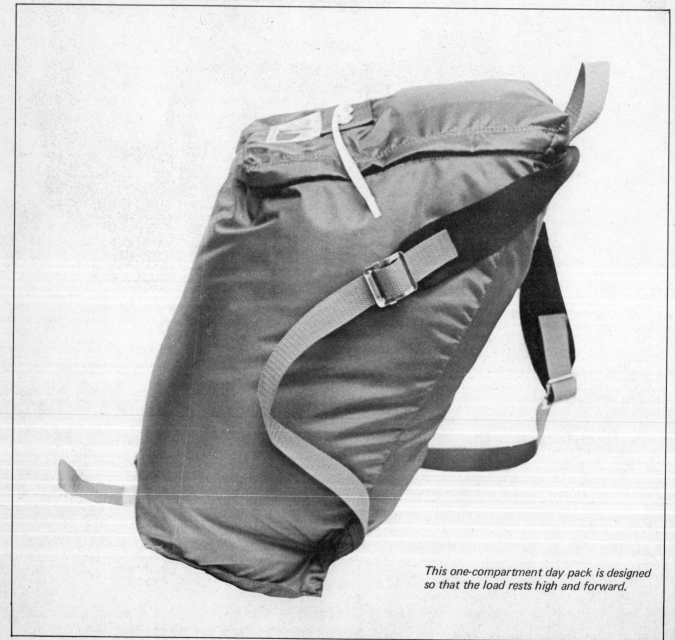

This one-compartment day pack is designed so that the load rests high and forward.

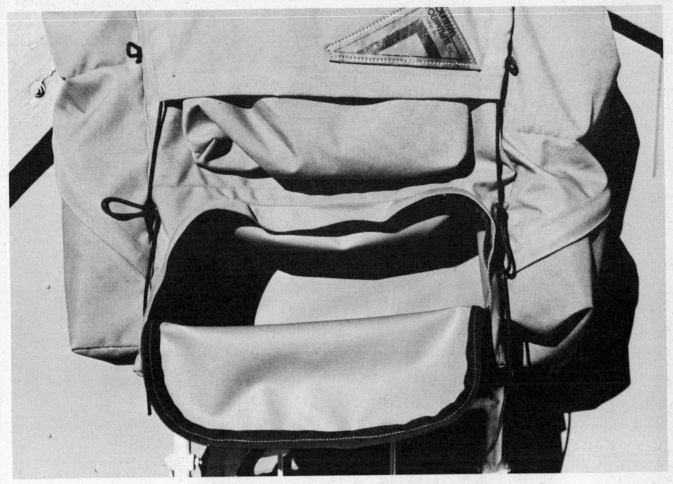

This pack is divided into two compartments, upper and lower, with access to lower through zippered flap.

experienced backpackers put their clothing in the bottom section and the sleeping bag in a stuff sack hung at the bottom of the pack. Food and cooking supplies go in the top divide and any special items, such as climbing equipment or the paraphernalia of the nature photographer, are put in the extra pockets on either side. A tent, poncho or the rolled-up sleeping pad and ground cloth are strapped to the top of the pack.

The general rule in packing is if it's heavy, put it high and close to the back. Lighter items are packed low and to the rear of the pack. This keeps the backpackers' center of gravity as normal as possible while carrying his extra weight.

This is considered the best packing method when using any of the frame-type packs. The fanny pack and day pack are smaller and more specialized in their use.

A fanny pack is a small satchel or pouch that is strapped to the hips and rests on the hiker's fanny. It is used primarily as a container for emergency survival gear and to carry extra ammunition or other items while leaving a hunter's hands free to shoot bow or rifle. The items carried

Shoulder-slung satchel could be emergency survival pack.

This external frame model is a hip-suspension system. It employs a wrap-around frame. Note wide backband.

in such a pack should be taken along by anyone who leaves his car or campsite for even the briefest stroll into the brush. An unexpected mishap, such as twisting an ankle in a hidden chuckhole, could turn a simple walk in the woods into real trouble if the hiker does not have his survival pack along.

Every hiker's survival gear should include a knife, first-aid kit, map, compass, water and food, flashlight and extra batteries, a complete fire-starting kit, a length of nylon cord and an assortment of fishhooks. Bow, rifle or pistol hunters might add extra ammunition for their

An external-frame backpack with hip band and frame extension holds sleeping bag.

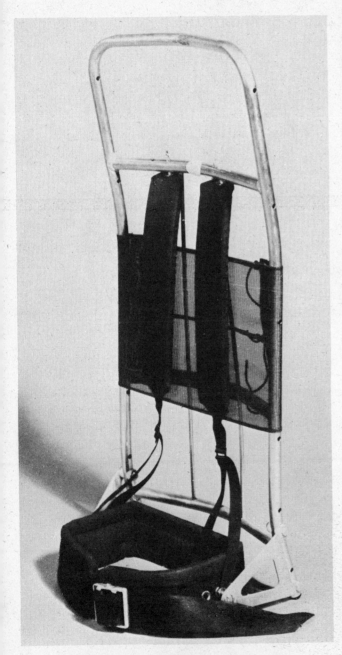

External pack frames are available in a variety of designs. This one uses adjustable hip-suspension system.

weapon and the necessary repair kit. With these items along, a lost or injured hiker has vastly improved his chances of being alive and whole when the search party finally locates him.

In picking items to fill these survival needs, the backpacker should be careful to stay within a three to five-pound limit. An overloaded fanny pack will drag uncomfortably on the belt fastener.

Fanny packs usually are made of the same lightweight material used for the larger styles. One feature the hiker should look for is a wide — one-inch minimum — nylon belt that will not cut into the waist. The unit should have a

Most pack compartments are held closed with a nylon-toothed, self-healing zipper to resist corrosion.

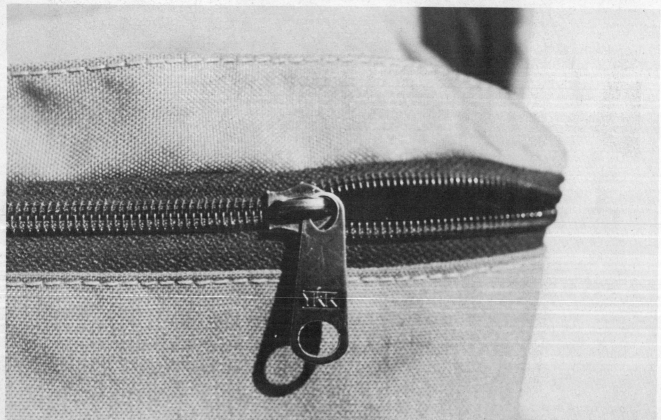

Placing zipper at top of fanny pack lets hiker swing it to front, remove one item without losing all.

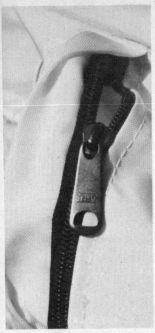

full-zipper closure on the top — not the side — to allow the hiker or hunter to swing the pack to the front and open it to remove needed items without dumping the rest of the pack's contents. An improvement would be the addition of a flap over the zipper to prevent it from being snagged by a branch and pulled open on the trail.

The fanny pack has no ready-made compartments but the backpacker can organize his gear by packaging it in smaller containers. Most commercial first-aid kits come in their own container but a homemade variety might fit in an empty Band-Aid box. A pair of socks placed in the center of the pack would serve to separate emergency rations from the rest of the gear in the pack.

When first using a fanny pack, many beginners will make the mistake of drawing the waist strap too tight. This can cause unnecessary discomfort and tempt the hiker to leave

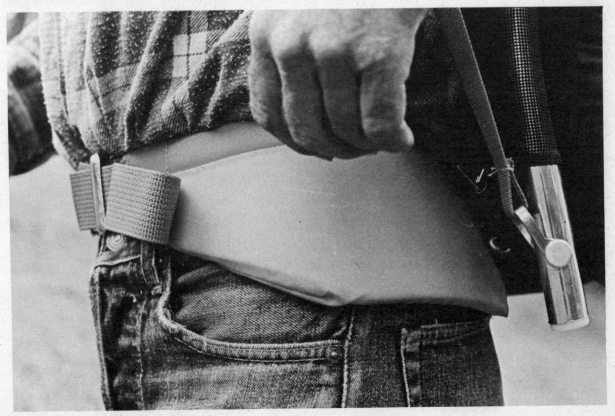

A pack which incorporates the hip-suspension type of load-carrying system
requires a well-padded and sufficiently wide hip belt to be comfortable.

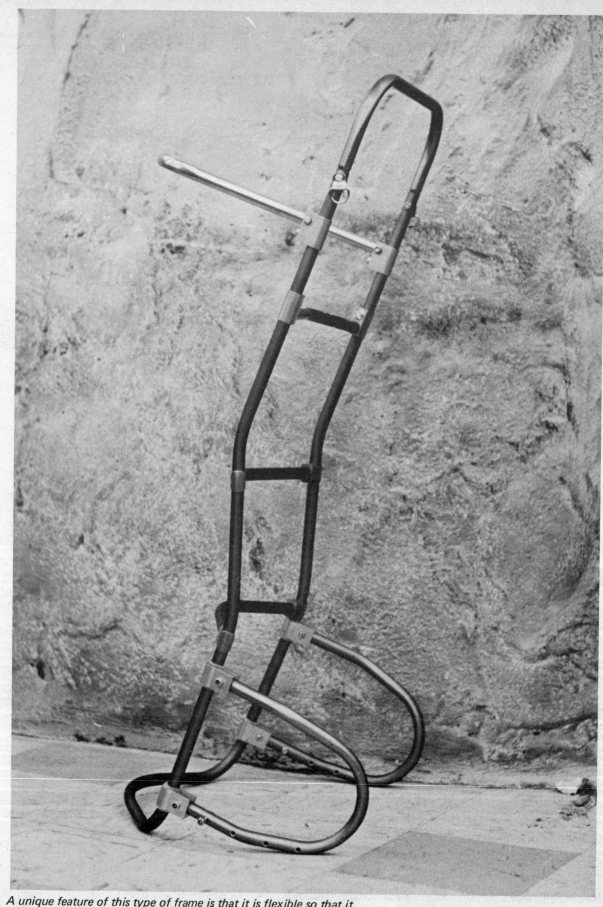

A unique feature of this type of frame is that it is flexible so that it moves with twists made by backpacker's body. Note hold-open bar.

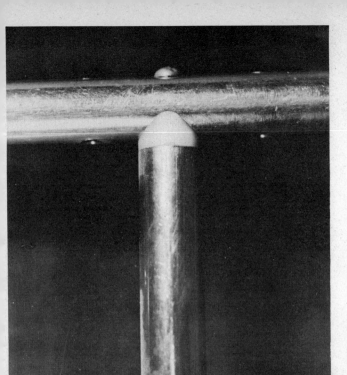

This exterior frame uses machined joints with a separate clamp to hold the pieces of the frame without slippage.

his emergency rations behind, which can get him in trouble in a hurry. Always leave enough slack in the strap so that the pack can be pulled around to the hiker's front with just a slight tug on the strap. Most fanny packs will have a snap-to-D-ring type fastener. Avoid those with a double D-ring fastener as this type is inclined to come loose frequently, obliging the annoyed hiker to retighten it every few strides.

After a few trips, a well-organized fanny pack becomes like those few extra pounds the beginning backpacker didn't know he had gained. It's there, but the hiker isn't aware of it until he looks back for it.

When the list of items a hiker considers necessary for a one-day trip exceeds the five-pound limit, the backpacker should look to the next larger size, the day pack.

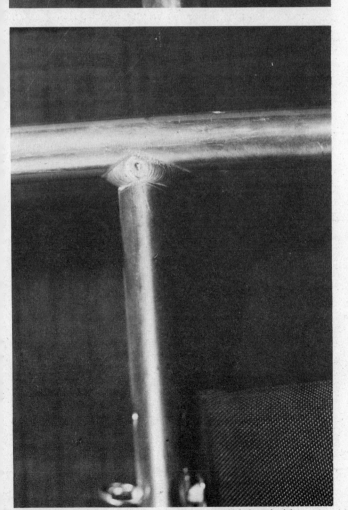

The better-constructed frames will have all joints held together with heli-arc or tig weld for more strength.

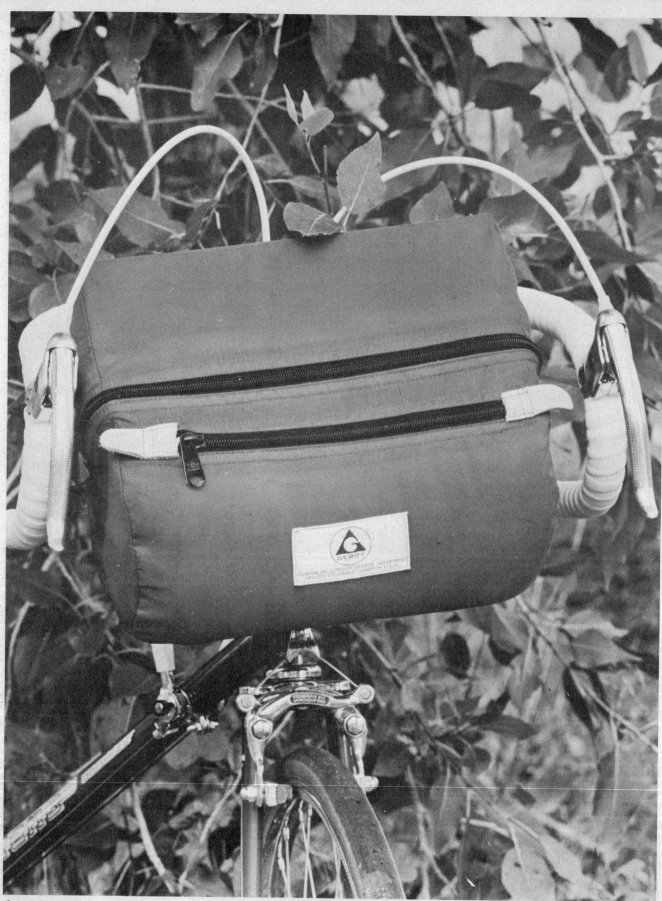

Specialty packs, such as this bicycle handlebar pouch, are designed for a single specialized use. When riding woodland trails, this is an emergency pack.

For a long biking trip, the saddlebags above would hold needed equipment.

This type of pack uses shoulder straps and, in some cases, a waist belt to support the load and prevent it from swaying and bouncing as the backpacker hikes along. It also fills the need of a hiker or hunter to carry needed camping gear and still have his hands free.

Many day packs are constructed in a teardrop style, and most have only one compartment in which the hiker must fish around for a needed item. Two-compartment styles are available, with the upper section separated from the lower by a sewn-in nylon wall. The lower bag will have a zipper on the back of the pack for easy access without opening the upper portion. The shoulder straps on a good day pack will be padded. Those without such padding tend to become uncomfortable even on a short walk.

The weight limit for a day pack is fifteen pounds as it does not include a frame to help support additional weight. While such a light load might seem too restrictive, a careful packer can carry enough to stay out as long as two days, if he includes a sleeping bag and camps near a clean water source. If the backpacker finds he cannot hold to the

A specialty pack such as the one above would enable man's best friend to help out with the chore of hauling along the necessary — his and master's.

fifteen-pound limit, he should graduate to the next larger pack, the rucksack, which was the type used by many a Boy Scout on expeditions until the frame styles became available.

Whenever experienced backpackers gather to debate the virtues of their sport and its related equipment, the inter-related requirements of form, fit and function will always be a part of their conversation. What is the intended use? One pack can serve many uses from a one-day hike to an extended expedition but many are designed to meet specialized requirements. Does the pack incorporate the desirable features of separate pockets and exterior lashing points? What is the best shape and design to allow proper weight distribution for balance and ease of carrying? Should it be a shoulder-slug type, one supported by the hips or one using both methods?

A hearthside conversation back at the hunting lodge is perhaps the best place for the beginning backpacker to pick up the best pointers on what to look for and what to avoid. Another good starting place is a camping equipment store where the sales personnel are themselves backpackers. Selecting the right store for the purchase of backpacking equipment is almost as important as getting the right pack. One actually leads to the other.

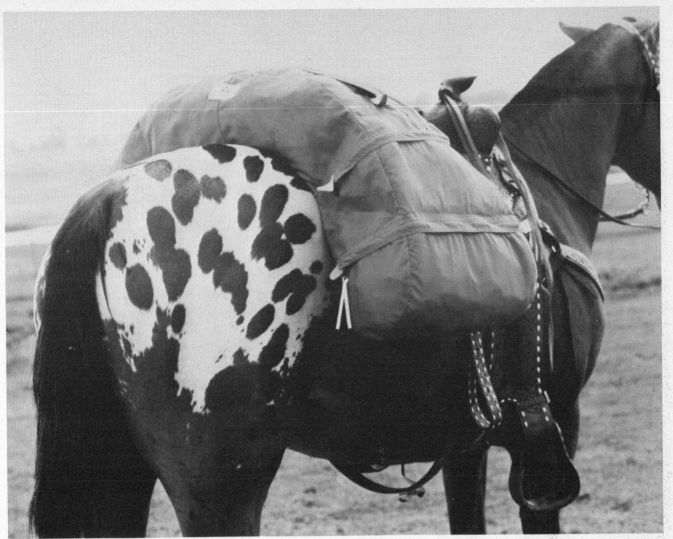

A prolonged stay in the wilderness might be managed with this horse pack. The backpacker could cover many more miles this way and his horse would be living off the land.

A good store for this type of equipment is probably one in which the owner is present. The buyer can get an immediate decision on returns or adjustments. There should be at least three of the major brand names included in shelf stock and a good selection of backpacking literature. A money-back guarantee on all but sale-priced merchandise is another good indicator as is a good quantity of merchandise and accessories. Most important is the attitude of the store personnel. If the clerk tries to push the buyer into a sale he isn't sure of, is not knowledgeable about the equipment or shows little interest in the buyer's camping needs, the best place to shop is at another store.

Cross-country motorcycle touring could be much simplified with these or similar saddlebags to carry required gear.

Motorcycle packs, like the other specialty items, are available in a variety of styles to suit the individual. With a suitable pack and a tent, the rider skips hotels.

The backpacking beginner has a whole new world of enjoyment ahead of him but he must also realize his responsibilities to others who share his new-found interest. The backpacker today is aware of the ecology of his outdoor playground and most plan their trip around the ethic of leaving nothing but their footprints. There is a large quantity of good ecology literature available and the backpacker's first step should be to familiarize himself with his environment. Once he has this basic knowledge, the next step is to gear up and head for the back country to try it for himself.

Penetrating the wilderness is not the only way to put a pack to use. Passengers on an across-the-lake ferry or tour boat could carry along swimsuit, towel and lunch, or some type of emergency medical kit to treat mishaps.

CHAPTER 5

CARE AND REPAIR

ALTHOUGH A BIT TRITE and most certainly time-worn, the expression, "A stitch in time, saves nine," is one that deserves serious consideration by anyone who back-packs.

If you spend any time at all backpacking, there is going to come a time when your equipment will break down while on the trail, miles from any repair shop. Without a little knowledge and prior planning, you could well find yourself up the proverbial creek without a paddle; or in your case, without any means to repair your equipment. A smart backpacker will heed the advice that is so freely given by the grandmothers of the world. A stitch in time may

save much more than nine...it may save you from having to backback into an area to pick up gear that was left behind because of damaged pack equipment. Besides, it might be gone when you return.

With the use of nylon materials in the construction of pack bags, straps and webbings, these parts of your pack normally will hold up for many years without breaking down on the trail. However, there are times when damage does occur to these parts and you should be prepared to fix them when it does. The majority of the pack frames today are made from aluminum, which is an extremely strong material and there is little chance of it ever breaking, or for that matter, rusting. It will sometimes turn a whitish color because of oxidation; however, this does not harm the frame.

Most frame breakdowns are caused by poor welding or joining of the frame sections. This can occur because of age or undue stress applied to the frame. For example, the undue stress of dropping your frame from a high distance onto a hard surface such as rock, can cause even the best joining methods to weaken and possibly break. It goes without saying that your pack should be treated with the same tender, loving care that you lavish upon your favorite hunting rifle or fishing outfit. A good pack is hardy, but it is not indestructible.

Should you have the problem of a broken frame on a trip, it can be repaired by simply using a stick of wood and some nylon line (an item that you should always carry with you). By placing the stick over the break and tying the nylon line around it, you can reinforce the broken area. This may not have great aesthetic value, but it will get you, your pack and your gear back home where the pack can be repaired by an expert.

For making repairs to the pack bag itself, an item that every backpacker carries, adhesive tape, is very handy. This also can be used in lieu of the nylon line for repairing pack frames. Another item now on the market, ripstop nylon material with an adhesive backing, can be used to repair tears in the bag. It is a good idea to have a package of this with you whenever you backpack. Even the worst tear can be mended temporarily using this material.

The biggest offenders when it comes to tearing pack bags are tree limbs and fence sections, both of which seem to have an uncanny knack for catching hold of an unsuspecting bag at the most inconvenient times. However, with the adhesive tape from your first aid kit or the nylon adhesive-backed material, you can repair your bag in no time and be on your way. In repairing a rip, you should never apply the tape or nylon material to the outside of the bag, since a patch applied in this manner tends to peel off easily.

The best method is to remove the contents from the section that has been torn and apply the patch to the underside of the hole. When you replace the contents of the section, they will help hold the patch securely. A handy hint in making this type of repair is to heat a rock in your campfire and, using it as an iron, iron the patch onto the bag.

Field repairs require a great deal of ingenuity and improvision on the part of a backpacker since rarely is he equipped with the proper tools and materials. There are, however, a few lightweight tools that are quite versatile and easily carried.

One of the handiest tools to carry would be a pair of long needle-nose pliers, similar to the ones used by fisher-

Repair of broken frame has been completed in this case by using one section of nylon line wrapped on bottom and inner strands of the line on the upper section of the repair.

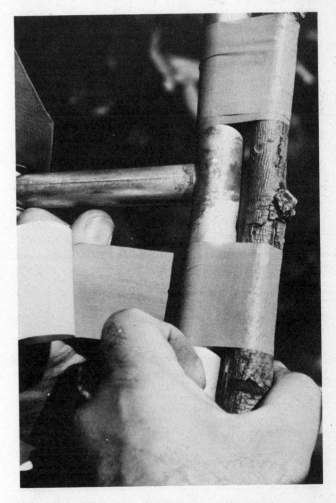

In this instance, a hasty repair is accomplished with the use of nylon ripstop tape. This also can be done in similar fashion with adhesive tape from first aid kit.

men. They should have the wire cutter section for cutting nylon line or wire. Often you can find scrap pieces of wire around camp areas or fence lines and these can be used for repairs. If you are really in a bind and cannot find any wire, sometimes there is spare wire around fence corners and gate posts that can be snipped off and used. However, if you have to resort to this source, it is advisable to ask permission prior to wielding your pliers. Otherwise, you are liable to find that you have more of a problem than a broken pack frame. There are ranchers who are known to carry a double barrel shotgun loaded with rock salt, and they often will shoot before asking questions. This wire can be twisted to make repairs to the metal frame sections and can also be handy for other uses on the trail or around camp.

Another tool that is a must for backpackers is the common Boy Scout knife, with its assorted blades. Most of these also are equipped with an awl or leather punch, which can be used as a drill to enlarge a hole in the easily worked aluminum frame. A word of caution here, however: aluminum is extremely soft and, if not careful, you can do more damage than repair. A tool along the lines of a Boy Scout knife is the Swiss Army knife, which is available though the Precise Import Corporation, 3 Chestnut Street, Suffern, N.Y. 10001. This is a far more sophisticated knife and is equipped with a small pair of scissors and a magnifying glass. There are those who claim that with this particular knife they can repair anything from a highly complex computer to a Swiss watch. This is open to speculation; however, it is an extremely handy item to have along on a backpacking trip.

One other repair item you should always carry is a simple sewing kit. With this, you can sew any rip that you may get in your bag — or in your clothing — whether or not you have any adhesive tape or nylon adhesive-backed repair material.

In making any type of repair on the trail, there is one thing that you should keep in mind. This is that these field repairs are temporary and as soon as you get back, you should take your pack to a qualified repairman. Few field repairs will hold up under long use and, if not properly repaired later, you will find that you may have the very same problem the next time you are out.

In the case of repairs to the pack frame, they almost always should be done by professional repairmen; unless you are an expert welder or repairman yourself, of course.

However, in the case of rips in the pack bag, these can, with a little effort and practice, be repaired permanently by almost anyone. All you need is a matching section of material and the use of a sewing machine. If you want to have a bag with a more mod appearance, you might try patching with different colored material. Eventually you will have a many-colored bag that will stand up to any patchwork quilt that your grandmother ever made. In selecting your patch material, you should insure that the material is as strong as that of which the bag is made; otherwise you might find that it will tear out again on the trail.

If seams tear out, these always can be repaired on the trail using your sewing kit, which you should carry with you habitually. If you don't have one, you can use fishing line for thread and improvise a needle. Or, if you have the needed nylon line, which is much too heavy for bag repairs, you can pull threads from the line to use in making repairs.

The most wear on a pack bag occurs around the hold-open bar where it wraps around the bag on the top section. Normally this isn't from wear on the trail, but is caused by the sliding motion when it is carried in the back of the vehicle. A way to alleviate this wear is to place the pack on

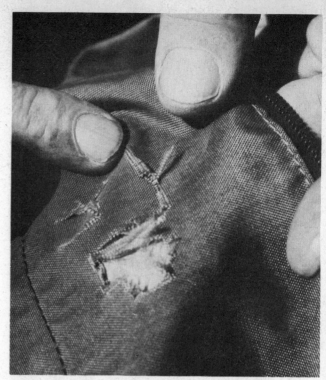

A piece has been ripped out of this bag, but it has been patched on one side with ripstop nylon tape. The tape has a sticky surface which tends to stop unraveling.

The outer surface of the bag also is covered with the adhesive nylon tape. When the two surfaces adhere in the holed-out space, they result in a strong repair.

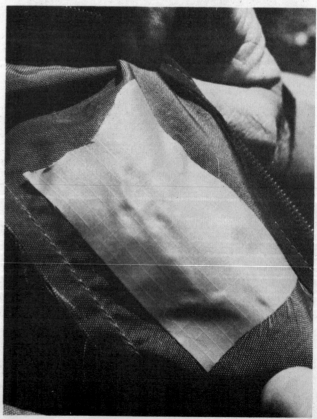

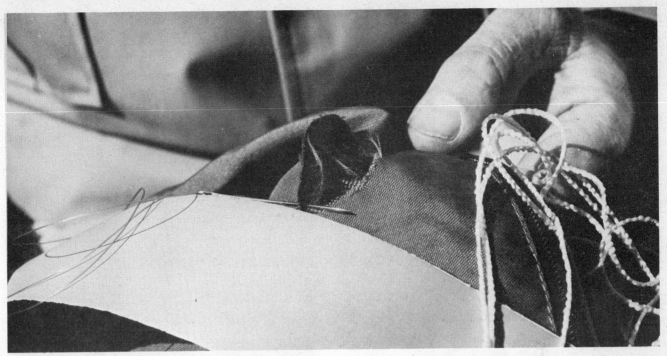

These are materials needed for major pack repairs as one might experience if a bear got to it. Included in the array are monofilament, ripstop tape, nylon inner threads from line and a heavy needle with a large eye.

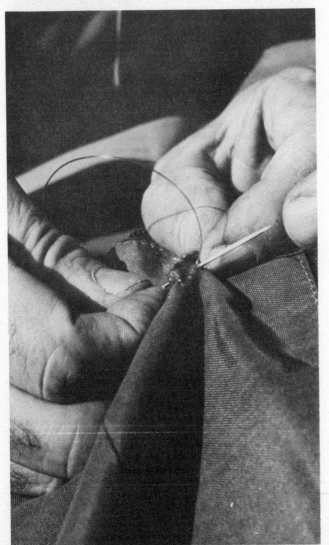

A temporary in-the-field patching job can be achieved on less serious tears or rips with the monofilament and the needle. But take large stitches so that there is plenty of material against the pull of the pack load.

the frame side when transporting it in a vehicle. If your bag is unduly worn around this area, you might check to see if you are guilty of placing the bag side down.

During a trip the shoulder straps, bag sections and the belts will become dirty. These can be cleaned by using warm water and soap. The water should be cool enough for you to be able to place your hand in without burning it. If the water is too hot, it may remove the waterproofing on the bag. If the bag becomes too dirty, you can remove it from the frame and send it to a dry cleaner. You should let them know, however, that it is waterproofed so that they will treat it properly.

Heat and direct sunlight can be quite harmful to nylon materials, so your bag should not be left in the sun for any extended period of time. Storage, between uses, should be in an area that is shaded and away from any heat source.

Whenever you return from a trip, you should check your bag quite thoroughly, both inside and outside. Remove all the contents and check the inside seams, the pockets on the outside, the zippers and the straps. Most buckles now used are not the toothed type, so they should not cause much wear on the nylon webbing used for straps. However, they should be checked to insure that they are not becoming separated, frayed or worn. If they are, they should be replaced.

Many inexpensive bags will begin to show wear in the seams after but a short time. To remedy this, you should sew along all the seams, using a sewing machine. If you ask nicely, you might even get your wife to do it for you, since you may break her sewing machine or at least you can give her the impression that you might. By sewing over the original seams, they become much tighter and stronger. This will extend the life of any bag.

Most zippers now are made of nylon and are self-healing. Should they become separated, you can run the closure back over them and they will come together. If you pull one end loose, you can use the needle-nose pliers to remove one or both of the stops on the end of the zipper and replace it on the unit replacing, of course, the stops as well. If you can't do this, you can always sew them together in an emergency.

If you tear out a zipper tooth, you can run the closure or slide to this section, and sew the zipper together so the slide won't come off. Of course, you will have limited access to that section of the bag, but at least it will remain partly closed and you can carry some articles in it.

Losing a pin or ring from the bag attachment to the frame is not too terribly important. There are three pins necessary in this type of frame-bag construction: one on the top, one on the bottom and one to hold the hold open bar to the frame. If you lose a top pin, you can replace it with one of the lower ones in a four or five pin style bag. Pins normally are not lost, but it does happen on rare occasions.

A good idea is to store your pack with all the contents in it, ready to go when you're ready for your next trip. If you have room, the best place to store your pack is in a warm

If a zipper becomes broken or torn while in the field, the zipper is moved behind the torn area, then inner threads from nylon cord are used to sew the zipper in such a way that it cannot be opened beyond stitches.

With the zipper sewn together just above the area of the tear, it still is possible to open it part way. This may not be convenient, but still is functional until such time as one reaches home and the zipper can be replaced.

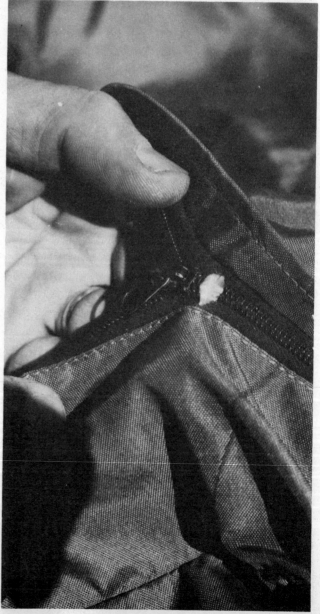

The inside threads from heavy duty 600-pound test nylon cord can be removed and used for many types of repairs to clothing, pack equipment in the field.

A nylon cord or even a rope may become frayed with use. This can be remedied by simply melting the fray with match.

The flame causes the synthetic material to melt, forming a hard shell over the cords that stops unraveling. The lariats used by today's rodo cowboys are of a similar material and are treated in same way before being used.

and dry closet. Or, if you prefer, you can make a rack for it and hang it in a closet or the garage. If you stand your pack up against a wall, the frame side should be placed against the wall, not the bag side.

One item that you should not keep in your pack is your sleeping bag. It should be removed from its stuff bag and hung over a hanger to allow air circulation.

The most important thing to remember in pack maintenance is to check your bag and frame at the end of every trip. If repairs are needed, take care of them then. It is much easier to make repairs at home, than it is in the field. However, you should always be prepared with needle, thread, adhesive nylon tape and long-nosed pliers, just in case problems should crop up while on the trail.

CLOTHES MAKE THE BACKPACKER...?

CHAPTER 6
Not Necessarily, But The Right Garb In A Specific Clime Can Add Much To Your Trip!

THERE ARE MANY factors that determine whether your backpacking trip is a success. One that often is overlooked, but has an important role, is the selection of the proper clothing. How often have you seen someone new to the outdoor life arriving at the rendevous point either overdressed or underdressed? Unfortunately, far too often.

One reason for this is that man, although he may vociferously deny the fact, is the most vain creature to inhabit this earth. We are being bombarded constantly with the "beautiful people" image...on television, in the magazines that we read...practically anywhere that we turn. Few people have not vicariously lived the experience of shooting the rapids, vividly told in photographs and text. Normally telling the story is an atractive young couple, sitting around a campfire sipping one of America's "favorite beverages." Their attire is form fitting and perfectly tailored, showing every beautiful curve and muscle with which they are so well endowed. An appealing scene for a Neiman Marcus Sporting Department ad, but their clothing is hardly practical for hiking fifteen miles over rugged, mountainous terrain.

With this constant subtle advertising campaign, it is no wonder that many beginning outdoor enthusiasts often find themselves improperly attired. Hopefully, this chapter will give some practical hints on just what clothing should or should not be taken or worn on a backpacking trip.

Clothing is a personal matter and no one person can establish any set rules on what is always appropriate and what is not. An item may work well for one person, while another may find another item that suits his needs better. Personal preference always will play a part, but in general most of the items mentioned in this chapter have proven themselves on the trail. The criteria for good backpacking clothes is that they be durable, warm and lightweight. The items discussed here have these features.

Warmth is an extremely important factor to consider in the selection of your clothing. Naturally, you can always carry plenty of clothing, but if you do, you will also have to sacrifice other items that might come in more handy on the trail. Clothing, like any other item, quickly adds up. Your goal should be the least that you can get by with, without sacrificing comfort.

Keeping warm, as mentioned in an earlier chapter, is a matter of common sense. However, there are some tricks of which many are not aware since we live in a temperature controlled world — with our central heating systems and air conditioned automobiles. For the most part, we can control

Backpacking clothes should be durable, lightweight and warm. The down jackets above meet all these requirements.

The ultimate in hiking attire for warm days could be that of the girl in the upper left photo, with a good pair of hiking boots added, of course. However, for all seasons the display shown above will meet all your needs and will easily fit in your pack (below left and middle). Below right: In using the layer system you begin with a good quality fishnet T-shirt.

the temperature to our liking. However, this is not the case in the backpacker's world.

One factor that many people fail to realize, although it's a rather obvious one, is that altitude is important to temperature. The higher that you climb, the colder you can expect it to become. Conversely, when you camp or hike in the lower desert country, you would normally expect it to be warm or even hot. However, many hikers are astounded by the cold nights they find in the arid areas.

If you are familar with the area or have hiked there before, you will generally know what to expect and can plan your clothing needs accordingly. However, if you don't know the area, you should always check with someone who is familar with the climate and seek his advice.

Even taking this precaution, with the weather being as unpredictable as it is, there is going to come a time when the conditions are going to be exactly opposite than what you had expected. If you don't believe this, ask any weather forecaster...there is no such thing as a one hundred percent correct weather forecast. Therefore, most experienced backpackers will use what is called the layer system of clothing.

Basically, the layer system is just what it sounds like... you start with basic underclothing and work up from there, one layer after another. Using this system, you either strip or add layers of clothes as the temperatures vary.

For warm weather hiking during moderate to hot temperatures, all you may want is a pair of hiking shorts

For additional warmth there are full length fishnet pants, which are warmer than the thermal underwear.

For keeping the feet warm and to protect them from blisters you should always wear two pair of socks.

and a polo-pocketed T-shirt during the day and, as the chill of the night descends, you would add slacks and a sweater or jacket.

For inclement or cold weather you will need another layer system. You would start with basic underclothing, add a second layer of the popular fishnet upper and lower garments, and then add a third layer of cotton or, preferably, wool garments. This fishnet material, which actually has large diamonds or holes in the material, acts as an air trap, keeping the air trapped between the outer layer of

wool or cotton and the body. Surprisingly, air is an excellent insulator and if you keep a layer of air trapped between the body and your outer garments, you will stay much warmer.

Thermal underwear can also be used in place of the fishnet garments. It has the disadvantage, however, of being heavier and bulkier.

If the day remains fairly moderate you may be able to get by with the fishnet garments or thermal underwear and a light cotton shirt. However, as night comes or the temper-

The second pair of wool socks provides warmth and acts as a cushion between the foot and boot.

A pair of outer wool socks, which can be ankle or knee length, completes the first layer of garments.

Beginning your second layer, you should select a pair of durable long pants. Wool pants provide the most warmth and remain warm even when wet.

Many backpackers prefer the more popular Levis, which are more than adequate, but are not as warm as wool for the more extreme temperatures.

A light, short sleeve shirt and boots complete the second layer of clothing for hiking during moderate temperatures. As it becomes colder, you can always add a sweater or a windbreaker.

ature takes a dive, you should add a heavier shirt. The best and warmest material is wool. It is heavier than cotton; however, unlike cotton, it has the advantage of staying warm even when wet. There are those who can't wear wool because of allergies or because of the itchiness of wool. For these individuals there is a combed cotton material — sometimes called chamois cloth — on the market that is excellent. Garments made from this material are normally more expensive, but are very durable and will last for years.

As mentioned earlier, your goal should be to carry the least amount of clothing that will offer maximum warmth and comfort. For example, let's assume we are on an extended trip at a moderate altitude during the fall when there is a full range of temperatures from warm days to chilly nights. You would build from the bottom layer of underclothing to the fishnet, to a wool shirt for your upper torso. Starting out in the morning this would be your basic attire. Fishnet garments are available in the long leg style, which will give you warmth for your lower torso. Again, wool pants are the warmest, but are often rather expensive. Some surplus stores have the wool pants used by the military and are excellent sources for warm hiking clothes at a moderate cost. Many hikers prefer the Levis, which are adequate and can be worn year 'round.

For colder climates and snow, you should add a down jacket, a wool hat and wool mittens. This ensemble will keep you warm under any conditions.

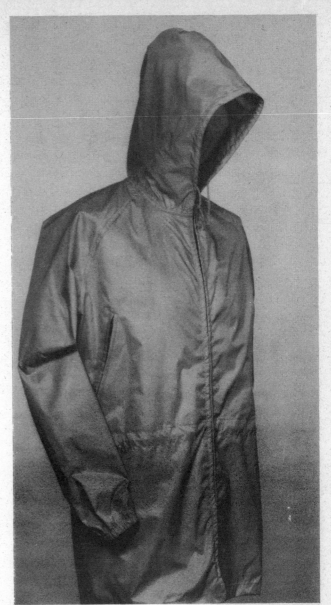

In rainy seasons or at high altitudes, a waterproof parka with a rain hood is almost a must. There are some styles that can double as a ground covering at night.

With this basic layer system of fishnet and wool, you can shed as it becomes warmer and put on a lighter shirt, or remove the fishnet altogether, if it becomes too warm. If the temperature drops, you start adding sweaters or heavier shirts to keep your upper body warm. If you are still cold after adding a heavier shirt or sweater, you should add a down jacket or windbreaker. If you use a windbreaker it should be of light nylon since lightness is important and all that you need is something to keep the chill factor down.

The legs normally do not become as cold as the arms, shoulders and chest area, so they should remain warm with the two layers that you already have, should the thermometer drop.

If there is any chance of colder temperatures, you should always carry a down jacket with you. They are light-weight and are about the warmest garment you can find. Most are made with nylon outer and inner surfaces and if the windbreaker is not enough, adding a down jacket should do the trick in almost any type of weather. As the day warms up, you can remove garments until you are back to the basic layer of garments.

One thing you should always remember is that when you move, you generate heat and when you stop this heat generation also stops. Like an athlete after a game, you should always make it a habit to put on a windbreaker or jacket when you make a trail stop. This will prevent you from getting chilled.

The body has a built-in thermostat that attempts to keep the body functioning at 98.6 degrees. If any of the internal organs become cold, the body reacts by drawing heat from

Above: Down jackets come in both men and women's
styles and varying weights. Below: Down cardigans
are extremely lightweight and provide good protection.

the extremeties such as feet or hands in order to keep the
inner body warm. The old saying, "If you want to keep
your feet warm, put on a hat," has more truth than myth
to it. This works and you can utilize this system to keep
your overall body temperature range comfortable.

The importance of socks was mentioned in the chapter
on boots; however, we will dwell upon them briefly here.
You should always use two pair of socks: a pair of heavy
wool outer socks and a pair of dry inner socks. The
outer wool socks should be long and reach almost to the
knee. With these you can pull them up to keep the lower
leg warm, or roll them down as it warms up. It is very
important to keep your feet warm and dry because if they
are cold, heat from the rest of the body will transfer to
your feet to warm them and your overall body temperature
will drop, making you cold all over. Most of us at one time
or other have experienced a chill all over when our feet
have become cold and the only way to warm up was to
start with the feet...once they were warm, we felt warmer
all over.

Wool mittens — the style with the four fingers together
— are best for keeping your hands warm. Gloves may be
adequate in mild weather, but if really in cold country,
mittens are the only thing to consider. With four fingers
together each finger can draw warmth from the other three
and the whole hand will stay warm. If it is extremely cold,
you can also slip the thumb out of its stall and place it in
with the fingers. These mittens do not allow much manual

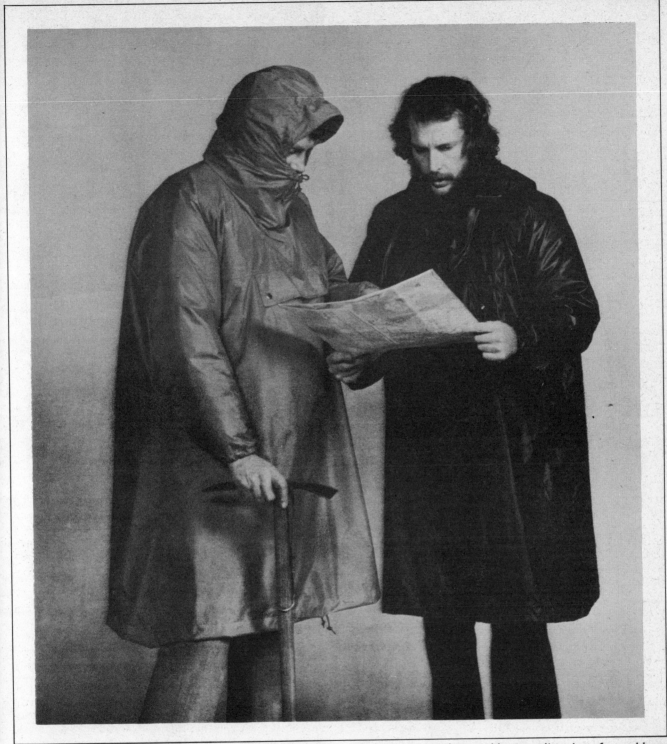

Rainshells offer the ultimate protection in rainy weather. Many styles are designed so that they will roll up and fit into their own pockets, making a small package for packing ease. Their durability offsets the cost somewhat.

dexterity, but they can always be removed if you have to adjust a strap or loosen a buckle. It is wise to use the old system of attaching the mittens to a string sewn to the sleeve of the jacket. This will prevent you from losing them and will make them readily available when you need them.

Wind is a very important factor in keeping warm. If there is little or no wind blowing it can be comfortable at a very low temperature, but add a little wind and the comfort range drops rapidly. This is called the chill factor and as a general rule of thumb, for every mile or knot of wind blow-

ing, you can subtract one degree from the temperature. For example, if the temperature is 10 degrees above and there is a ten-knot wind blowing, you would have a chill factor — temperature affecting the body — of zero degrees. The thermometer may register a temperature well within the comfort range, but with a wind blowing you will feel much colder than the mercury would indicate.

There are nylon mittens on the market that could be called windbreakers for the hands. These help prevent chafing and soreness to the hands caused by the wind.

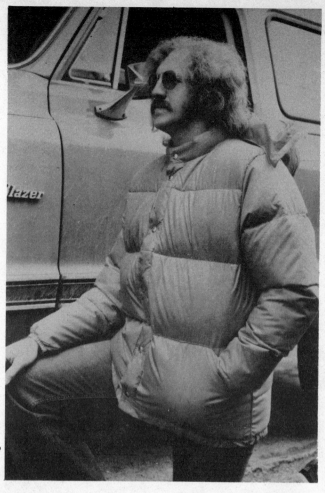

Some styles of down jackets have a hood that can be worn down (right) for warm weather and for colder weather they can be pulled up to protect the head and lower face region, leaving only the eyes and nose exposed.

Sometimes a windbreaker and wind mittens will be all you will need in order to keep warm while hiking, but you should have a jacket to put on when you stop.

If you are one of the fortunate types that do not chill easily, a down vest instead of a jacket might suffice. In fact, even with a down jacket, it is sometimes wise to also carry along a vest. These can be purchased in many styles and price ranges, but you should insist that it is long enough to cover the kidney area in the back.

A vest that comes only to the waist all around isn't worth putting in your bag: look for one that will come to the crotch. The cost is normally not that much more and it offers much more protection. An alternative is one that has a flap that extends down past the waist in the back to protect the small of the back and the kidney areas. It is your choice whether it snaps or zips.

This type of vest under a windbreaker may be all that you need in moderate temperatures. Add a down jacket and you are ready to face any weather. Some consider a vest an added item, but it is made of nylon and is not heavy or bulky.

Remember that when you are selecting clothing, you must fit all of your clothes into the pack on your back and they must last for several days. You certainly can't carry all the clothing items you might take with you on a car camping trip. Even if you go out for a several-day trip, you normally will not need a change of outer garments, slacks and shirts. You should take along a change of underclothing and perhaps an extra pair or two of socks, both the outer woolen socks and the inner lighter socks.

For example, a list of needed clothing for a fall trip without snow might look like this: Two pair of woolen socks, two pair of wick dry socks, a full set of fishnet long johns, a cotton T-shirt, a wool outer shirt, wool pants, a nylon windbreaker, a down vest, a down jacket, a floppy hat for day wear, a stocking cap for night or colder weather, nylon wind mittens, polaroid sunglasses, and a pair of hiking shorts, if you like.

Some advocates of hiking shorts feel that they are a necessity; however, if hiking in a wooded area, they can leave you with some mighty sore and scratched legs.

One item that you might consider is a pair of suspenders for holding up your pants. Many packs have a belt system for carrying the pack. The belt used with the pack and the belt normally used to hold up your pants can make a chafing point and give you sore hip bones. If you use a pair of suspenders you will have only the pack frame belt around the waist. Suspenders also allow air to circulate more freely since they don't constrict the trousers at the waist as a belt does.

You should buy your backpacking clothes with two things in mind: the amount of weight and how much warmth they provide. Fishnet garments store more compactly than thermal underwear and nylon down jackets and vests easily stuff into small areas, yet provide maximum warmth with minimum weight. If you have a choice between wool and cotton, you should always select the wool garments.

Plan your clothing needs in advance and don't take more than what will easily pack into your pack bag.

You now have protected your body from the neck to the toes, but we have not talked about any means to pro-

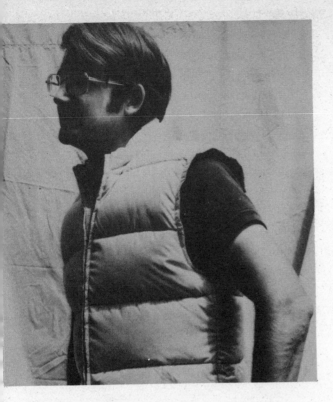

tect the head from the cold. You should always have a hat with you. For cold weather many hikers prefer the old style stocking cap that can be pulled down around the ears for protection or it can be rolled up above the ears if it becomes warmer. This again should be made of wool for the greatest warmth. Stocking caps also make excellent head warmers at night when curled up in your sleeping bag.

For those who do not like the stocking cap style, there is a ski style ear warmer on the market that many hikers prefer. These are nothing more than a band of wool that fits around the head and you can regulate the ear coverage to keep them warm or allow them to cool off. When you cover your ears you will generate more heat than what you might expect. Often just covering the tip of the ears will be enough to keep your head warm.

A hat with a brim should also be included in your clothing layout. Each person's vulnerability to sunburn differs, but even a person who tans well should take at least a baseball type cap along. However, if you are extremely tender skinned, a better hat would be the floppy style felt hats that have a full brim, but are flexible enough to be worn with the pack behind the head. If you have a ten-gallon Stetson cowboy hat, leave it at home...it is not a backpacker's hat. The stiff brim will come in contact with the pack behind you and it will be pushed down over your eyes continuously. A similar western style hat with less body could be used by pinning the brim in back a la Aussie style. This type would shade the ears and the eyes, and would certainly add a bit of flare to your outfit.

One item often overlooked and very necessary on the trail is a good pair of sunglasses. In snow country they prevent snow glare, which can cause snowblindness in extreme cases. Even without snow, sunglasses will protect you from water glare and wind. They also help prevent dust and small bits of rock from blowing into the eyes.

Today there are many styles on the market that are quite effective and moderately priced. The plastic polaroid styles are good for glare and cost very little. If you wear prescription glasses you should wear the flip style sunglasses to protect you from glare and to keep your other glasses from becoming dirty. If you hike into a very dusty area or an area where there is blowing snow, you might consider the full goggles used by skiers to protect their eyes.

One item you should consider, especially in high mountain country, is rain gear. This can range from the simple plastic poncho, which can also double as a ground cover at night, to the full two-section plastic suits with a hood attached. Afternoon showers are common in the mountains, so you should always be prepared for wet weather.

The simple poncho costs little and can be used and discarded as a disposal item. A plain plastic rain coat will keep the body dry, fold compactly and take very little room in the pack. There are rain suits on the market that cost little and have a set of trousers with suspenders and a jacket with a hood attachment. These also fold compactly and can be used once or twice and discarded. Your floppy hat might not be the best thing for rain, but it does keep your head from getting wet.

If you expect showers, you should also plan to cover your pack. Most good bags are waterproof but after considerable use, the seams will sometimes leak and the contents of the pack can become wet. This can be prevented by simply covering the entire pack with a thirty-gallon trash can liner. Two or three of these liners will fit into a pocket of the pack, taking little space or weight.

Your boots should be waterproofed with wax or similar material so the feet should remain relatively dry. If it is chilly, you can always add a vest or windbreaker under the rain gear for warmth.

Rain gear is probably the easiest item on your clothing list to forget, so you should add it to your list now and leave it in your pack, without removing it each time you return. By leaving it in the pack, you will always have it when you need it.

POINTS WELL TAKEN

CHAPTER 7

Full Knowledge Of Points Of Your Compass And Maps Can Cure That Lost Feeling!

To obtain an accurate reading with a lensatic compass care should be taken to hold the compass steady. Above is the most acceptable hold position.

HAD COLUMBUS BEEN afraid to leave the shore, he would have never discovered the new world. The same applies to you. If you are afraid to leave, in your case, the well traveled road or path, you will not discover your new world — the world of nature as it was intended to be...raw, roughed and wonderful.

However, Columbus was a wily old fellow and knew that, even with the power of the Queen of Spain behind him, he should not venture forth on a sea that supposedly ended in a bottomless pit, without some means of finding his way home. Consequently, by using the stars and a crude form of chronometer (a simple clock) he figured out a means to determine his direction.

This was probably one of the first uses of the concepts that later resulted in modern day compasses. Had he not, for all practical purposes he could well have sailed off the end of the earth, since the chances of his ever returning would have been somewhat unlikely.

As a backpacker, you should take a tip from this early explorer and never venture off the road into an unmarked area or one unknown by you without a compass and topographic map.

Often you will hear oldtimers say that they would never use a compass; that their compass is built into their heads. If this is the truth, they are fortunate. Most of us, although we may never become lost, find that there are times when we become turned around and lose our sense of direction.

With a compass, a topographic map and a bit of innate instinct, this situation can be rectified quickly. Only the very young or very foolish wander off into an unknown area without means of finding their direction should they inadvertently become "turned around."

Compasses basically fall into three classes...all of which will do the job, but some of which are a little more sophisticated.

The first type would be a simple needle with a compass rose under it in a carrying case. The case may be brass or the ever increasingly popular, plastic case; with this case housing the needle and compass rose. The metal units have a lever to dampen the swing of the needle when the hood of the case is closed. The hood is used primarily to protect the glass over the needle and at the same time keep the unit clean.

The plastic models normally will be filled with a liquid such as alcohol or glycerine, which will not freeze in extremely cold temperatures. Purpose of this liquid is to help slow the swing of the needle while taking a bearing. This is a handy time saver, but is not necessary and is not always found in your cheaper models. The price of these simpler models will run from approximately one dollar to five dollars, depending on its construction. The scale of degrees on this compass will read clockwise from zero moving around the dial to 360 degrees. This type of compass will be more than adequate if your budget is a bit tight.

Another type of compass is the military or lensatic compass. This has the same clockwise degree scale, but has the added feature of a sighting system for taking a bearing on an object at a distance. Another feature allows you to look at the scale at the base of the finder and read the bearing with the aid of a small lens in the viewfinder. This is extremely handy and this model as a rule is a better com-

A Silva Ranger model is excellent for map work. It has a declination setting that can be locked in for an area with a screwdriver. This compass usually is used by the more serious-minded off-trail hikers.

The close contour lines of the topo on the left indicates an extremely rough and high area. This is an area that should be avoided by most hikers.

pass. It does cost a few additional dollars, but some find that it is much easier to use. Others will find that the extra gadgetry only confuses them and is more of a hinderance than an aid.

The third version of the pocket compass is used by the forestry service, surveyors and other professionals. This compass has the degrees going counterclockwise on the dial and is used in a different manner than the other two types mentioned.

If you plan to do serious work in the field, or want to

By using your compass and the magnetic declination angle on the standard map (to left of the compass in the photograph) you can adjust your compass reading to find your true direction. All topos will have this diagram.

lay out lines or other map and compass problems, this compass should be your choice. This model is often called a cruiser compass. However, if you are a beginner, you are better off staying with one of the first two types described. The cruiser is mentioned only so that you can distinguish the difference should you desire to purchase a new compass and are not familar with this style.

Many beginners will purchase an excellent compass, then allow it to rest at the bottom of the pack, never used. Not only can a compass be a necessity sometimes in an unknown area, but practicing with it in a known area can become a great sport. By doing this, you become thoroughly familar with how it works and when the day comes when you really do need it, you will have no problems.

Before getting into how to use both a compass and a map, let's first discuss the simple use of a compass. This is where you want to simply get from Point A to Point B, then return to Point A. This is a relatively simple process.

Before leaving your car or base camp, remove the compass from your pocket and, holding it steady, take a reading. If you have the model with the swinging or rotating marker such as the lensatic model, you can set it to point in the direction of camp on the reciprocal heading. This means that when you leave camp, for example, you may be going north and to return to the camp, all you need to do is go south.

This sounds simple. However, once you leave the road or camp, you may not be able to travel in a straight line due to impassable creeks, downed timber or other types of obstacles. To reach your destination, you may have to go around them, in a direction that is entirely different from that which you originally intended.

If this happens you need not worry about true north or other situations you will encounter in map reading. All you need to do is follow the arrow as you lay it out. To do this, when you meet an obstacle and must go around it, take a

With a good compass and topographical map, a hiker can always find his way, no matter what terrain he encounters.

An inexpensive compass is normally all you need. This one would not be good for map work, since scale is in five-degree increments. It will get one from point A to B, however.

reading on the compass; move approximately one hundred steps or whatever it takes to get around the obstacle; clear the obstacle and use the reciprocal heading to return the one hundred steps or more to the original line of direction.

You may not have to count your steps if you have a good landmark to use for direction; however, if you don't, you may forget to use the compass and you may find yourself in deep trouble. The landmark may become obscured by fog, a hill, a line of trees or almost anything that can block your view.

If you do not know how far you have gone off course, it is difficult to get back to the original line of direction, especially if the landmark you have chosen is no longer visible by the time you are able to to get around the obstacle. It is always best to use your compass and if, when you get around the obstacle, you still can see your landmark, well and good: You will have a double check. Once back on the original line of direction you can continue on your way.

There are no set rules for the use of compasses, but the one discussed is the easiest and the best for just getting from one point to another without using a topographic map. The use of a compass in conjunction with a map will be discussed later in this section.

Many backpackers are afraid of becoming lost in the mountainous areas, because they are so vast and are rarely traveled. Here you can spend the entire outing without ever seeing another person, which is what backpacking is all about in the first place. So mountainous areas should not be avoided strictly because of a fear of becoming lost. This is why you have a compass and if it is used properly, you should have no difficulty finding your way no matter what the terrain.

Other hikers prefer the mountainous areas, because should they be in a forest area for awhile, when they come out into a clearing they can use the mountains as a land-

mark. When they went into the forest the peak was on the left for example, and upon emerging into a clearing it is now in front or to the right of them. By zeroing in on the mountain and hiking in that direction, they can find their way back to their original line of direction.

These people also should use their compasses, because if you do much backpacking at all, there is going to come a time when there is nothing in the terrain that can be used as a landmark. In this situation, the only thing that is going to get you heading back in the right direction is a compass.

A phenomenon which often occurs and can give a backpacker some trouble, is that anything that is iron or steel in your pack can have an effect on the needle in your compass. If you carry an ax or anything with a large mass of iron close to the front of your pack where it is near your compass, it can throw your compass reading off. Most pack frames are made of aluminum and will not affect the needle, but anything that is of iron or steel in the pack definitely will, if too close to the compass.

Should you find yourself continuously ending up to the right of your objective, you should check whether you have something metallic on the right side of your pack. If so, it should be moved to the back center where it will not affect the needle. This metal mass deviation should not be confused with compass declination, which will be covered later. The deviation is an error in your compass reading caused by an abundance of natural ore in the area, or as mentioned, a metallic mass in your pack.

This deviation of the needle works by the inverse square law theory. This means that, if the metal object is one foot from the compass, it will deviate quite a bit and be obvious to the user. However, if the metal object is two feet away, it will exert four times less attraction on the needle and the needle will not swing in its direction quite as noticeably.

If you move the object three feet behind you, it would then have nine times less attraction, so it would be barely or not at all noticeable.

If your compass continues to behave erratically, check

A simple direction compass with a folding cover is the type used by most backpackers. The cover protects the sensitive insides from dust and dampness.

for metal in your pack and, if there is none, then you can assume that the needle is being affected by a natural ore deposit in the area.

Stars are another means to determine your direction and they can be helpful in checking the accuracy of your compass. If you are out after dark on a clear night, you can check the compass deviation by finding the North Star and sighting the compass on an object or imaginary object at the base of the star. If the needle is not pointing north on the dial, however many degrees you are off is your compass

Compasses come in all styles and price ranges, and the style you select should depend upon your needs and budget. A simple one is quite adequate for the beginner.

Higher priced compasses will have added features and will normally have a cover to protect the rose. A cover is not absolutely necessary, however.

*When inadvertently turned around, it's time for
a short break and a quick session with your compass
and map. With these you will soon be back on course.*

deviation and you can adjust your direction accordingly.

Some compasses have luminous dials for night use, but, if yours does not, you shouldn't worry. Luminous dials are fine for military night maneuvers, but for the average person lost at night, the last thing he should do is to move. It is best to make yourself as comfortable as possible and wait for morning, unless, of course, an emergency necessitates your trying to find help.

A compass that is going to be of any use should have a graduation of degrees not less than units of two. A graduation of one degree is difficult to read and one that is five degrees will not be accurate enough, but will have a variation that will throw you off your target point.

The most common style of compass used by backpackers is the pocket compass, but there also is a wrist compass available. A disadvantage of this style that you might want to consider is that it becomes covered by your jacket and is difficult to read. There is also the possibility that it might be caught on a limb and be pulled off without your knowing it. In fact, it might not be a bad idea to carry two compasses in case one might get lost.

Some compasses have grid scales that can be placed on a map for reference. These are helpful, but for the compass to have them it must be bigger and the larger size is sometimes more of a hinderance than what the grid lines are worth.

MAPS AND WHAT TO DO WITH THEM

Almost daily somewhere across the nation the following headline appears in a newspaper: *Missing Hiker Found*

After Intensive Four-Day Search. You could well be this hiker, and unless you are particularly desirous of this type of instant notoriety, it would pay to learn something about map reading, along with learning how to use the compass.

To most of us, reading a road map presents no great problem. However, the map used in backpacking has little similarity to the common road map that you can pick up at your local gas station.

Of course, there are some similarities. For example, both may show the same roads and towns, but the backpacker's map shows a great deal more...it shows the actual topography of the area.

Most backpackers use a topographic or United States Geological Survey map, often referred to as USGS topos. This type of map offers the hiker all the information he needs to find his way in the back country, and they are easily obtainable.

A word of caution concerning these maps: Often these topographic maps are ten years or older and do not show current roads or other man-made structures. Should you be hiking and run into a road that is not on your map, don't be concerned; chances are the road was built after the map was published.

Naturally, it is a help if they do contain the roads, and many maps will; however, the primary purpose of a topographic map is to show the contours of the terrain. They are made from aerial photographs of the area and by using stereoscopic viewing methods and special machines, map makers are able to project the actual contour lines on the map. Topographical map making is a rather complicated

*Some topos will indicate distance in both miles and feet,
as well as contour intervals. The magnetic declination
diagram is also shown very clearly in the map above.*

procedure and a discussion of it has little place here.

When looking at a topographical map, in the lower left-hand corner you will find the date that the aerial photograph was taken. You will find that many are made in the mid-Fifties and early Sixties and one should keep this in mind when moving over unknown terrain. The rivers, streams, hills, valleys and mountains will be shown, but more than likely many of the present roads and other man-made structures will not appear. Use the map for determining the terrain, and shift with the roads and other structures as you come upon them. One time through the area and you will be familiar with these also.

The U.S. Forest Service and the Bureau of Land Management (BLM), also publish maps, but many times these will not have the contour lines. They will have streams and drainage systems, but not the contour lines of the terrain.

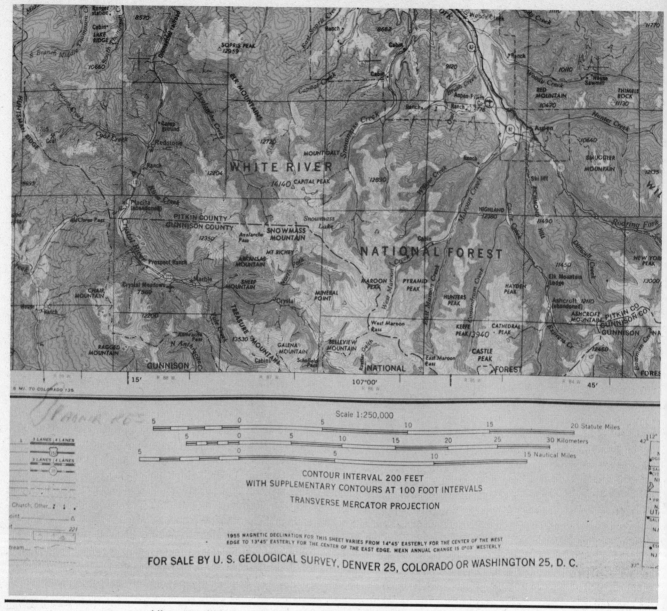

All topos will have a distance scale in the lower margin.
These normally are in either feet or miles; however,
some maps will have both measurements for more convenience.

These should be used only when the other type of maps with contour lines are not available.

Many stores that carry engineering supplies will carry topographic maps of various areas; and some sporting goods stores in small towns will have them for their local area. However, you should not rely upon these sources, but should plan ahead and order your maps through the offices listed at the end of this chapter. In ordering these maps you should always remember to give the exact quadrant or area you need.

An inexperienced map reader may be overwhelmed when he first looks at a topographic map. To him the map looks like a bunch of mysterious squiggly brown and green lines drawn in no apparent pattern. However, with a little knowledge these soon begin to take on some meaning.

The first thing you should check is that you have a map of the right area, which is written in the lower right-hand corner of the map. Maps are normally named by landmarks

or particular areas: for example, Cannibal Plateau, Colorado quadrant. Just left of the quadrant name is a map of the state in which the section map appears and a dot that represents where the section is located within the state map.

Moving to the left of this, there is the scale for that particular map. These scales run from 1:1,000,000, a small scale map, to one of 1:20,000, a very large scale map. There will be a distance line marked off in scale for miles or feet and in some cases both. This is an aid in plotting map distances before starting out. For example, prior to leaving, you can determine your night's campsite by using the maps to plot the distance and your average miles covered per day.

An important item on the map is the magnetic declination diagram normally shown in the margin towards left of the map. This will have a star with a straight line representing the North Star and a line to the right of it or left of it, depending on the area, to denote the magnetic declination

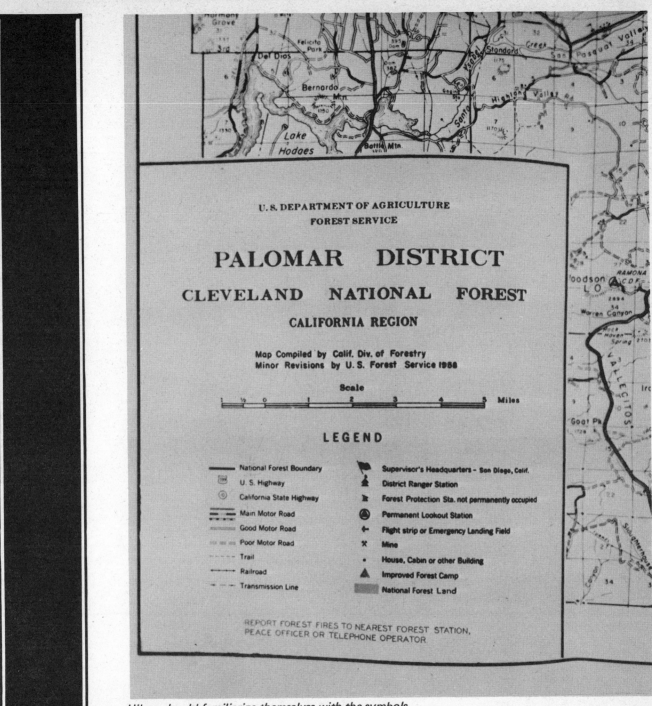

Hikers should familiarize themselves with the symbols used on the particular map that they are using. All maps will have a legend in the lower margin. To save time on the trail, you should study them before starting.

you must apply to correct your compass in order to use the map for true headings. Another line with a GN will also appear, which represents the Geographic North. The North Star is actually one degree to the east.

The diagram is used to compute your true direction by compass on that particular map. There are a few basic rules to follow in order to do this.

To change magnetic to true heading you will add east declination and subtract west declination. If you want to convert from true to magnetic, you will subtract east and add west. This appears confusing, so let's use a map of a western state as an example. The topographic map has a

declination angle at the bottom of the page, which shows true north by using a star and a straight line, as mentioned above. The declination for this particular area for example, shows a fourteen-degree east declination from true north. A reading with the compass will give a magnetic north and, if this is followed, you would end up fourteen degrees too far east. To convert magnetic north on the compass to coincide with true north on the map, add fourteen degrees to whatever reading is obtained on the compass and you will be back on course.

Along the edges of the map will be latitude and longitude markings, but the hiker will have little need for these

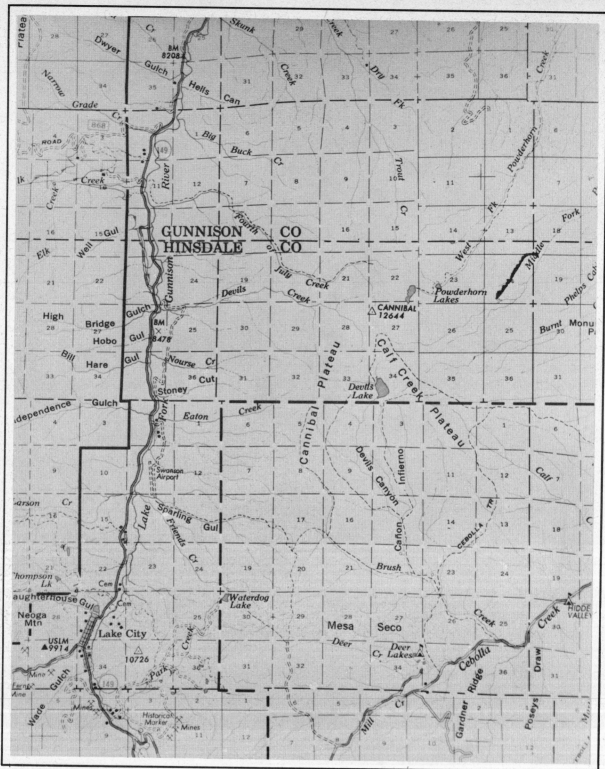

Maps published by the U. S. Forest Service are handy, but they do not have the contour lines that are contained on the topographical maps. They can be used, but to get a true picture of the terrain, a topo is much better.

markings.

In the middle section along the edge will be the name of the next quadrant that matches your map. If you plan a long hike or one that may take you into the adjacent quadrant you should have both quadrant sections with you. These can be cut and taped together to make one large map or they can be used individually.

On the face of the map, one will find the actual terrain markings. These will show you the features of the terrain such as streams, peaks, rivers and forests. In addition, once you have learned how to read the contour lines, you will be able to predetermine the slope of the terrain, which is the beauty of a topographic map. It saves one from hiking many miles only to find that you have run into an impassable peak or cliff. By using the contour lines, one can plot his course to go around these obstacles prior to setting out

Small scale maps will give a large area, but are difficult
to read. Sometimes it is better to get large scale sections
of the same area. These can be taped together or used singly.

and this can save many miles of backtracking.

In looking at a topographic map, you will notice that areas are shaded in various colors. These colors play an important function in map reading. Black stands for man-made objects, such as roads, towns and buildings. Blue represents rivers, creeks, lakes and other bodies of water, as well as permanent snow and ice. The color, brown, is used for all contour lines, except those in an area of permanent snow and ice. A darker brown line is used for altitude checks and will have the altitude written in small print alongside the line. An area shaded in green represents a forest area, with lighter shades of green used for a sage or lighter foliage area. A tufted green area indicates marshes or a swamp area. Red is used for subdivision boundaries and more important roads.

A quick look at a topographic map will tell you where the timber is; where the water and roads are; and with a careful study of the contour lines, you can determine the steep areas that should be avoided.

When the brown contour lines are close together and it's difficult to tell them apart, it means that you are looking at a virtual cliff face. Unless you are a rock climber, this would be an area to avoid.

Where the contour lines are farther apart, it means the slope is more gradual and the walking should be easy.

By using these contour lines and taking compass bearings before setting off on your jaunt, you can preplan your entire trip.

Should you get turned around, a good way to find your location is to check the contour high points on your map (peaks), then look around you for these peaks. By using them as a reference, you can determine where you are in relation to your map. You should use two or more check points, since this will enable you to better pinpoint your actual location.

Topographic maps also show jeep roads, pack trails and some even include hiking trails. There will be times when you find a trail that is not shown on the map. The reason for this is that often where there is too much traffic on a particular trail, these trails will be left off the map in order to help lighten the traffic in the interest of ecology.

By preplanning with a topographic map, you can mark

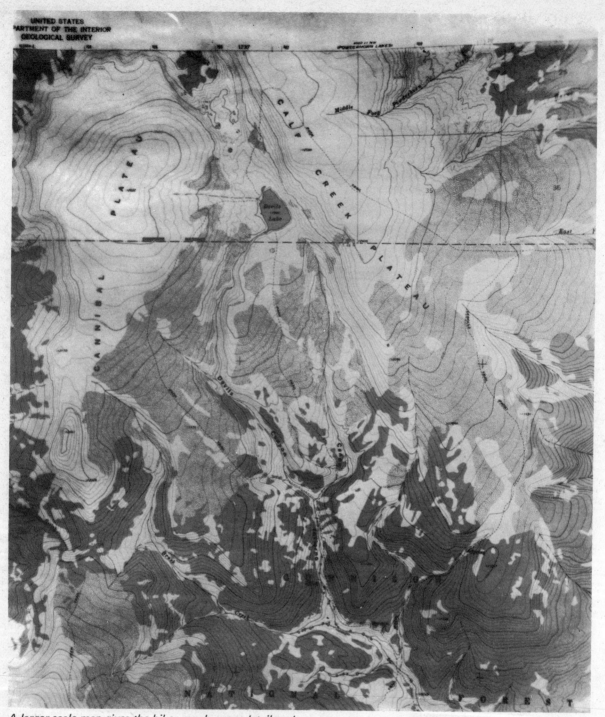

A larger scale map gives the hiker much more detail and a better idea of the terrain. The map above is a large scale, which shows the contour lines very clearly.

each day's hike before you leave. However, if you plan to camp at a stream shown on your map, take along a canteen and keep it filled anyway. These streams can be dry during certain times of the year or it may have dried up completely since the map was made. You should never rely completely upon your map without obtaining current information from other sources. A good source would be a local game warden or forestry service office in the area where you plan to hike. It is also a good idea to check in with them and let them know who you are, where you plan to go; how long you plan to be there. If something should happen and you are late in returning, there will be someone

in the immediate area who might become alarmed and come looking for you. With this in mind, be sure to advise them when you are leaving their area.

Much of the back country is laced with trails. These often are marked on your map, but there are times when they are not, for various reasons. Ranchers will use trails to move their livestock and these normally are not marked on the map, but often are confused as hiking trails. If you are somewhat familar with the area they are no problem. If not, be careful not to take one, thinking it's the hiking trail on your map and wander way off course.

As stated earlier, topographic maps are made from aerial

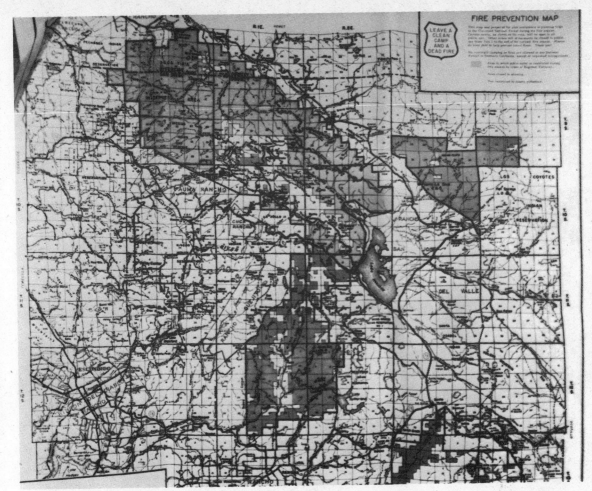

The Forestry Service map above shows the drainage
system of the area, but without the contour lines of
a topo, it gives too little information on terrain.

photographs of an area. If you have the interest and the time, you can purchase such aerial photographs before your trip. These usually will be about nine inches square and will be sent to you as a contact print. There is a data section at the bottom of the photograph, but that is all the reference material there is.

You can take two of these vertical prints and by using a stereoscopic viewer you can see the full area in a three-dimensional view. This can be helpful if you know how to read aerial photographs, but for the average hiker they are difficult without some training. However, the aerial view affords an idea of what goes into making a topographic map. It takes hundreds of photographs to make one topographic map, so it could turn into a costly project if you attempt to get all the photographs for a large area.

The following are sources where you can obtain maps — for USGS Maps east of the Mississippi River:

Washington Map Distribution Center,
U.S. Geological Survey,
1200 Eads Avenue,
Arlington, Virginia 22202

For USGS Maps west of the Mississippi River:

U.S. Geological Survey,
Federal Center, Building 41,
Denver, Colorado 80225

If you don't know the exact quadrant area you need, you should ask for the index of the state in which you are interested. USGS will send an index map that has all the quadrants available in that state. When you receive this

larger map, which is too small a scale for use, you can pinpoint the area you need and order it by quadrant designation. It takes time, so you should plan well in advance. The quadrant maps cost about fifty cents each.

Another source of maps, although they are not topographic maps, is the Department of Agriculture. These are used by the Forest Service, which is more interested in land management than in terrain features, so they do not have the contour lines. They do show access roads and all man-made structures, however.

These maps are free of charge from specific national forests, wilderness areas and range districts. To obtain the maps you should ask for brochure No. FS-13, "Field Offices of the Forest Service." This brochure contains the ten regional offices from which maps may be obtained. These are usually in short supply, so be reasonable in your request. The address is:

U.S. Dept. of Agriculture,
Forest Service,
Washington, D. C. 20250

If the use of aerial photographs sounds interesting to you, they may be obtained from the Map Information Office, U.S. Geological Survey, Washington, D.C. 20242. You should ask for the free publication, "Status of Aerial Photography." This booklet will tell you where to obtain the photographs. They are often in the hands of the company who contracted for the aerial photographic work and the prints must be made on order, so you should allow plenty of time for them to arrive.

CHAPTER 8

FEEDING THE INNER FURNACE

ON A SATURDAY MORNING of vivid greens and browns under a startlingly clear and cloudless sky, the weekend backpacker leaves the weather-beaten forestry station, crunches across its gravel parking lot and trudges down a shadow-speckled slope toward the crystalline stream he will try to follow to its source.

Myriad items of clothing, bedroll, maps, first-aid kit and canteen dangle from the aluminum frame or bulge the sack to its seams as another week-long city dweller joins the continually swelling ranks of those discovering a new world of recreation and pleasure in the out-of-doors.

The dream of stolen minutes at his desk in the shiny, glass and steel cocoon has come alive, and the backpacker is off to face the elements with only what he carries on his back to give him that surviving edge over every obstacle his chosen mountain can throw across his path.

As close to nature as he will come, the backpacker is still, in a sense, a machine. His body will take in fuel, in the form of the food he will eat, and break that fuel down and convert it to heat that will enable him to fight off the chilling effects of high altitude. From that basic fuel also will come the energy he needs to top off that final forty-degree slope to the level clearing where he will spend his first night of freedom.

If the backpacker is knowledgeable and experienced in the hazards he may face, and has stocked his fuel supply accordingly, it is almost certain that he will find little to stop his complete enjoyment of the wilderness world he

Trail End Charlie loads up cans for the long trek.

prefers. He could find himself facing unnecessary danger if he does not.

The backpacker should pay at least as much attention to planning his trail menu as he does deciding what to have for supper each day after work. There is one critical difference in how he will make his culinary decisions — he must take into account the fact that four sturdy walls and central heating are conspicuously lacking at a mountain campsite. This means that the health-conscious, perhaps dieting city dweller must become the voracious glutton who will burn off what might otherwise be considered excess calories, feeding the ravenous internal furnace that will keep his body at a healthy temperature in spite of the night's cooling mountain air.

The body moisture he lost as he sweated his way up a shifting, rocky slope or eased his awkward weight around a glassy, wet rock face, must be replaced or the backpacker could find himself facing the effects of dehydration and, possibly, heat prostration.

A human body exposed to wind, rain and the colder temperatures of the higher altitudes can require as much as four times the amount of nourishment needed to sustain it at sea level and in the milder climes. Away from his protective apartment, the hiker's natural heating system will radiate away heat ten times faster than normal as he struggles

Preparing for a long stay in the wilds means turning to the light weight and compactness of freeze-dried or dehydrated supplies to fuel heat-producing inner furnace.

Mealtime On The Trail Can Be The Day's Healthiest Highpoint

Most freeze-dried dishes use two-to-three cups of water. A water bag, used by backpackers, holds 3-5 gallons.

*Hearty trailside meals give family hikers necessary
energy to meet the demands of outdoor recreation.*

up a steep incline and fights off the chilling effect of clothing dampened by a sudden, brief rainstorm.

On his present weekend jaunt, the backpacker can easily
meet his dietary needs with the canned meats, vegetables
and fruits he picked up on his way home from work Friday
evening. His favorite cheese spread and a package of crackers will give him a quick source of protein and a bread
substitute to munch while he waits for his dinner to heat.
On the trail, he can maintain his energy levels by snacking
on the small packages of raisins, dried fruit, beef jerky and
candy he stuck in various handy pockets before leaving his
car.

He won't be going far in the brief time he has and he can
set an easy pace on the smoother stretches, so he doesn't
have to worry about the bulkiness and heavy weight of
canned goods. He has also offset the constant weight problem of all backpackers by eliminating the need to carry
pots, pans and plates. His canned meal can be cooked in its
own container and eaten right from the can with the plastic
fork and spoon that fit handily in his shirt pocket. Cutting
jobs will be handled with his pocketknife. When he finishes
his meal, cleanup chores will be a simple matter of tossing
the empty can in the fire to soften it, making it easy to
flatten and drop in the bottom of his pack to be carried out
on the return trip to civilization.

When he throws that last stick of wood on the fire and
rolls up in his sleeping bag, the backpacker feels the con-
tentment of a full stomach and will sleep comfortably
through the night's temperature drop as his body furnace
breaks down its replenished fuel supply to keep him toasty
and relaxed until breakfast time.

In the morning, after starting the day with a hot meal
simply prepared, the weekend woodsman can leave his
campsite in almost the same state he found it. To break

camp, he just buries the ashes of his morning fire, slips hi
eating utensils back in his pocket, drops the empty can
from breakfast into his pack and sets off down the trai
toward home, thinking about what a great weekend he'
had and how he really will find that stream source when he
takes his vacation this year.

Canned goods have seen the weekend backpacke
through nicely, but a month from now when his vacation
comes due and he sets out to find the source of that stream
in earnest, the problems he will have to consider and the
answers he finds for them will be radically different.

With additional clothing, tent, emergency supplies and
perhaps, a few luxuries like a citizen band radio, weigh
begins to become a critical factor in the amateur explorer'
calculations of what and how much he will be able to take
along on this extended expedition.

One area where he may be able to cut down his weight
worries is in the type and form of the foods he will need.
The experienced backpacker knows that an adverse environment, such as the cooler air of the mountains or the radica
temperature extremes of the desert, is no place to skimp on
the basic proteins, carbohydrates and fats his body requires,
not just to stay in good shape, but even to survive the rigors
of the out-of-doors. At the same time he can hardly consider it practical to cram a three or four-week supply of
groceries into the nooks and crannies left by the shoulder-
numbing array of gear he already must fit in a one-man
pack.

Though canned goods might be a good way to meet the
necessities for the first couple of days, they will probably
take up too much room to be truly efficient as the backpacker settles into the third or fourth day of his odyssey
and his appetite increases accordingly.

At this point, the would-be one-man Lewis and Clark

Crackers and cheese spreads, sausages give protein; raisins, dried prunes are quick-energy trail snack.

Most sporting goods stores stock freeze-dried or dehydrated foods for long-range hunters, hikers and campers. Choices range from steak to chicken, dessert.

begins to think hard about all the conveniences he's struggling to get away from. He knows he is going to be out in the wilds, far away from his well-stocked refrigerator and the local supermarket. He can hardly pick up the phone and call his favorite Chinese restaurant for egg rolls to go; even if he had a phone, just thinking about the long-distance charges would kill any chance he had of enjoying his hard-earned vacation. He's going to be doing all his own cooking, but he does that anyway, with little trouble thanks to modern developments like instant potatoes, powdered soup and dehydrated — hmm.

Check the cupboard, he thinks. Freeze-dried peas and corn, dried fruit from last weekend's hike; even powdered cake mix — don't really need that. Nobody is going to haul a gas range up any mountain trail just to make a cake that will go bad in a couple of days. Efficient simplicity is the key.

Make a list. What is available? Is dehydrated meat worth the trouble? Do they make this type of food just for back-packers? Who carries the stuff and how do they distribute it? Call Jerry; he makes his living climbing mountains. Wait a minute. A quick finger stroll through the yellow pages and a couple of calls to local sporting goods stores gives most of the needed answers.

Sure, he is told, there are a dozen or more companies that process and distribute freeze-dried food packs. Some sell their products through retail outlets, such as a sporting goods store or market; some deal directly through the mail; and some use both channels.

Buying off the shelf gives the prospective Daniel Boone a chance to see what he is getting before he pays for it and also means that he will have it in his hot little hands as soon as he can arrange the necessary financing. If dealing with a mail-order company, the camper will have to plan his excursion well in advance as most of the mail-order houses can take as long as four weeks or more to deliver the goods. Another disadvantage of shopping through the mail is that some companies will substitute items they do not have in stock with some oddball tidbit that does not even go with beef stroganoff, or whatever the original order included.

Whether prowling the local market or ordering by mail, the long-distance hiker will find that there are about as many varieties from which to choose as there are palates to make the choice. This includes endless combinations of individual dishes or prepackaged dinners for two to six people. A freeze-dried dinner can include every course from soup, entree, salad, main dish and vegetables to a variety of desserts, including milkshakes.

Chicken, fish and even steak can all be included in the long-distance explorer's menu, along with rice, beans, corn, apples, blueberries and noodles with their flavors enhanced by fruit sauce or gravy.

These freeze-dried edibles come in forms ranging from simple ones in which you just add boiling water and wait to complex culinary operations that require two or more cooking pots, three forest fires and a series of complex mixings that could give a chemistry major a nervous breakdown and send the average camp cook weeping into the brush. Obviously, the backpacker with a hearty appetite is going to think twice before tackling a seven-course dinner while isolated high in the Sierras, but the trail gourmets of the boondocker set may find their heart's desire in reconstituting turkey tetrazzini or shrimp creole over a pile of fire-blackened rocks with just water and their handy-dandy spice tray from which to work.

The big decision the backpacker will have to make is how much trouble he wants to take to fix his meals, how long after quitting the trail he can wait to eat and how many pots and pans he is willing to wash up afterwards.

The true culinary connoisseur of the woods might well be willing to lug the extra weight of pots, pans, griddle, ladle and tasting spoon as he goes jangling and clanking through the trees, but the rescue party that has to go in after him when he collapses from exhaustion might not

for example, which boasts a beef stew dinner for four, costing about $3.50, while a can of similar stew might cost seventy-nine cents at the local grocer. The difference is that the four-climber dinner might weigh sixteen ounces, while the can could drag the hiker down with as much as five extra pounds in his pack.

There are some less expensive brands, but this gets into another area where home experimentation can pay off before the backpacker on an extended trip has to live with, or think he would rather die than eat, the results of modern science.

Many of the economical brands can result in palate-pleasing experiences when their printed directions are observed, despite the camper's temptation to anticipate preparation times and dig in before the food is properly cooked. One way to avoid ruining what could otherwise be the high point of an invigorating day is to lean hard on trail munchies, such as candy or fruit, and to have some high-protein or energy snack handy, like cheese spread and crackers, when the distraction of setting up camp has diminished and hunger pangs start to gnaw. The quick fixing of powdered chicken noodle soup or a hot cup of instant tea or coffee with a hefty lacing of sugar can do a lot of appetite appeasing while the main dish is being pre-

Freeze-dried dishes are available as either full course meals for two-to-six hungry backpackers or as on-the-trail snacks. Some can be eaten cooked or dry.

appreciate having to carry him and all his cooking gear back down the mountain.

To avoid falling into this beginners' trap and to have some idea of how the miracle goop is going to turn out, it might be a good idea to try preparing some of the freeze-dried dinners at home, where there is always the family fridge to provide the necessaries for a filling Dagwood sandwich if the grand experiment fails. If nothing else, the gastric results of such a recourse should be enough to take the would-be trail chef's mind off the tremendous bundle of loot he blew on the mess that is now oozing all over the top of his stove.

The cost of the new freeze-dried comestibles is one of their serious drawbacks. As a comparison, it is not uncommon to find a foil packet from Mountain House or Seidel's,

pared. The hot liquids can also help a sweaty hiker offset the effects of dehydration as he rests in the cooling mountain air after a long march.

Something to keep a sharp eye peeled for when stalking the supermarket aisles to stock up on supplies for the hazardous trek is the validity of the portion sizes that are listed on each company's freeze-dried offering. While some dishes accurately predict that the reconstituted chicken and rice or whatever will comfortably fill the camper's inner recesses, most firms that process these products fail to consider the appetite-sharpening elements of fresh air and vigorous exercise.

A workable rule of thumb is to buy double the recommended portions; if the packet claims enough for two, buy for four, etc. This can mean double the number of foil

George Modern Convenience hauls along everything, including kitchen sink.

Some freeze-dried meals can be elaborate culinary chores while others need only boiling water. The camp cook can decide how many pots he or she wants to carry up the hill.

envelopes pouching out the contours of the hiker's pack, but this situation can be alleviated by repacking the purchased ingredients in larger plastic bags. Be sure to tape the correct label and directions to the right plastic bag of unidentifiable powder or granules when repacking, or certain inevitable problems — like broiled chicken covered with powdered gravy that turns out to be lime jello — may arise.

The hard-core individualists of the backpacking fraternity may decide to try mixing separate dishes in various unheard-of combinations. This may certainly cut down on the number of four-man dinner packets that will have to be fitted in a limited amount of room and could give the backpacker a way to save a little money on the necessary. This is, however, another phase of individual experimentation

that should be carried out prior to leaving home for the outer reaches before the experimenter's best intentions change him from the clean-shaven epitome of youth and cheerfulness into a creature that bursts from the dim, dark forest, covered with hair and mad at the world. All the mouthwash and antacid lozenges in the world will not help a victim of reconstituted sweet-and-sour sauce accidentally mixed into the eggs Benedict.

In deciding what kinds of food to take, the backpacker cannot dismiss the possibility that an emergency situation may keep him out of touch with civilization longer than he plans to stay. A broken leg, sprained ankle or unexpected severe weather conditions may block him from a timely return to a place where he can replenish depleted food supplies.

Such a situation can be easily faced by the well-prepared backpacker. Having listened with a smile to the old-timers who disdain the use of modern foodstuffs in favor of more familiar iron rations, the contemporary woodsman still remembers how his grandfather told of American Indians sustaining themselves on the move against cavalry troop expeditions for months at a time on a ground corn substance the old man called Rockhominy.

Early settlers, he is told, used Rockhominy as a bread substitute on their long journeys across the plains and over snow-covered mountains, and explorers kept their packloads to a minimum by carrying Rockhominy as their basic food supply. Corn is not a complete food, though, he is warned. Diseases such as pellagra plagued early mountaineers who depended too much on corn bread and pork.

Used as a basic food, trail munchy or emergency ration, though, Rockhominy is hard to beat for a lightweight, easy to prepare, yet filling means of meeting dietary needs on the trail. A mouthful with water or eaten dry will absorb moisture in the stomach and provide a comfortably full feeling between meals. For a hot meal, Rockhominy can be used to make a thick, hot mush that will release its energy gradually and prevent the hiker from growing tired while on the march. A handful of dried fruit and a little Rockhominy could be the ultimate in high-energy yielding trail munchies.

With a couple of quiet questions around a late-night fire, the budding explorer learns that Rockhominy is easy to make and to keep on the trails. The dried, shelled corn can be purchased at any health food store at a negligible price. The corn kernels are toasted in the oven at 350 degrees for about thirty minutes, or until they are the color of crisp bacon. The corn is allowed to cool, then is crushed by whatever convenient means falls to hand. The crushed bits should be small enough to swallow, but not ground to dust. Once prepared in this fashion, the Rockhominy can be stored and carried in whatever container the hiker chooses. Parching the corn in the oven bakes out replaceable water, thus removing excess weight, and precooks the corn to give it a nutlike flavor. The drying effect of the heat acts as a preservative, so the hiker does not have to take any special precautions in storing the Rockhominy until it is needed.

Another trick the more experienced trailhounds might pass on to beginners is a high-fat-yielding drink known as Grand Canyon Java or Sherpa tea. Fat, one of the three basic fuel sources for the inner body furnace, seems to be the hardest nutritional requirement to fill on the trail. Only pemmican meal seems to provide adequate supplies of fat, and then only in the jerky-fat version, not in the nut-fruit variety. Grand Canyon Java can provide this missing, needed fat in a hot liquid that gives the hiker a quickly prepared source of external heat in addition to satisfying body fuel requirements.

This trail concoction can be prepared by mixing an ounce of powdered milk, an ounce of sugar and an ounce of margarine with a sprinkle of instant coffee. The dry ingredients can be mixed prior to embarking for the hills and the margarine carried in a squeeze tube. Heated in a cup of water, Grand Canyon Java can be the quick-filling warm-up to the evening meal that gives the hungry camper the patience to let his regular meal cook thoroughly before eating, instead of chomping down some half-raw glop.

Another appetite appeaser for the iron-ration set might be the Breakfast Bar made by the Carnation Company. Designed to provide twenty-five percent of recommended daily nutritional allowances when eaten with an eight-ounce glass of whole milk, a Breakfast Bar could serve as either an on-the-trail snack or as the appetizer to the evening meal.

One item that is sometimes overlooked by the backpacker in planning his trail menu is some form of bread substitute. This can be important, not only from a nutritional point of view, but in terms of convenience as well. Bread can be an important source of energy and the starch which can provide needed carbohydrates to the inner body furnace. Small sandwiches, made with the wide variety of canned meat spreads available can be a quick, palate-pleas-

ing relief from the drier forms of trail munchies. Such meat spreads are packaged in containers that are small enough and light enough to be relatively inoffensive to the weight-conscious backpacker.

With this answer to trail chow needs comes the problem of keeping the bread in an edible state on the long cross-country trek. Most commercial loaves will harden or grow great, green beards of mold before the first week on the trail has passed. So, the long-distance woodsman must turn to other sources for the necessary nutritional elements and the conveniences of sandwich makings.

One answer that many hikers in the western parts of the country turn to is the corn or flour tortilla passed on to them by their neighbors to the south.

To prevent the same storage problems that preserving regular bread would present, the tortilla toters can premix the basic ingredients of flour or cornmeal, baking powder, shortening, and salt, store them in a plastic bag and wait until mealtime to add water and cook.

For the trailhound who wants to keep such baking chores to a minimum, there are ready-made crackers, cookies and breadsticks which offer the same carbohydrates but may be too small to make a man-sized sandwich. The choice, again, boils down to how much work the outdoorsman is willing to put into feeding his face while roughing it in the uncharted wilds.

Once all major and minor culinary decisions have been made, the prospective prospector must then figure out how to fit his exotic masterpieces in among his extra clothing, boots, compass and comic books. While repacking his collection of foil packets into more convenient sizes, the backpacker must consider how many hungry hikers will be feeding at each meal — if he is alone, the individual commercial packets may suit him perfectly — and the order in which each meal will be served. The first night's offering should go in last, so as to be on top.

The camper who manages to arrange his menu so that it

Fat Mr. Hungry's diet could slim him down to a skeleton.

Commercial trail snacks can help tired hiker over hill.

One small tip on timing might be to heat the instant coffee or tea in one pot first for a quick, right-off-the-trail warm-me-up, while the main meal is bubbling to palate-pleasing completion in the second pot; then reuse the first pot to put any desired after-meal treat on the fire while the camp chef kicks back to enjoy his culinary efforts and unkink the muscles he knotted up on that last tricky bit of cliff face.

A teapot or nonelectric coffee pot might seem to be an unnecessary frill to some would-be mountaineers, but to the caffeine or tannic acid addict it might well be a mandatory item which could relieve the impatient cook of the necessity of waiting for half his cookware to be freed so he can prepare his favorite dessert. It might also give the tired camper the provision of that all-important after-the-meal cup of coffee with which to relax while recounting the triumphs of the day.

Properly planned, these little esthetic considerations can do much to contribute to the backpacker's enjoyment of his vacation. Left to chance, or the whims of the moment, they can pile up on the order of that boating adage, "Every-

Some camp cooks are professional procrastinators and can put off clean-up until residue is crusted to pot. Eventually, though, the washing will have to be done.

requires the least amount of preparation is still going to have to deal with one unavoidable problem. Having eliminated the weight and bulkiness of canned goods, the backpacker has also eliminated their handy containers, and must provide himself with some kind of equipment in which to combine and prepare his modern-day sustenance.

This can be anything from a collection of antique odds and ends from J.C. Penney's to the complete aluminum kits which offer a variety of cookery combinations. Whichever road he travels, the backpacker who goes the freeze-dried route is going to have to take some kind of pot with him. If he goes the way of the curio shop, the backpacker should remember that his cooking utensils are going to have to fit in a small mountain pack with a large mountain of gear. His boiling pot for those miracle preparations that are on the simple side should have some kind of removable handle. See how handy those can lids were? If the handle is permanently affixed, it will make packing the pot exceedingly awkward.

The packer will have to be guided in his selection of cooking necessaries by the number of pots and pans needed to reconstitute his chosen variety of freeze-dried dinner or dish. Like the home-bound housewife, he will want to have every part of his meal ready at the same time, or as close to it as he can manage with only one fire, so the entire meal can be served while it is piping hot, not eaten one lukewarm dish at a time.

To manage this, even the most back-to-basics camper will probably want at least two pots, one for the complete freeze-dried dinner and one for coffee, tea or his dessert.

Removable pot handles make packing a less awkward job and can help prevent burns from fire-heated handles.

thing goes wrong in sets of threes." Such a trio of disasters could ruin a camper's whole trip.

One thing that can spoil a nature lover's good mood in a hurry is to hike miles into the wilderness to an isolated spot, rustle up and wolf down a sumptuous repast, then stretch out by the fire to relax, only to have his wandering eyes fall on the blackened pots he must sooner or later do something about. Depending on his skill at procrastination, he may be able to put off the inevitable until that last little bite he just couldn't cram down dries to a thick crust in the bottom of the pan but, eventually, he is going to have to give up the comfortable nest of his sleeping bag for the stultifying chore of cleaning up the mess he has made. He cannot just pitch the crusted pot into the nearest creek because he knows there will be another time when he will want that pot to repeat his last campfire masterpiece.

He must also consider the fact that, if he should ever meet up with the next half-a-dozen campers who use this spot after he has left, they will probably ask him why he abandoned that pile of dirty, crusted hardware in the middle of their nice, clean stream, and beat him half to death when he smirks and mumbles "Too much trouble to clean up, I guess."

With these considerations in mind, the advantages of holding the number of cooking items to a minimum become obvious, and the backpacker planning an extended journey into the wilds will find himself with less on his mind, and considerably less on his back, if he makes the effort to plan for his needs, compromising between 'druthers and dragdowns as he assembles the pack on which his life in the wilderness will depend.

There is still another essential item needed by any camper or backpacker who turns to freeze-dried or powdered foods to reduce weight without sacrificing nutrition. Almost every premixed food calls for one or more cups of water to reconstitute the moisture that is removed during the freeze-dried process. Some dried foods, such as fruit or nuts, can be eaten without adding water, but an all-dry diet can get tiresome in a hurry to any hungry backpacker. This means that an ample supply of water is essential no matter what kind of trip is planned in whatever type of terrain.

Water is also necessary to make cleanup chores easier and for drinking purposes to help replace lost body fluids. Almost everyone has heard from childhood the motherly admonition to drink at least four glasses of water a day to stay healthy.

In town, as well as in many so-called isolated country areas, water is piped in and is as easy to come by as turning a spigot. This is also true of many mountain areas, where streams and creeks fill with winter's high-altitude snows and flow downhill toward the sea. Desert campers, though, will probably find themselves in areas where water is at a premium; not available at all for miles in the lonely stretches of parching sand that make up much of the Southwest.

When camping or hiking in these areas, or in mountain parks where many streams have become polluted and the water is labelled as not safe for drinking even when boiled, the backpacker will have to add a heavy weight of water to his already staggering load.

This will also be something for the shopping adventurer to think about as he tries to decide between a freeze-dried steak dinner that needs three cups of water to be made edible and a side order of corn that only requires one or two cups of water.

As a gauge, two campers will probably use as much as 3½ gallons of water a day to meet all their drinking, cooking and minimal washing needs. The smart backpacker will probably forego shaving and use a damp cloth instead of a bowl of water to wash up with. At eight pounds to the gallon, the single backpacker can count on adding about fifteen extra pounds to his minimum load — if that doesn't correct any posture problems, nothing will. Excess weight will be self-correcting as the water is used each day, hopefully at the same rate or faster than the backpacker's shoulders tire from the load. The smart backpacker will still wind up carrying some of that water back down the trail, leaving his emergency rations untouched until he reaches a campground or farmhouse where he can count on replenishing his supply.

The backpacker who runs low on water in an area where there is no more should consider turning back early to avoid being found a week later as the search party follows the buzzards to what is left. No matter how beautiful the spacious scenery may be, it can't possibly be worth spending three weeks in the hospital with needles and tubes stuck into every available limb; or not being able to come back next vacation time, due to being baked to a crackly crisp

under that gorgeous cactus blossom the hiker just had to push his luck to photograph.

The experienced or cautious backpacker will know to stay within the range he allowed himself at the beginning of his trip. When he packs in enough food and water for a five-day hike, he knows to start back about noon of the third day so he will be back within range of immediate resupply when his provisions are exhausted. When planning how much food and water to take along, the backpacker will probably allow an extra two or three-day supply for an extended trip of a week or more, knowing that, if he should slip on a wet rock face, get caught under a falling tree, or just find an old chuckhole the hard way, he will have enough of the necessary to stay alive and healthy until he is missed, searched for and found.

In planning his regular menu, the backpacker will keep in mind the type of terrain he or his party will be hiking through. If he knows there will be steep hills to struggle up, he will increase his supplies accordingly, since he is going to be hungrier after a hard climb than after a stroll to the corner and back. He will want to know the prevailing

Simplest cook kit may have as few as three pots and some backpackers can make do with one.

temperature. Hiking in the cooler air and high altitudes of a mountain range will mean a bigger appetite and a need for more heat-producing body fuel.

A desert trip will mean stifling heat during the day and drastic temperature drop at night, with a need for hot, filling dishes for the evening menus. What normally unexpected dangers could keep him from getting back to civilization within the planned amount of time? These will decide how much food and water to allow for emergencies. Naturally, the backpacker will want to carry enough food and trail munchies to last until he expects to be back; he will know how far he will be walking and climbing each day and how hungry such exercise makes him.

The backpacker will have shopped around at hardware and sporting goods stores and assembled the type and amount of cookware gear he prefers and he will be conscious of what his cleanup problems will be and have

A more elaborate collection of cooking equipment can rival the contents of the home kitchen cupboard. Above is a compromise to bridge the gap between trailhound and gourmet.

enough water to meet those, plus his cooking and drinking needs.

He will have picked out his favorite freeze-dried foods and trail snacks and be familiar with the requirements for fixing each dish.

As a regular visitor into the untamed reaches, he will know that he must eat the kinds of foods that will provide his body with the basic proteins, carbohydrates and fats that are needed to keep him healthy enough to enjoy his sojourn in the wilderness.

To provide himself with the necessary external warmth and to heat the food that will feed his inner furnace, the backpacker will turn to an outdoorsman's most versatile tool — fire. Besides warming him and providing a means to boil the water the backpacker needs for that freeze-dried specialty, fire also gives off light, keeps woodland wildlife from raiding the backpacker's camp and creates that relax-

ing atmosphere in which trail companions can kick back and banter their day's experiences.

The inexperienced camper might think nothing of learning how to lay out the foundation of such a simple thing as fire. To him, it is only a matter of striking a match. What he forgets is that he is not just turning a stove knob or flicking an emery wheel against his lighter flint. The outdoors fire must be prepared properly or it will either constantly go out or not light at all. The unconcerned act of striking a match can get complicated in a hurry in a high wind.

The simplest type of campfire is built by laying some flat rocks in a rough circle. This prevents the fire from spreading to nearby shrubs or that comfortable blanket of pine needles. The rocks also give the camp cook a level place to put his pots and pans, and reflect the fire's heat to make cooking more efficient. In the center of this rock circle, the backpacker places a handful of pine needles, some shredded tree bark or dried grass. He builds a tepee of tiny twigs over this tinder and, crouching down with his back to the wind, strikes a match.

Cupping this tiny flame between his hands, the camper then touches the match to the side closest to him, putting the flame up under his tinder so the rising heat will ignite it. If he is properly prepared, he has progressively larger twigs and branches at hand, and he patiently adds them to his fire one or two at a time. If he piles on too much wood too quickly, the blaze will be smothered and he will have to start over. With patience, the backpacker will slowly build up his fire until it is burning strongly.

The camper who proceeds to pile on half his wood supply to create a blazing furnace will probably find himself forced to stand far back from it, being crisped on the front of his body while his backside hangs out in the cold night air. The backpacker can easily avoid this and save himself the effort of stumbling around in the dark to gather more wood, by building a small fire that he can squat next to within easy reaching distance for handling his cooking utensils and stand over to be warmed on both sides at once. The smaller fire will also save the tired camper the effort of scraping a thick accumulation of soot off the bottom of his pot or pan during his after-meal clean-up chores and will let him stretch a small wood supply through the night.

One way to make more efficient use of a fire is to lay the rocks in a keyhole shape. The blazing fire at the big end of this arrangement is used for heat and light, while the camp cook scrapes coals from the main blaze into the smaller end to use in preparing his gourmet specials. This method reduces soot-scraping chores even more.

Being always conscious of his responsibility to preserve the natural environment of his favorite hiking country as much as possible, the backpacker who prefers a wood fire for his camp needs will probably carry along a small, leak-proof container of alcohol or wood spirits to make easier the job of cleaning the soot-blackened rocks he used to contain his cheering and useful blaze.

A growing movement among ecology-minded backpackers to avoid wood-burning fires has resulted in a bur-

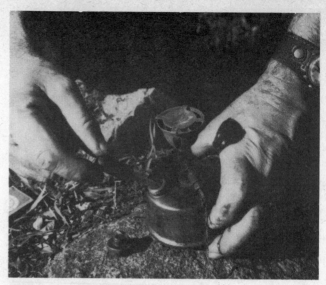
White gas stove needs priming with each use. Be careful.

Fuel from reservoir goes in priming vent.

Fuel is ignited. Pot and favorite dish come next.

Joe Rough-and-Ready goes for the basics.

geoning collection of commercially manufactured camp stoves designed especially with the weight-conscious backpacker in mind.

These stoves use white gasoline, propane fuel cells, or the popular jellied alcohol canisters that fuel the collapsible Sterno stoves. The basic, one-burner Sterno stove folds flat and the cans of fuel weigh a little less than a can of Vienna sausage. The liquid or compressed gas stoves do not pack as easily, but experience has shown that white gas burns more efficiently at high altitudes, making cooking easier and wood gathering unnecessary above the tree line.

The variety of designs and weights of these stoves is almost endless, and the decision of which to use will be

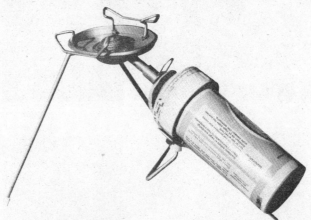

Some backpacker stoves use disposable fuel cells.

dictated by the backpacker's financing and his taste in what looks easier to pack in and use. One advantage of the white gas or liquid alcohol stoves is that the backpacker can fill the built-in reservoir, eliminating one or two extra pint cans of fuel that he will have to take with him. The pressurized gas types are fueled by nonrefillable, sealed cells; depending on the stove's design, the backpacker can apply the same room-saving principle by attaching his fuel cell to the stove before packing. The camper should be sure that the stove is packed in such a way that the feeder valve cannot be rubbed open by other gear in the pack or fuel will leak out, wasting his money and creating a possible danger of unexpected fire.

Care should be taken to pack extra cans of white gasoline in such a way that adequate ventilation prevents the accumulation of fumes which could be accidentally ignited inside the pack. Some pack frames have a built-in tank for fuel, but backpackers using this type should be careful to check for leaks before starting out.

The backpacker who uses any kind of fueled stove should remember to set his fuel supply well away from any combustion when he sets up his camp. Extra cans of fuel, especially the pressurized types, should be stored in the shade of the camper's tent or buried well away from the cooking site until needed.

Like any potentially dangerous, but useful tool, fuel canisters and fuel-type stoves are easy to use and convenient to the camper who does not want to help nature along by burning dead wood, or who is in an area where fires are not allowed. They must, however, be treated with the respect they require for safe operation and the full enjoyment of the benefits they provide.

There are several types, sizes of one-burner stoves for the backpacker. If using fuel cells, pack out empties.

CHAPTER 9

BEWARE THE ELEMENTS

The Wonder Of The Outdoors Can Lull The Unwary Into One Of Nature's Many Traps

Some families have strict rules about snacking between meals. That's fine for weight-watchers and mothers concerned that their children eat the proper foods at mealtime. On the trail, however, high-energy snacks can help the backpacker fight off the detrimental effects of cold, wind and rain. Dried fruit, raisins, candy or any sugar source is best.

IT IS A BREATHTAKING summer Sunday afternoon and the bearded, bedraggled hiker grins at the thought of how his city friends would react to the shabby appearance he must present. His boots have been scarred by his fight to get across that almost perpendicular slope of loose, sandy shale, and the right sleeve of his muddy, plaid shirt is ripped where he caught it on a low-hanging tree branch. His hair has not been combed for two days and his chin stubble is starting to itch. His knapsack, lightened by the weight of the four meals he ate cold from cans, sways and bounces almost unnoticed on his shoulders as he sets the mile-eating pace of the born woodsman on the last, four-hour stretch of his weekend hike away from it all.

An hour and a half later, he lays gasping by the edge of the stream he would have sworn he had passed at least forty-five minutes ago. His shirt and jeans have been torn in several places by his aimless stumbling and falls, and his efforts to get his pack off are blocked by a strange stiffening in his arms and shoulders.

He can't understand how he got so weak so quickly. He has been getting out into the woods every weekend since a friend reintroduced him to the wonders of the great outdoors less than a month ago. It was kind of clumsy for him to slip on a wet rock and end up splashing around in that muddy stream — was this the same stream? But with the weather as nice as it started out — it is getting cooler since

Rain parkas will keep the outdoors enthusiast dry and warm in the face of a surprise rain shower. The large pockets of this type of jacket give plenty of places to stow trail snacks and such emergency gear as fishlines, snakebite kit, fire-starting kit and trapwire. A well-designed hood prevents body heat from radiating from ears, face and neck.

that unexpected overcast moved in — he figured he would be dry long ago. His clothes should have dried, but that last bit of uphill trail did bring out a little sweat. Why had he started back up the hill when he had to get out of here and be ready for work Monday morning?

He chuckles to himself, thinking how his boss would react if he walked into the office looking like a reject from "Robinson Crusoe" and the effort warms him briefly, but it doesn't last long. His body is wracked its whole length by another bout of the chills and shivering he thought had finally stopped. It had been damned hard trying to get up that sandy slope with his body shivering violently every fifteen feet. Each attack had cost him half the distance he

covered between chills, but he'd finally gotten over the top, only to find that he must have been wandering in circles the whole time. He doesn't understand. His sense of direction is usually pretty good. What the hell is h-h-hap-p-pen-n-ni-n-ng? he wonders. Wish the damn shivering would stop at least.

Better try to get up and get going, he reasons. Got to be back home before this afternoon. Now what's wrong with my legs? They're so stiff. Can't really move them. Maybe if I just rest a while.

His hands fumble in the rocks and dirt of the creek bed, and the flash of reflected sunlight draws his eyes to his watch. It can't be only eleven o'clock, he thinks in a sudden

A woolen sweater will still retain body heat even if wet by perspiration or a dip in a creek. Other fabrics will not.

surge of panic. It's almost dark now. It is his last coherent thought before the blackness takes him.

Twenty-four hours later, a searcher with the rescue party from the forestry station, where the young hiker got his rough directions Friday afternoon, spots a flash of color against the grey of the creek bed and leads the party to where the novice woodsman lies stiff and cold at the water's edge. His body is taken back to the station and a doctor summoned to find out why he died. The resident ranger has been in the field for a couple of years, but he never heard of anybody dying of exposure overnight.

The doctor hasn't either, but he begins to suspect what caused the young man's death when he sees that he carried no jacket, that his clothing has been wet and that his body temperature is only eighty degrees.

On a frozen strip of snow-covered Oklahoma highway, a police patrol unit stops to aid the driver of a stalled sedan. The officers are startled to find that the driver, a young woman sitting under the wheel, is dead. Her mouth and eyes are open; the cause of death is thought to be exposure to the bitter cold of the nighttime hours she had unexpectedly spent in her car. It is only after the car is towed to a garage with the body still at the wheel that police notice a pulse and quickly call for medical help.

It is found that the woman is still alive, but her body temperature has dropped to seventy-one degrees — twenty-

seven degrees below normal. If she continues to live, it will be a miracle.

There might seem to be a gaping difference between the backpacker who heads into the wilds unsuitably clothed and equipped and the commuter whose car has broken down on a deserted highway in the middle of Winter, but both face approximately the same risk of death due to what is most commonly called exposure.

This condition can strike almost without warning and before its victims may realize they have a problem. Especially vulnerable is the hiker who takes to the hills in just a short-sleeve shirt and jeans because it is so calm and sunny outside, or because he only plans to be out on the trail for a little while.

Weather can change drastically, and unforeseen delays have more than once caught an otherwise well-prepared traveler in his shirt sleeves facing a surprise downpour that drops temperatures into the low fifties or sixties.

Such temperatures alone probably would not present any real danger, but they can and have been fatal when combined with such factors as wet clothing, a light breeze and inadequate nourishment to fight the chill factor present under such conditions. This chill factor can be the death of an unwary hiker or any person caught out-of-doors unexpectedly in adverse weather for a prolonged period of time.

There are several elements which combine to cause the condition known as exposure, but the one that will most always be present is what physicians call hypothermia — the rapid and prolonged loss of body heat by a person who might otherwise be in little or no danger.

With proper preventive measures, the risk of falling victim to hypothermia can be minimized, but it must still be kept in mind, along with the other necessary considerations of watching the trail for chuckholes or loose rocks, keeping an eye on the other party's pack for loose straps or falling gear and maintaining a steady, unfatiguing pace that all members of the group can sustain.

The outdoorsman must keep an especially sharp eye out for the symptoms of hypothermia as it is often mistaken for simple exhaustion and can strike in unexpected situations. Backpackers have fallen victim to hypothermia in temperatures as high as fifty degrees.

A fatal case of hypothermia could well begin at the backpacker's home where, since he is running a bit late to meet the other members of his hiking party, he decides to skip breakfast, figuring he can make up the lost meal by snacking on the trail. By doing this, he is not ahead of the game, but has left himself vulnerable to elements that can combine to ruin his whole weekend, thus reducing his chances of surviving a surprised or planned overnight stay in what he might consider only mild cold.

What he has done, in terms of how the malady will attack his well-being, is to pass up his first chance of the day to replenish the basic fuel from which his body's internal heating system would produce the heat the camper needs to maintain his body's normal warmth during overnight temperature drops.

Like the fire around which the tired trailhounds will spend the night, a human body generates, circulates and radiates heat produced by the breakdown of proteins, carbohydrates and fats from the food the hungry hiker wolfs down. Like the fire, a body's supply of fuels must be replenished at regular intervals for its heat-producing system to keep the body temperature at healthy levels.

A great deal of the heat produced within the hiker's body is radiated away through exposed areas of skin, such as the face and hands. More heat is lost each time the hiker exhales into the thin mountain air. This lost heat must constantly be replaced by the body's internal furnace, so the body's internal and external temperature will be maintained.

When the hiker is properly clothed, and so protected from most weather changes, the radiated heat is confined close to his body in a thin layer of air trapped between clothing and skin. This trapped air keeps the outer layers of body tissue warm without depriving the inner tissues of their heat, much like a home furnace's heat is confined in ducts which channel warmed air between a building's outer and inner walls.

As with home-heating ducts, once heat has been produced by the body, it is circulated along the blood-carrying arteries and capillaries out to the body's extremities; the fingers, toes, etc. When parts of the body become chilled, heat is moved from the body's central core, out through the arterial heating ducts to replace it. In order for this lost heat to be replaced as it radiates from, for instance, the hands and face, the hiker must continually provide his internal heating system with the fuel from which it produces life-sustaining heat.

With a reduced supply of raw material to produce heat, the body's immediate reaction on becoming chilled is to reduce the flow of heat-carrying blood to surface vessels all over the body, and reserve what heat remains for the body's inner core of vital organs. In conditions of cold, dampness and wind — even as little as two miles per hour — the temperature of fingers, toes, face and other exposed skin areas may drop rapidly to as low as fifty or sixty degrees Fahrenheit, while the body's internal core maintains its normal ninety-eight to ninety-nine-degree temperature.

The body's internal heating system is further aided by a layer of subcutaneous fat which acts like the spun fiberglass inside a house's walls to hold in the heat produced internally. Women have a slightly thicker layer of this subcutaneous fat than men and are thus slightly better equipped to resist cold than men. This means that the negligent backpacker's wife or girl friend could wind up having to carry him back down the mountain if he has not taken the time to protect his internal heat supply from a surprise rain shower or snowstorm.

Freezing temperatures are by no means necessary for the outdoorsman to find himself in trouble. A hiker or backpacker who has fallen in a snowbank, been drenched by a sudden, brief rain or waded a deep stream without changing clothes can suddenly begin to shiver uncontrollably; the first sign that the hiker may soon become a victim of hypothermia.

To prevent his problems from getting worse, the backpacker should immediately change into dry clothing and treat himself to some warm food or liquid, such as soup, tea or coffee. A further preventive measure would be for the camper to wrap himself in a sleeping bag prewarmed by another member of the party until he is thoroughly rewarmed.

At this point, the hiker's treatment would probably be only a matter of inconvenience and possible annoyance to his better-prepared trail companions. Should the condition go undetected or treatment be postponed until the party reaches its first night's planned campsite, it will become considerably worse.

While insulated by dry clothing, the hiker's body has little trouble preserving its natural heat, provided the hiker has fed it the fuel it needs for the task. The undernourished backpacker, though, will begin to feel uncomfortable as the outer layers of his body begin to chill. Once wet by stream crossing or excessively dampened by perspiration as the hiker sweats his way up the trail, most fabrics will lose their insulating abilities and allow body heat to escape as much as ten times faster than normal, causing the hiker's body

Thermal jackets keep warm air circulating next to outer skin surfaces to help the backpacker maintain a healthy temperature. Lost heat because of poor clothing can be trouble.

temperature to lower rapidly. Such a steady loss of body heat can go unnoticed by the backpacker and may get to the danger point before it is even recognized by the backpacker or his buddies, if they are not aware of the possibility of hypothermia.

Warning symptoms of hypothermia occur in a recognizable pattern, though this pattern may vary slightly with different individuals. As the backpacker's internal body temperature drops just two or three degrees, the victim will begin to shiver uncontrollably, as all his muscles contract involuntarily in a struggle to create heat with muscular movement. The hiker will shake steadily, as though he had a palsy, at first. However, as his body grows colder, the shivering will begin to come in violent waves that become so distorting that the hiker may not even be able to perform simple tasks, such as striking a match for a badly needed fire or buttoning his jacket against that treacherous breeze. As the hiker's inner temperature drops still further, the shivering will come in more and more violent waves. The camper may lose all coordination, have difficulty speaking and begin to stumble and fall.

The backpacker who takes shortcuts at mealtime will find his thinking even more impaired as his capillaries become restricted and blood is drawn away from his extremities, including the brain, to help preserve warmth for the inner organs. He will have difficulty following conversations and, at this point, his friends might laugh and tell him that he must be tired, it's time to turn in. If none of them thinks to check more closely, they could find him dead in his sleeping bag in the morning without even the general expo-

Insulated pants, jacket and hood, wool mittens and boots large enough to permit the wearing of two pairs of woolen socks will help protect the backpacker in freezing weather.

Eventually, the hypothermia victim begins to see his fading world through a dim haze as he dreamily watches the ground come up to smack him in the face.

He cannot be roused and may begin to cough up a white, foamy fluid. Shortly afterward, if he is not found and helped, his heartbeat and respiration will slow and, finally, cease and the victim dies.

In extreme cases, a hiker or climber may progress to the passing-out stage in as little as thirty minutes. In most cases, though, the chilling process moves more slowly and there is usually plenty of time for the victim's companions to discover that their friend is in trouble and give him some help.

On the trail, this involves three key resources. Most important is preventing further heat loss by stripping the victim of his sweaty clothes and getting him into warm dry ones. The victim should then be laid in his sleeping bag inside a tent or other shelter, out of the cold. His lost body heat must then be replaced from outside sources, starting with a fire, then getting him to drink and eat some hot liquid or food, especially hot soup, tea or coffee heavily laced with sugar. The sugar and dried fruit or candy will give the trail casualty a quick source of rapid, heat-producing energy to aid rewarming.

The rewarming process is slow; it may take as long as six to eight hours for the victim to be completely rewarmed. Once he has recovered, the victim should be taken back to civilization as quickly as possible with his friends taking care to prevent him from getting chilled again.

The most important precaution anyone who gets into the outdoors can take to prevent such a needless brush with death is to be aware of the possibility of hypothermia and of the climatic conditions of cold, wetness and wind that may cause it. The hiker or camper who wears adequate clothing will be better able to fight the effects of blustery weather. It is better for an outdoorsman to wear more protective clothing than he might need and have to take some of it off and carry it than to wear less than he might need to stay healthy and alive and be caught without.

The hiker or backpacker should be wearing at least one set of outer clothing made of wool, the only fabric that retains some of its insulating powers when wet. Dry woolen mittens and a down-filled parka with hood in place can protect the backpacker against cold, wet weather and can help prevent heat loss.

One of the outdoorsman's major concerns should be to supply himself with adequate and proper foods and liquids. Carry enough food and water to last the trip and keep some in reserve for possible emergencies. Lean hard on trail munchies for quick energy and to sustain body fuel levels. Don't skimp on camp meals as a hiker's body will need three or four times the normal amount of fuel to sustain itself while climbing a steep incline in the cold.

The backpacker should make it a habit to carry emergency shelter in the form of a small mountain tent or heavy-gauge plastic tarp, even on a short trip.

A sprained ankle can cause an unexpected delay in the hiker's scheduled return to civilization and shelter from the elements can be the difference between staying alive to be found, or being carried out in a body bag.

When in camp during chilly weather, keep moving. Chop firewood, walk around or do light calisthenics to produce heat with muscle movement.

Back in the city, a program of physical conditioning and a steady diet of protein and carbohydrate-rich foods, such as meat, eggs, some vegetables and cheese, can help improve the would-be trailmaster's circulation and give his body a reserve of the heat-producing basics it needs to maintain a healthy body temperature outdoors.

Staying fit, maintaining a steady fuel reserve and wearing

sure as a readily recognizable reason. If one of them laughingly suggests that the stricken camper get out of his sweaty clothes and put on dry ones, drink some hot soup by the fire, then get into his sleeping bag, he may knowingly or unknowingly save his friend's life.

By this time, the fasting hiker should realize that something is wrong, but he may not because of the reduced function of his mental faculties. He may not be able to help himself if he does know what is wrong, for as he continues to lose more body heat, the shivering has probably stopped, but his muscles have begun to stiffen.

As his body continues to cool, he loses most of his muscular coordination, and his limited contact with his surroundings is lost as respiration and pulse are slowed, and he enters a zombie-like stupor. An alert trail buddy should notice that the victim is having problems at this point and not allow his friend to go wandering off into the brush alone, even to answer an urgent call of nature. The victim of hypothermia just might keep on going until he walks off a two-hundred-foot-high drop in the dark.

proper clothing can make outdoor activities safer and more enjoyable for the backpacker, and can help prevent him from having added problems during an unexpected or lengthy exposure to the elements.

If most outdoorsmen have never heard of hypothermia, even the rankest novice should be aware of the common-known danger of frostbite, especially as he heads up into snow country for a weekend of hiking, skiing or hunting.

Frostbite rarely traps the experienced and suitably equipped outdoorsman who knows its dangers. Most of its victims are from the ranks of the ill-prepared, inexperienced and perhaps careless first-timers or persons who are caught outdoors unexpectedly in freezing weather. It is just as possible for a housewife in the eastern or midwestern snow country to lock herself out of the house and become frost-bitten before neighbors can find her as it is for some care-lessness or accident on the trail to catch the unwary hiker by surprise. Either could pay a high price for a simple mis-take.

Frostbite is the result of prolonged exposure to freezing temperatures that will actually form ice crystals between the cells of an unprotected hand, ear or face. The symptoms of frostbite first appear on the extremities and its victim probably really stuck his chin out for it. The first sign that the novice backpacker may pay the ultimate price for clumsily dropping his gloves in that beautiful, ice-trimmed stream will be a reddening and slight swelling of the affected tissue accompanied by an initial biting cold feeling. When this biting cold turns to numbness, it may feel like a blessing, but the victim's problems are far from over. He is, in fact, in even worse trouble; that lack of feeling is, or should be, telling him that the first layer of nerve tissue has begun to freeze and he better call a halt and build a fire to get his hands rewarmed while he can still use them.

Unnoticed and unchecked, this freezing of the hiker's flesh continues; more swelling becomes evident and the initial redness turns to a violet color. If not treated, the outer tissues form a hard, wooden-feeling crust over the not-yet-affected inner tissues and the frozen outer skin takes on a yellowish-white tint.

By this time, the victim should be more than aware that he needs help. If the surrounding cold has numbed his brain to the point where he doesn't notice his condition now, he will discover it in a hurry as the freezing moves deeper into his body.

As the tissues continue to freeze, the victims's skin be-comes puffy, tight and shiny and takes on a rose-violet coloration. Blisters begin to form as the secondary layers of tissue begin to feel the effects of freezing cold.

Untreated at this stage, the blisters soon burst of their own volition; the affected tissue begins to scar and peels to the secondary layers. Stopped at this point, there will still be some permanent damage and the injury can take as long as six months to partially heal.

As the affected tissue continues to freeze, the broken blisters dry and blacken and the dead skin sloughs off. Lack of oxygen due to restricted circulation in the frozen capil-laries causes the skin to turn ashen in some areas, blue in others. Restricted circulation also causes swelling, a loss of mobility in the affected limb and infection leading to gan-grene. Skin graft or amputation of the frozen arm or leg is almost a mandatory part of treatment for this advanced stage.

Unlike hypothermia, frostbite is not usually fatal, but a frostbite victim might well have suffered from hypothermia in a milder climate; vulnerability to one stems from much the same causes as the other. Poor physical condition, un-healthy or erratic eating habits and excessive exposure to

wet, cold and windy weather in poor clothes for the type of climate all can make any hiker susceptible to frostbite.

There are two types of frostbite and distinguishing be-tween them is vitally important as the proper treatment for each type varies widely. Mild frostbite, or frostnip, involves only the first and possibly the second layers of tissue in the frozen area. Reddened or yellowish-white coloration of the frostbitten fingers, ears, cheek or chin, and a feeling of hardness over softer, unaffected tissue are good indicators that the frozen hiker is suffering from frostnip. A solid area of hardness under discoloration of a rose-violet hue proba-bly means the victim has graduated to the more serious deep frostbite. If unsure which type it may be, the best bet is to do nothing. Seek the advice of other, more experi-enced campers or get the victim back to camp and get outside help.

The doctrine of do-nothing also applies when deep frost-bite has definitely been established. Attempting to rewarm the frozen area out on the trail may leave the victim's al-ready damaged limbs open to becoming refrozen during the retreat march. Frostbite victims have been known to walk on frozen feet for hours or even days, but if their feet were rewarmed on the trail, they would have to be carried out. Wait to begin treatment until the victim is back in camp, where the rewarming process can take place without inter-ruption until professional help can be arranged.

Frostnip, on the other hand, can be treated as soon as it

Thermal booties for wear in camp and when sleeping, and leggings to prevent snow or water from wetting feet prevent heat loss from the hiker's main equipment.

Down vest, stocking cap and heavy woolen socks will keep this hiker warm as he proceeds to check for the safest way up the rock face. The deep pockets in the vest are a good place to renew lost warmth to hands; stocking cap protects head and ears.

is discovered, preferably as soon as possible after the tissues have begun to freeze. Treatment involves immersing or copiously drenching the injured area in water heated to between 108 and 112 degrees Fahrenheit (Lacking a thermometer, dip an elbow in what should be lukewarm water). Be careful not to rupture any blisters that may have formed. These blisters can form a natural protection for underlying layers of tissue that have not yet been affected. The temperature of the heated water should be in the recommended range to provide for rapid rewarming without further injury to the victim. Contrary to a popular old wives' tale, using cold or cool water to gradually rewarm the frozen part may cause additional harm to already damaged tissue. Do not rub snow on the affected area as additional cold and friction will only increase the damage to the frozen, perhaps blistered tissue. Rewarming must be accomplished quickly, but do not use the dry heat of a fire or water heated to over 112 degrees as the victim will be unable to feel the excessive heat and might be further injured (Dry heat draws moisture from already dehydrated cells). It would be the ultimate irony to be suffering from blisters caused by too much heat and those caused by too much cold simultaneously, but the victim would probably be too busy hurting to appreciate the joke.

Rewarming will be accompanied by a tingling and burning sensation in the affected area, along with the appearance of a mottled purple discoloration which will indicate renewed blood circulation as capillaries begin to reopen. Blisters may form once the rewarming process is completed, and care should be taken not to break them since this will cause additional tissue damage.

Promptly treated, tissue which has been frostnipped should recover with no permanent damage. Deep frostbite, again, is another matter and extreme care should be taken to distinguish between frostnip and deep frostbite before any treatment is given.

As with hypothermia, or any injury or disease, the best possible treatment is prevention. Frostbite is an exceptionally tragic affliction, especially when the victim loses his hand or foot as a result, because it is one of the simplest outdoor dangers to prevent. Where experience and presence of mind can aid in the quick treatment of frostbite, a good jacket, woolen mittens, heavy trousers and woolen slacks will keep body heat next to outer skin layers, preventing the chill that can lead to freezing. A woolen ski mask can stop heat loss from face and head, and prevent possible freezing of ears, nose, cheeks and chin.

Crossing over streams and creeks may not seem as adventurous as fording against the racing, white water, but the precaution can keep the hiker's most important piece of equipment — his feet — dry and healthy. This is the easiest precaution the backpacker can take to keep a sneaky bit of outdoor discomfort known as immersion foot from ruining an otherwise perfect weekend in the boonies.

Immersion foot became all too familiar to American troops during World War I, when they found themselves forced to stand in cold, rain-filled trenches for days or weeks with no opportunity to change soaked boots and socks, or dry their feet. It affects campers, hikers and backpackers today when they allow their feet to remain in wet, cold boots and socks so as not to call an early halt on that extended march.

Wet clothing draws heat away from the hiker's body rapidly; almost ten times as quickly as dry clothing will allow. Inside a wet boot, this produces an effect similar to the cold dampness that can bring on a case of hypothermia; a loss of body heat which causes the capillaries that normally carry heat to the toes to constrict, reducing the flow of blood — and of replacement heat — to outer foot surfaces.

Sunglasses protect this hiker against snow-blindness and water glare. Full hood and turned-up collar hold warmth.

This creates an effect similar to the damage done by deep frostbite, and the initial symptoms are much the same; a feeling of damp coldness that gives way to numbness. In the initial stages, only the skin surface tissues are affected, but an untreated case of immersion foot can eventually cause damage like that of frostbite to all of the toes and the ball and heel of the foot.

Treatment for immersion foot is the same as for frostnip except that a well-wrapped canteen of heated water or a well-wrapped heated stone should be used as the source of external heat so that the foot remains dry. Saturated socks can be hung on a stick and dried over the campfire at the same time for later use, but the backpacker should put on fresh, dry socks once he has rewarmed the wrinkles out of his feet.

As with frostbite, the prevention of immersion foot is considerably easier than the treatment, and simply involves keeping the feet as dry as possible. Immersion foot presents little danger on a short hike, but backpackers on a prolonged trip through rain, wet snow or marshy landscape should make it a point to stop every six to eight hours, build a fire and dry and rewarm their feet before continuing.

Waterproof boots roomy enough so that the hiker can wear two pairs of woolen socks are the best idea for keeping the feet dry in damp country or rainy weather. Another easy precaution is for campers to wear their pants cuffs outside their boots to prevent rainwater from draining down inside them. On the trail, the hiker should bounce on his toes or wiggle them occasionally as he walks to keep the muscles of his feet from cramping in the confinement of his boots. When the backpacker sets up his hiking schedule for wet country, he should allow time to stop along the way to change his sweaty, marsh-soaked socks whenever his feet begin to feel damp.

Outdoor activities can be fun and help improve the enthusiast's health, but not if the outdoorsman becomes careless and allows the adverse effects of the environment to sneak up and ruin his body.

The prepared backpacker thinks first of his survival.

ON A SUN-SPECKLED stretch of sandy, rock-strewn mountain slope, a lean, tanned young hiker lies slumped against a weather-greyed, rotting tree trunk, moaning and tossing his head from side to side. His face is discernibly pale beneath the dirt he collected during his fall, and sweat beads streak his pain-contorted features. Gradually, the moans grow fainter as the hiker slows his aimless gyrations. His rock-scraped, bark-scrubbed hands cease to twist and roil the rocky soil in which he lies amid the wind-tossed, summer-seared weeds and grasses that hide him from easy view.

His breathing had been quiet after his body's automatic defense mechanisms had compelled him into unconsciousness to give him a time of relief from the agony of his injuries. Now, his bruised chest muscles begin to send stabs of pain through his upper body; his breath comes in sharp shallow gasps as the curtain of darkness that had dropped over his vision lifts abruptly. Lines twist and bunch around his blistered, bleeding lips and his teeth snap down with an audible click to stop the scream that bubbles in the back of his dusty throat.

His eyes open wide and cringe almost shut again as his skyward glance is met and overpowered by the glistening rays of the afternoon sun. He lowers his gaze to the sight of his denim-covered legs, almost hidden in the brown-green-red-grey-black kaleidoscope patterns of the heavy, matted groundbrush that caught and halted the plunging downhill tumble that turned an easy summer stroll into a potential death trap.

Hooking his elbows back over the fallen timber that serves as an impromptu rest, he starts to pull himself away from the piercing rock edge that has all but numbed his left buttock. This motion is stopped almost before it begins as agony lances through the hiker's body, forcing a nasal grunt over the wall of his self-control.

Trembling slightly, the hiker forces himself to lean forward, and gently pulls aside the wild grass that covers his legs. He sucks air through clenched teeth at the sight of his left leg, twisted outward at an angle that would be impossible if the bone between the knee and the ankle were not broken cleanly in half.

He relaxes against the log and decides just how much trouble he is really in. A brief flush of panic has given way to taking stock of his resources. The hiker checks through his pockets, inventorying the few souvenirs of civilization that may be his only means of surviving his moment of carelessness.

One shirt pocket holds a sweat-dampened book of matches and a crumpled pack of cigarettes. There are plenty of branches within arm's reach, so he can make a fire to fight off the chill of the rapidly approaching night, if his matches dry properly.

CHAPTER 10

YOUR ENVIRONMENT AND YOURSELF:

THE BACKPACKER'S GREATEST ENEMIES

Hiking alone can be the greatest test of a backpacker's outdoor survival knowledge. The lone woodsman depends solely on his own skills to procure needed food, water, shelter and emergency care. If hiking alone, be ready.

He sees that there are none of the summer berries he knows growing within crawling range. If he knew some of the edible varieties of the flowers and grasses growing within easy reach, he could add a bit of greenery to the can of Vienna sausages and the now-melted candy bars he stuck in his jacket pockets before leaving his base camp.

His canteen is probably hiding under a bush somewhere, but that is no real problem. He can get water and, maybe, some brook trout or salmon from the foaming mountain stream that splashes invitingly less than a hundred feet downhill in the gully at the base of the slope. This is providing it hasn't become polluted — he has no water-purification tablets with him.

His first problem, though, is to do something about that mangled leg. As it is, he pays for every movement with a renewed throbbing that jumps through his leg and streaks the length of his bruised body each time he tries to shift a bit. Some kind of painkiller would sure make his life a little easier right now.

He reaches for the heavy knife he wears on his hip, but his hand fumbles at an empty sheath. He sighs in disgust. He must have lost it during the fall. Now he will have to try to make some kind of splints with his bare hands. The trouble there is that a branch or stick big enough in diameter to make a good splint will also be too thick for him to

break off by hand in his weakened condition. A small hatchet would be the answer to the hiker's prayers and a folding camp knife would help to replace the one he lost getting into this mess.

He has to figure out something pretty quick. If his leg becomes infected, as it will if he isn't found soon, he has no antibiotics to delay the slow poisoning of gangrene. He might use various herbs as a substitute for more civilized medicines, if he knew what to look for and how to use it, but he never had any interest in botany.

There is, of course, the challenge of staying alive long enough for gangrene to become a problem. When the evening dew forms, he has no tarp or any kind of shelter to keep himself and his clothes from becoming soaked and leaving him open to any number of cold-weather diseases.

The hiker sees no way to resupply his meager food supplies, even as he watches half a dozen squirrels leaping about the branches of a tree just twenty-five yards away, and listens to a family of wild rabbits rustling under a tangled thicket within a stone's throw of where he lies. He wasn't carrying his fishing tackle and another search of his pockets reveals that he does not have so much as a straight pin or any piece of metal from which he could rig a hook, even if he had a piece of line. Neither does he have any wire or twine from which he might fashion a dinner-trapping noose or rig a small-game trap or snare.

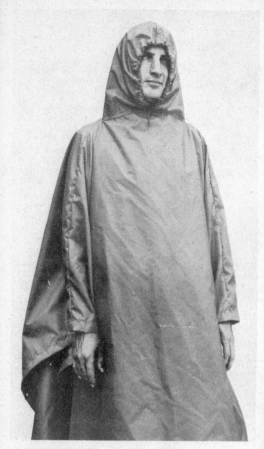

A plastic poncho can shelter the stranded backpacker from elements. Object is to stay alive to be found.

A well-planned emergency survival kit will include food, water, a shelter tarp, twine or wire, fishline and hooks, a mirror or signal light, flashlight, first-aid kit, multi-bladed pocketknife and the most complete fire-starting kit the backpacker can assemble.

A small belt pouch can serve as a trail munchies grab bag or survival pack.

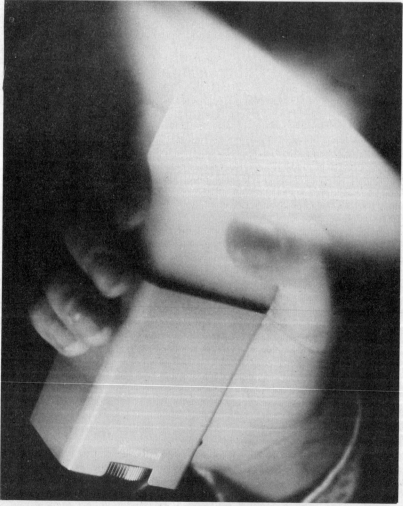

A bright signal light can lead searchers to the stranded camper or attract the attention of aerial spotters during nighttime hours.

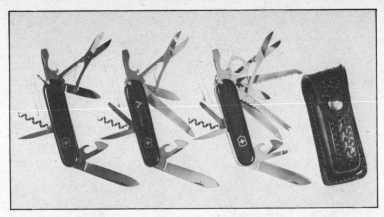

Multi-bladed knife in secure case is many tools in one.

When that sandy bank at the edge of the trail unexpectedly gave way, the hiker tumbled and thrashed down some three hundred feet of mountainside before he came forcefully to rest against the log that now pillows his shoulders. In the heavy foliage of this vertical terrain, it will be almost impossible for searchers to spot him so far off the hard-packed trail that will be the starting point of their search, and he has no mirror, whistle or anything with which he could attract the attention of a ground party or any aircraft that might be flying low over this isolated place. A skilled tracker might decide that the broken gap in the trail shows the place where someone went over, but the same marks also could easily be mistaken for a natural slide. The soft soil that might have preserved readable signs of the hiker's accident is now scattered and hidden among the rocks and weeds that dot the hillside, though some of it did manage to find its way down the back of the hiker's neck.

If the hiker is able to get a fire going, he can hope that searchers will see the smoke. However, a fire large enough to attract attention in a vast mountain range might well turn on the stranded trail casualty, and by the time his charred remains can be found, it is likely that one lost hiker will be the least of the Forestry Service's troubles.

The hiker stranded in the wilderness cannot depend on help from the civilization he has gone to such trouble to leave behind. The search party that sets out after a missing camper — when somebody finally notices that the camper is missing and reports it — will probably consist of men who know the country, know how to organize such an undertaking and know what to have with them when they find the injured man. In a pinch, though, a rescue party could be any persons who happen to be handy when the word is passed that someone needs help in a hurry.

The outdoorsman has achieved his heart's desire. He is strictly on his own, broken leg and all. Knowing the unforgiving nature of his chosen environment, he still got careless and may yet pay the final price for his mistake.

All of this puts the hiker in the classic position of adding insult to injury as he remembers how he carefully sifted and selected his equipment and supplies from a dizzying array of backpacking possibilities, then lugged the bulging result up ten miles of steep trail so he would have everything he could possibly want or need, all neatly arranged inside his specially made, strong-but-lightweight tent or set out in handy places around his cookfire. Having gone to this expense and trouble, he is now stranded five miles farther up the hill, with less in his pockets than he normally carries to work. There's something wrong somewhere.

This outdoor enthusiast has fallen into a trap that every person who ventures into any wilderness area should avoid like the plague. Being aware of the fact that everything he adds to his list of what to take will be that much more of a drag on his progress, the weight-conscious backpacker will try to avoid duplicating any item he plans to take along. This line of thinking could easily backfire when the rugged individualist finds himself separated from that shoulder-creaking load he so lovingly assembled, with anything from a poor sense of direction to a moment of awkwardness at the cliff's edge to keep him from getting back to the gear on which his life depends.

On an extended trip, the question of duplication does not arise, because most of the items that should be in every backpacker's emergency pack will probably be needed as a matter of course when living in the wilds for more than a couple of days. Even on a short outing, the hunter who intends to just step across the creek for a closer shot at a distant deer, the fisherman who doffs his portable living quarters and wades into fast-running shallows, and the photographer who leaves his pack for a difficult climb to an award-winning scenic view should each take a few extra seconds to pick up and take along a small satchel of the basic necessities in case the unexpected should happen.

A fanny pack or light satchel that can be slung over the hiker's shoulder will hold everything the outdoorsman should need to handle the day-to-day necessities of isolated circumstances.

A well-stocked emergency pack should weigh no more than ten pounds and probably will be as light as five pounds, when supplemented by other items the woodsman should have in his pockets or on his hip. Most of the needed gear will weigh no more than a few ounces, but any of it could be worth many times its weight in gold if the backpacker doesn't have it when his life may depend on it.

Being cut off from civilization, the woodsman will want to be able to live off the land as much as possible. An indispensable item that should be included in every survival pack is a handbook or written list of the annual and seasonal plants and fruits that a stricken outdoorsman will find edible. Such a list can be obtained from local forestry personnel or residents. The backpacker should already be somewhat familiar with the most common edible varieties to be found in the areas where he regularly travels. He will know how to recognize the flowers and leaves, which parts of the plants are edible and which should be avoided, at what time of year each is ready to pick and how to harvest and prepare them.

The backpacker should carry at least a two-day supply of canned or freeze-dried foods which he can thin out over as many as five days by using natural foods he finds at hand. Even the desert can supply nourishment to those who know where and how to look, but the hiker preparing for possible emergencies should not count entirely on living off the land unless he has absolutely no other source of food

Knowing edible plants can allow trail victim to add to food supply.

available. A two-day supply is about right in terms of weight and in providing the backpacker an opportunity to become accustomed to the natural foods, if he has not already done so.

This is a necessary consideration for any potential Euell Gibbons whose digestive system is accustomed to the processed groceries that fill every supermarket shelf. Most newcomers to the outdoor scene, and many experienced campers, who have not tried munching a tasty dandelion or grubbing for wild turnips, will find themselves suffering some stomach upset the first few times their system has to make the change-over from commercially processed vegetables to the natural tubers and grasses. Using the civilized foods to which their bodies are accustomed to supplement a diet of wild flowers and natural grains will help ease the backpacker's transition pangs.

One way to anticipate this possible trouble is for the weekend outdoorsman to pick a few of the edible plants he finds along the trail, take them home and add them to his normal daily menu on a regular basis. Then, should the time come when the backpacker finds himself totally dependent on such foods for his survival, his system will already be somewhat used to them, leaving his mind free to concentrate on getting out of his wilderness predicament without the constant distraction of irreverent interruptions.

A proper survival pack should include a small, handleless pot for boiling edible plants, but in its absence, the hiker should be handy at constructing an oven by digging a square pit and lining it with stones or putting a flat rock to use as a skillet. Other smooth stones could be used for grinding the naturally harvested grains and softening tuber edibles prior to cooking.

No one, no matter how familiar he might be with nature's abundant vegetable garden, should have to depend solely on his grain-harvesting abilities for healthy eating in a tight situation. If the backpacker in trouble has included a twenty-five-foot roll of flexible eighteen-gauge wire, a supply of single-barb hooks, an assortment of small to medium-sized spoons and about fifty feet of strong nylon cord in his emergency pack, fresh meat and fish for his

With a small plastic bottle, backpacker can refill main water supply from creek, stream or have an emergency supply in his survival pack if water bag is punctured.

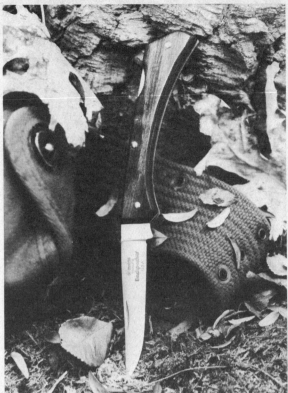

Above: The woodsman's basic tool —
a good knife. It is used to shave
kindling strips, carve fishhooks and
game traps, and to cut bandages or
smooth off rough splints. Left:
A topographical map can direct
lost hiker back to highway and help.

survival larder are a simple matter of finding a likely game trail or stream, and a little judicious carving.

The hunter carrying a rifle, sidearm or bow will include an extra box of ammunition or an extra quiver of arrows in his survival gear and should be able to supplement his emergency supplies by taking small game or waterfowl as he needs it. He should not, however, kill more than he can eat or preserve in an edible state if he finds himself unexpectedly isolated from his base camp for an extended period of time.

The knowledgeable survivalist will include the woodsman's basic tool — a knife — in his survival pack to supplement the one he normally wears on his hip or to replace it should it be lost. This can be the long-sheath type or, preferably, some version of the multi-blade folding camp knife that provides everything from the basic cutting edge to fork, spoon, scissors and tweezers, which can be used to remove painful splinters or cut makeshift bandages or wrappings.

Anticipating that some kind of accidental injury may cause a delay in his return to civilization, the backpacker will want a first-aid kit handy at all times. The contents of this kit will vary according to individual preference, but any list of first-aid items should include a snakebite kit with anti-venom serum, various-sized sterile gauze pads, tape, some kind of disinfectant, a razor blade, a pair of tweezers and a plastic — not cloth — stretch bandage for wrapping sprains or securing splints.

Darvon, or some other pain-reducing drug, and antibiotics may be included at the individual's discretion, but the woodsman should remember that he is not a physician and should take care to learn of any allergies that he or a trail companion may have before handing out capsules.

The backpacker should carry enough water to meet his cooking, drinking and cleaning needs, plus a little extra to cover emergencies. Two of the standard one-quart canteens or a water bag fit comfortably on the hiker's hips or pack and should see a mountain camper through until he can find that next sparkling stream. The backpacker's survival pack should include its own water supply, which can be contained in a small plastic bottle or a pocket-size metal hip flask that fits in a small satchel without taking up too much room. The outdoorsman who sets up camp next to a creek or pool should remember to take water with him when he leaves his campsite in case he does not return when he expects to. Every camper should have water-purification tablets or one of the commercial water-purification kits to enable him to supplement his water supply from surrounding sources.

Fire is one of the most useful tools that the backpacker has at his disposal. A well-laid fire will provide heat to protect the camper against the temperature drops of nightfall or the chilling effects of rain or falling snow. The backpacker who is cut off from his nice warm sleeping bag is going to need some way to keep himself warm and to cook whatever source of nourishment his ingenuity and knowledge of the outdoors manages to turn up. To ensure that he has at least this much of an edge on survival, the backpacker should have as complete a fire-starting kit in his survival pack as he can fit in with the other necessities.

or the sudden chill of a desert night, the backpacker who leaves his base camp to stalk a wild moose or find salmon should have with him some form of plastic or rubber tarp that he can use to rig a temporary shelter. The backpacker who wants to travel really light is not going to be bothered with toting a bulky sleeping bag up and down mountain trails on an afternoon hike.

In a survival situation, a lightweight tarp, which will easily fit folded in the bottom of the hiker's survival pack, can pinch-hit for tent and sleeping bag as a potent weapon in the backpacker's battle against the elements. Erected on the windward side with part of the camper's supply of light-weight cord, this makeshift shelter will reflect the heat of a controlled campfire, keeping the tired camper comfortably warm on both sides, instead of too hot on one side and too

Left: Old-fashioned, strike-anywhere kitchen matches are best for the fire-starting kit. Paper matches or the smaller kitchen type aren't as dependable. Below: A commercial fire-starter is handy when wood is wet.

This fire-starting kit should include large-size kitchen matches in some type of waterproof metal container. They can be wrapped in tin foil, and this may be an even better practice, because the metal containers are subject to rust and may be difficult to open with chilled hands. Smaller kitchen matches or the paper type are not good substitutes for the larger brand, as they usually require special abrasive paper to set them off, whereas the old-fashioned, larger types will strike on just about any surface from the sole of a hiking boot to a piece of rock. Also necessary is a supply of punk or ready-made tinder that is easily ignited. These and the fire-starter cubes available at most camping goods outlets will make starting a fire a lot easier in a damp forest or against high winds.

A small magnifying glass should be part of the fire kit, for use as a substitute for matches in a pinch. The magnifying glass can be kept in the first-aid kit, doing double duty as a fire starter and for use with a pair of tweezers in removing troublesome slivers or cactus spines that a pocket-knife or fingernails will not get out.

Another good fire starter is the commercially made Metal Match, offered by the Ute Mountain Corporation, in a kit that includes ready-made tinder. Added to this should be a supply of short, thick candles, known as plumbers' candles, which can be used in drying wet tinder or as a long, steadily burning match that will reach under a tepee-type fire and resist an untimely gust of wind. This method of fire starting can also help a camper preserve his limited supply of matches during a long stay out. A small supply of dry kindling can make the whole process of obtaining warmth and light and preparing food a lot simpler for the hiker caught out in rainy or snowstorming weather. A piece of flint can be useful if the backpacker's matches have gotten wet when he tripped and fell in that icy stream.

Although a fire will help stave off the cold mountain air

A plastic tarp becomes instant shelter with poles cut from surrounding saplings and twine from survival kit. Without poles, it can serve as an impromptu sleeping bag or makeshift poncho to keep hiker dry in the rain.

cold on the other, as he catnaps his way through a bitter winter night.

The most important gear a lost or stranded backpacker can have in his emergency satchel are the odds and ends he will use to find his way out of that predicament or to attract the attention of outside sources of help. These items should include a small hand mirror or, perhaps, a policeman's whistle with which the accident victim can signal a low-flying aircraft or direct the members of a search party to his location. Every backpacker, especially if he is hiking in unfamiliar territory, should have with him a topographical map of the area he is exploring and a good compass with which he can find his way back to civilization after he has gotten turned around tracking that eight-point buck or checking out that overgrown trail.

Depending on where he has decided to wander, the wilderness survival expert may have decided to strap on and take along some kind of small caliber sidearm or one of the recently developed collapsible .22 caliber rifles. These rifles are designed so that the broken-down pieces fit inside the rifle stock and the weapon can occupy an unobtrusive corner of the hiker's main pack. If the backpacker's carving skill is such that some kind of weapon is a necessary substitute in a survival situation, perhaps this is the answer to which he should turn.

In deciding on this method of procuring his survival sustenance, the backpacker preparing in advance for trouble on the trail should consider where his trip will take him, remembering that taking this piece of civilization will also mean hauling along the legal restrictions against concealed weapons that apply on any city street.

Those wilderness areas under the control of the National Parks Service, and those designated as primitive areas with many entrance and operating restrictions include in their regulations a hefty rule against the destruction of any animal or plant life even under emergency survival conditions. All firearms and weapons, including traps, spears, snares and fishing gear of any type must be broken down in such a way that they cannot be used to harm animal life, and the natural foods enthusiast is forbidden to munch the grass as well. If that sounds like typical bureaucratic gobbledegook, try this: Title 36, Parks, Forests and Public Property; Chapter One, National Park Service, Department of the Interior; Part Two, Public Recreation; Paragraph 2.11.

National Forestry Service areas, which do occasionally overlap National Park responsibilities in traditional government agency fashion, are covered by regulations which prohibit the discharge of any firearm in developed or primitive campgrounds, but forestry officials say they will provide appropriate absolution for a starving victim in wilderness areas under emergency conditions.

In the state parks and recreation areas of California, the destruction or harvesting of animal or plant life is prohibited by a variety of regulations, but the official consensus here also is that these would not be enforced in an emergency situation. Such provisions would prevent the backpacker from trying out his favorite survival foods under nonemergency conditions, however, so his digestive tract will just have to take its chances should he find himself in trouble.

Other states may have similar laws or regulations protecting wild animal and plant life. The backpacker's best bet, if he anticipates having to live off the land, would be to call his state's regional forestry headquarters to learn exactly what his state's restrictions are and whether or not these restrictions will be waived in an emergency. The backpacker might also look into what state fish and game laws he might violate in the course of trying to stay alive until a rescue party can find him.

The backpacker in trouble might logically decide that all bets are off when it comes to basic survival, but the sad fact is that logic and law can sometimes be miles apart and a $500 fine might be necessary to bridge the gap between them when the wilderness casualty eventually returns to civilization to face the music for his regulatory misdeeds. Don't assume anything. Check the sad facts first, then decide how dire the situation could get and whether or not that firearm is really an advantage.

Even a moderately skillful carver can easily avoid this survival-cramping hassle, at least in the wilderness areas where improvisation is permitted. A neatly trimmed sapling strung with fish line, hook and spoon will bring in almost any variety of fish found in most streams and lakes. For the more stubborn or wily species, grubs or worms dug from the moist soil along the shore or taken from under an overturned log should bring about the necessary cooperation.

There are a number of possibilities for the forgetful hiker who leaves his base camp without taking his survival pack along. In such desperate straits, the woodsman can weave a makeshift line from any long, slender weeds, reeds or grasses, starting with three or four stems of unequal length and adding a stem as necessary. This method will eliminate any weak spots in the resulting line that might part under the stress of landing the backpacker's catch. For a hook, the improvising outdoorsman could choose from a number of different types that can either be carved to smoothness or, lacking even a pocketknife, broken from a thorn hedge and used au natural.

The simplest of these is the ancient gorge, used for centuries by many Indian tribes and primitive societies in all parts of the world. The gorge's size depends on the size of fish the backpacker intends to land, as the whole thing must fit inside a fish's mouth, yet not be small enough for him to spit out once he takes the bait. To make the simple gorge, cut a small twig 1½ to two inches in length. Cut a notch around the middle of the twig and taper each end to a point.

Lacking a knife, the stranded backpacker could break such a twig off to the desired length and sharpen the points on a piece of rock. If he could not manage to employ a sharp-edged piece of stone as a crude but effective carving knife, he would have to take the chance of losing his gorge if it should work loose from his handmade line while the fish is struggling. Once the gorge has been smoothed sufficiently, bait is impaled on each end and the line, perhaps weighted by a rock tied onto it in lieu of the split shot that was left behind, is tossed out in hopes that the right-sized fish will happen along.

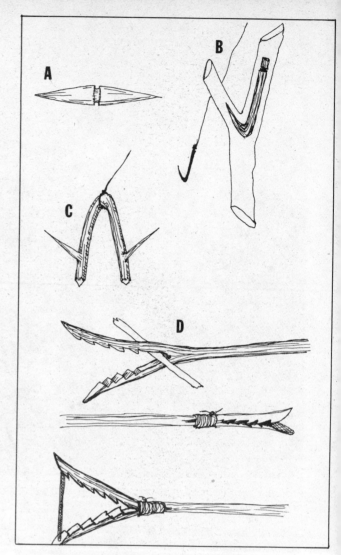

The gorge (A), the briar gorge (C), and a fishhook (B) carved from a branched twig are possibilities open to a moderately skilled carver. The fishing spear (D) and its variations require handiness with a blade.

Any briared brush or vine offers another alternative to this simple device in the form of a bend in the branch where two thorns are almost opposite each other on the stem. Cutting or breaking the vine off below the two thorns gives a ready-made and somewhat more flexible variation of the gorge. The backpacker's line is tied at the middle of the bend, preferably in a carved notch to keep it from slipping. Bait is added and the result is hopefully cast upon the waters. The erstwhile fisherman must tend the line carefully when using a gorge and be ready to pull back sharply at the first sign of a nibble thus forcing the gorge sideways in the struggling fish's mouth so the fish cannot spit it out or work it loose before the hungry fisherman can haul him to shore.

The impatient or perhaps injured backpacker who does not or cannot tend his fish lines could make use of any limber tree limb that he finds growing out over the water. Attaching his line and bait to this type of improvised pole gives the survival fisherman what has become known through the years as a treeline. This type of tackle works best if left overnight and its catch taken in for the first meal of the day. The flexible limb will keep the necessary ten-

A collapsible fishing rod can make the stranded backpacker's life a little easier by providing him a more
familiar way to hook onto that aquatic appetizer. Some
specially made poles break down to as little as 18 inches.

sion on the line to set the gorge, but added insurance may easily be had with a little refinement on the improvised hook.

This particular construction requires a bit of handiness with a carving knife, but with a little luck and a lot of patience even the novice carver can shape out a normal hook from the crotch or bend where a small branch joins a limb. Cut one fork about half the length of the other and make this the pointed end of the wooden hook. Notch the longer end after getting the hook smoothed off and tie the nylon fish line in this notch to prevent it from slipping off when the fish strikes. Cut a vee-notch on the inside of the straight part of the hook, near the line notch. Take a separate twig and fashion a point on one end, then cut the other end off at the same angle as the vee-notch. Fit this end of the second point into the vee-notch and bind tightly with nylon line, with the second point resting just inside the hook and pointing down. When a fish takes the bait impaled on the hook, the second point acts as a barb — in safety pin fashion — to hold the fish on the hook while the backpacker pulls it to shore. If used with a treeline, this type of hook will hold the fish until the carver gets ready to haul in his breakfast.

For the backpacker who wants immediate results from his food-gathering labors and does not want to wait for the fish to bite, there are a number of workable variations possible for a fishing spear. This implement can be as simple as a strong stick with a point cut on one end, or a more complex arrangement that features a split green sapling with notches or teeth cut in the mouth of the split that will grip the intended fryer and allow the spearfisherman to toss his wriggling prey onto dry ground with a flick of his wrist.

One way to improve on the simple sharpened point is to start with a limb that is thick enough to allow the carver to add a single barb to one side of his spear point. This would make removing the fish a time-consuming, or if the hiker is in a hurry, a messy gutting chore unless the trail casualty thinks to simply run the spear on through his catch and let it drop off the other end, which has no barb to impede its progress.

The isolated backpacker who has a knife, but is not skilled in its use might simply tie the knife to the end of a sapling to make his fishing spear. But in using such a construction — or any nonbarbed point arrangement — the survivalist should be careful to jam the spear point all the way to the bottom of the water to prevent his catch from slipping free and escaping before he can get it to shore. The hapless hiker might feel a bit foolish to lose the survival knife he carefully included in his emergency gear in such a careless fashion.

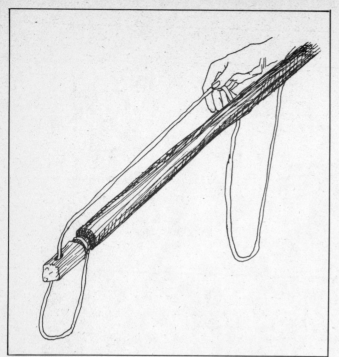

A catchpole, such as is used by snake handlers, can be the backpacker's means of catching a duck or field grouse if he is adept at stalking.

The simplest form of game snare can be set up across a likely game trail. The rabbit or squirrel runs his head through the loop, which collapses and holds him.

Rather than splashing around in a rocky creekbed, wetting what is probably his only change of clothing in the process, the wilderness survivor might prefer to remove his trousers and boots long enough to wade in and build himself a fish trap that will gather in his breakfast for the spearing.

Such a trap can be constructed downstream in the shallows close to shore, and might be either a curved wall of stones that will trap any fish feeding in the shallows by the simple device of blocking its return to deeper water, or a more complex operation, made of thick branches sharpened and driven into the creek bottom in a three-sided box arrangement with additional screens placed at either edge of the open fourth side to guide the fisherman's prey into his trap. Fish corralled in such a manner can be speared and flipped ashore, or the backpacker can collect his meal by heaving a heavy rock against the surface of the pool inside his trap, then removing the stunned fish by hand.

These elaborate methods are extremely time-consuming. Therefore, the fisherman working for an emergency meal should probably carve the notched, jaw-type spear used successfully for hundreds of years by the Indians.

This weapon can be fitted together in either of two ways. The carver first finds and trims out a fresh, green sapling or tree branch, then carefully cuts a split in one end between eight to ten inches deep. The place where the split ends should be bound tightly to prevent the stick from splitting further. The carver then puts a temporary wedge in the base of the split to hold it open while he cuts a series of notches in each face of the split. These notches should be cut with their points angling in toward the base of the split. Taper the open ends on one side to form the two penetrating points, then place a small twig in the mouth of the split to hold it open. When the carefully wading fisherman spies the trout and lunges frantically to stop his prey from dodging aside, the body of the fish should knock the twig aside, and the teeth will hold the fish until the lucky hiker can get it back to his campfire.

The other variation of this may work a little better as the propped-open jaws of the spear may not close tightly enough over the captive fish if they are jammed into the stream bed. To make this more effective spear, split the green sapling and notch the inside of the jaws as before, but now insert a permanent wedge into the base of the split and bind the split stop. This arrangement is strictly for impaling, as the jaws are not held as far open as with the first type, but with the twin barbs cut on either point, the fish cannot struggle loose.

For the survivalist who takes the phrase "living off the land" literally, that roll of eighteen-gauge wire and his pocketknife are the tools that, when combined with a little imagination will enable him to have fresh meat until he is found or has recovered from his injuries enough to make his way back to civilization.

The woodsman who is not immobilized by injuries, and who is a skilled stalker, might turn first to the simple-to-make and easy-to-use catchpole noose, which is a long, limber sapling or branch with a collapsible loop fixed on one end. The catchpole noose is made by cutting a small, round hole through one end of the chosen pole, about two inches from the end. The same end is notched and one end of a length of wire is wound around this end and twisted tightly. The other end of the wire is pushed through the hole and pulled toward the other end of the pole. This end of the wire is held by the stalker as he moves quietly behind a field grouse, quail, duck, raccoon or whatever and slips the wire noose over the unsuspecting prey's head and jerks it tight, then holds on grimly until the trapped animal stops struggling.

This is basically the same type of snare used by snake-handlers to lift a single specimen out of the terrarium without the risk of being bitten by the other snakes in the cage. This snare can provide a similar service for the hungry trail casualty by saving him from being lacerated into long uneven strips by a raccoon or rabbit that emphatically believes it has better things to do than grace the hiker's dinner menu. Anyone who has ever tried to cuddle a cute,

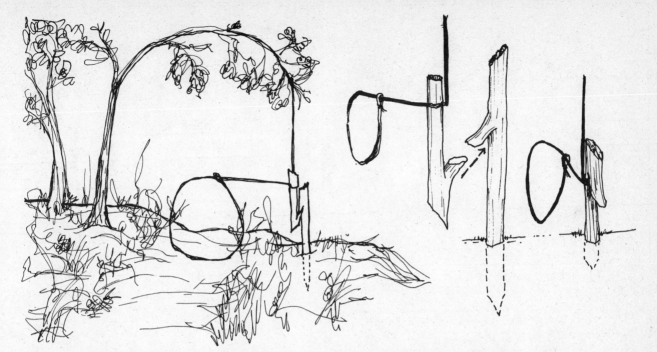

A reliable trigger for a more effective snare can be fashioned by trimming a branch as illustrated. The animal hits the noose and its struggles pull the retaining stick from its holder, hoisting the game aloft.

supposedly harmless wild rabbit while wearing a short-sleeved shirt can testify to the effectiveness of this wee creature's hidden claws, and the raccoon has long been known as a fierce fighter, bringing teeth and claws into play when cornered.

The length of the catchpole protects the hunter from these hazards and still supplies him his meal, provided he is strong enough to handle the explosion of frantic energy at the end of that ten-foot rod. That length is recommended for the catchpole. To make it much longer will cause it to be awkward to handle even in an open field, where a quick switch from left to right without becoming entangled in high grasses could mean the difference between eating and going hungry.

For the city-bred, and therefore noisier, weekend woodsman, stationary traps and snares, which are easy to make and set, are probably a more workable answer to the problem of surviving an unexpected hitch in the hiking schedule. These can be built along any recognizable game trail and can be used with or without bait. Baited or not, the snare or trap will have to be at least partially concealed to be effective. With the abundance of foliage and ground cover available in any forest, and the use of a little imagination, even the novice at survival should have little trouble collecting his meals.

Probably the simplest game trail snare to make is the one that starts with two forked sticks, one driven into the ground on either side of the trail, with a notched crosspiece resting in the forks. One end of a length of wire is wrapped around the notch and a small loop is twisted in the other. The wire is brought back through its own loop to form the lariat-type opening into which the unsuspecting animal will run. The resulting opening should be large enough to fit over the animal's head, but not so large that the animal just runs right through it and continues on its way. This loop is held open by bracing it with the branches of small plants growing along the trail. The poor vision of most forest creatures should make this enough concealment. More might interfere with the operation of the snare and cost a

too-clever woodsman his dinner.

A more elaborate arrangement might be contrived by bending a flexible sapling over and tying the trigger wire of the snare near the top of its trunk. A simple release for this type of snare can be carved by notching two small sticks and wiring one to the end of the trigger wire and the other to a stake in the ground. The notched pieces fit into each other in a fragile enough manner so that when an animal disturbs the loop, the trigger piece slips out of the anchor piece and the unsuspecting prey is airborne. This trap does not need constant attention; the animal it snares will simply hang around, waiting to be collected.

The simple box propped up by a stick is one of the best-known bird or ground squirrel traps, but it is awkward in that most birds are wary of going under any type of overhang. Unless the trapper is willing to spend the balance of the day lying in wait with tripcord in hand, it is necessary to take the time to carve out a complicated figure-four trigger. An obvious drawback of this type of trap is that the trapper could use a week's supply of grain getting his prey accustomed to feeding under the shadow of the box. Even when the game is cooperating, it is still necessary to use some kind of bait that might better serve to thicken out a stew made from snared game.

The unlucky hiker who finds himself in trouble on his first trip out may not have the slightest idea of how to go about emulating the Indians, but he can still use the natural materials around him to prolong his survival until he gets help.

A simple throwing stick or even a large rock can be used to net a meal from a flock of water birds that comes into shore to feed at dusk. If the camper finds that this device doesn't function as he would like, he can always add it to his supply of firewood and search out the tasty possibilities offered by any bird's nest or that clump of watercrest in the shallows of a handy pond.

Freshwater clams are easy to locate by their airholes as the meandering hiker strolls along the shore of a pond or lake, and some edible lichens can stave off hunger pangs.

A bed of logs will give the stranded backpacker a dry bed on which to lay his survival fire. Wet wood won't burn.

A wall of logs built on the windward side of the fire will reflect heat back toward the sleeping camper.

A knife blade struck against flint will produce needed sparks to get a fire started if matches were left behind.

A magnifying glass, camera or binocular lens can be used to focus sunlight on tinder for a slow but effective burn.

The fire drill can be used in either of two ways to start tinder smoldering. The backpacker who anticipates trouble will learn at least two matchless fire-makers.

The fire saw can also be used effectively if the proper wood can be found. A bit of carving skill is needed.

The fire bow is the most effective of the friction methods, but requires a supple limb, a bit of carving skill and a length of cord for the bow.

An improperly laid fire will either not light or will continually go out. Proper construction and a little patience will yield a better, longer lasting result.

The camper who prepares for survival before he needs the information will have made a quick reconnaissance of his neighborhood library to learn which land and water plants are edible, during what seasons shellfish can be added to his supplies and the potentially harmful varieties of animal and plant life whose consumption would only add to his problems.

The prepared outdoorsman may combine his taste for socializing with a bit of learning by cultivating the acquaintance and conversation of the old-timers who have lived in the area he plans to explore and who may know a few tricks their grandfathers used to stay alive in the area before the local retail outlets were even set up.

Once the stranded backpacker has collected the makings for his wilderness meal, he then has to put to use man's oldest and most useful tool for survival — fire. If he has left his survival gear — including his fire-making kit — back down the trail, he can still start up a blaze with materials he can take from his environment, providing he has taken the time to learn the various ways and means, and to practice them at home before his life depends on them.

A good fire starts with selecting the best wood for the type of fire the hiker needs. A midday fire should be small and use less wood of a type that burns fast and hot and makes good coals. An evening cookfire that will also be used for heat through the night will require a good bed of coals and the use of progressively larger sticks of hard-to-ignite but slow-burning fuel, unless the tired camper intends to stay up all night and use half the forest to feed a blazing, inefficient furnace.

Hardwoods work best for an all-night coal bed, which would be laid out by placing two oak or maple logs alongside the hot coals of the pine or juniper cookfire. Staying with the fire until it has burned down to coals will keep the camper from waking up with his clothes on fire because he rolled too close to the cheery blaze. The perimeter logs will provide fuel that the heat from the coals will eat into, making a safe sleeping fire for the exhausted outdoorsman.

A piece of flint scraped against the steel blade of a pocketknife or struck against a piece of stone will eventually provide a spark that can be softly fanned into a starting blaze in the bottom of an old, dried mouse nest or bird

nest. During daylight hours, a piece of magnifying glass will also bring quick combustion of tinder slivers to get things started. The fire drill, the fire saw and the fire bow, used by many Indian tribes before their introduction to matches, will require more patient work, but the end result, with proper technique, should be the same.

Such desperate measures will work only if the camper is completely familiar with their use. If he is, he knows that good tinder is a must and he will either collect the needed material along his route or gather a double handful of pine needles, break up a few cones or scrape the pitch from a maple tree to gain the necessary.

Once he has his basic materials, the survivalist must select a safe site for his fire and lay it so it can be ignited and contained with a minimum of effort.

The best method is to surround his fire site with flat rocks on which he can lay his improvised cooking gear. Keeping in mind that his intention is not to send the whole forest up in smoke, the camper arranges his fire bed so he can use one fire to meet all his campsite needs. He will construct his shelter of pine boughs or whatever, and place his fire in relation to it, so the fire will not ignite his sleeping place.

When he has his fire site picked out, his materials together and a small bed of tinder laid, the camper must then decide which fire-starting method he is most familiar with and construct the necessary tools to accomplish it.

Any of the friction methods will require a fire board, split from a small limb about six inches in width and twelve inches long. The board can be longer, but should not be so awkward that the camper cannot rest it comfortably with one end on the tinder and the other against his knee, or hold it down with his foot to prevent it from slipping. He must then fashion a fire drill by smoothing a short length of wood to one to 1½ inches in diameter. The camper then cuts a groove the length of his fire board and tapers one end of his fire drill to a point. Rubbing the tapered fire drill briskly in the groove of the fire board will produce friction-heated powder that will eventually ignite properly dried tinder. Once tinder has begun to smoke steadily, it should be fanned gently, resulting in the first bit of flame.

Another way to produce this friction is to cut a notch in a length of high-friction wood and rub a vee-shaped stick back and forth in the groove until a bit of spark is produced. This is the fire saw.

Preparing the fire bow is a lengthy process, but this is a sure way to get a fire going. The fire drill should not be rounded in this method, but should have octagonal faces along its length. The end is rounded and blunt, so there is a larger area in which friction can be produced. Cut a flexible limb and string it with a piece of cord, which can be anything from a tangle of string kept in a shirt pocket to a cord braided from the cloth of the camper's shirt. Loop the slack in the string around the fire drill and place the end of the drill in a notched piece of wood under the tinder. Using a knothole or flat rock to steady the drill, whip the bow back and forth to spin the fire drill in the notched wood, and blow gently on the resulting smoldering tinder to get the blaze going. Add progressively bigger pieces of wood to build the fire up to needed levels.

The camper should keep in mind that he will have to obtain his tinder from the lower, dead branches of trees in wet weather and should remember to build his fire on a platform of logs when laying it out on snow, ice or wet ground. A wet fire drill or fire board can make things difficult, but the only way to avoid this is to have dry fire-making materials — preferably matches, starter cubes and tinder — wrapped in a plastic bag and tucked in a shirt or jacket pocket before starting out.

A rough shelter of pine or evergreen boughs can be set up by bracing a long pole in the crotch of a tree.

A plastic tarp with its corners pinned between four piles of rocks will provide shade to a stranded desert hiker.

A makeshift tent can be rigged with a plastic or rubber tarp and line.

Sometimes a lost hiker will luck into abandoned shelter. Look for snakes, rodents before bedding down.

The backpacker in trouble may find himself stranded for as long as a week or, perhaps, longer. He will need more than a good fire to avoid falling victim to the elements; this means constructing some type of temporary shelter under which he can avoid becoming wet and chilled by rain, snow or wind until help arrives.

This can be anything from a large sheet of plastic to a lean-to of branches. The camper will be limited in how elaborate a shelter he will need by how long he expects to be out, how well he can move about and the extent of his imagination in terms of refinements.

The recommended tarp can be used in a variety of ways to build a lean-to, a pup tent or as a ground cloth that the backpacker can use in lieu of a sleeping bag. Without such a tarp, the hiker can still fashion shelter by propping or tying a long tree branch into the crotch of a nearby tree. The hiker can drape pine or evergreen boughs against the main pole on both sides and weave in cattails for added protection from the wind. The stranded backpacker will have his own ideas of how his shelter should be arranged for comfort, convenient entry and exit, but all will probably have some kind of ground cover to keep the camper dry and warm, even in inclement weather.

The backpacker caught out in the wilderness with the bare essentials — if he remembered to strap on his emergency fanny pack — will find that there is one artifact of civilization that is a lot more convenient to have than not as he fumbles his way through the process of setting up his survival camp in the fading light of approaching darkness. The regular-size flashlight and extra batteries and bulbs he probably debated including in his survival pack will more than make up for their weight and bulkiness as the stranded camper locates tree limbs strong enough to support his shelter; searches for, breaks up and gathers enough wood to last through the night; and follows the elusive sound of running water to that weed-covered creek nearby.

In these areas, and in the making of splints or a litter to support damaged limbs or carry out an injured companion, the isolated backpacker finds that another item of survival gear becomes more than worth its weight in usefulness as he employs the small hatchet he carries in a belt sheath at his waist to trim out his tentpoles, fashion a crude crutch or chip away at a fallen tree root for the big piece that will burn throughout the night.

The easiest way for the backpacker to survive in the wilds is not to let a moment of carelessness put him in a life-or-death situation that could easily have been avoided. Watch for soft places, loose rocks and chuckholes in the trail, especially when traveling through open, overgrown country. Spend some time on one or two-day hikes, getting to know the country; its danger as well as its delight, what plants and animals can provide food in an emergency and how to lay hands on them, how to find and purify water and the use and language of compasses and topographical maps. Get to know the residents, if possible, or get a detailed briefing on the area from forestry personnel on dos and don'ts of their area.

Be familiar with various ways to build and start a fire, with and without matches. Study and practice first-aid treatments for shock, broken or sprained limbs, how to stop bleeding and the procedure for administering mouth-to-mouth resuscitation.

Carry some kind of survival kit that includes basic items for providing oneself with food, heat, shelter, medical care and the means to find the way out or to attract the attention of searchers.

When the mountain-climbing or desert-crawling vacationer deals himslef into nature's vast poker game, he must remember that every game is different. His survival depends on knowing the house rules and betting accordingly.

As he moves his body from sheltered apartment to the harsh, open conditions of weather and climate, the backpacker must realize that he will have to find substitutes for the shelter, food and warmth he takes for granted in the city. There is considerably more than a ruined weekend at stake if he doesn't cover all bets before sitting in on the high stakes contest of man versus his environment.

A well-prepared backpacker will find living off the land no problem and will be able to limit the damage of accidents.

Chapter 11
TO ENHANCE THE GOOD LIFE

A Few Non-Essentials Can Give the Backpacker a Better Way to Go

With the bare essentials all accounted for, some nature enthusiasts may want to add in a few non-survival items.

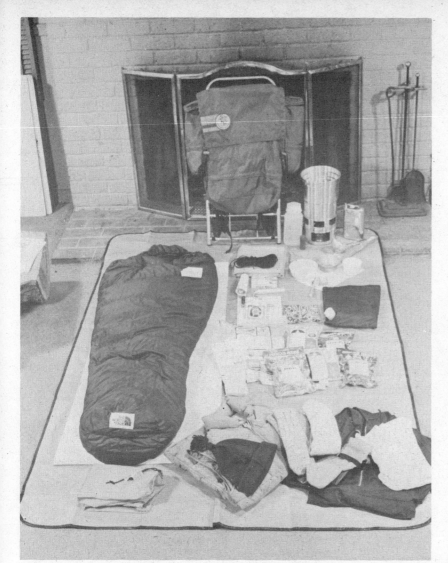

A picture of all his gear laid out on a tarp could serve the backpacker as a reminder of some things he missed last time.

SIERRA SOUTH

100 Back-country trips in California's Sierra

by Karl Schwenke and Thomas Winnett

Wilderness Press Trail Guide Series $2.95

Commercially-produced guides to the better backpacking areas could be matched by the homemade variety.

WHEN THAT WEEK-LONG trail-hiking marathon has given the backpacker the firm muscle tone and the snap and vigor of his early youth, he may want a few visual reminders of the hours of agony it took him to earn that tanned leanness, so he will not get lazy and grow himself another potbelly. He may want to remember that picturesque view as he stood at the edge of two hundred feet of open space, the terrain he conquered to get there and the friends who were along. He already may be planning his next trip and have a few equipment additions and deletions in mind that he learned from some bitter, or at best better-not-repeated, experiences on his last trip out. The family camper may want a few souvenir snapshots of his wife and kids against the background of that breath-taking forest or the tallest tree in the valley.

When last summer's vacation has faded into misty memory, the backpacker who adds just a couple of extra items to his checklist can bring back forgotten details to share with friends or to refresh his recollections of a certain stretch of trail by glancing through the color pictures or slides he snapped along the way with his trusty Instamatic.

A fixed-focus, fixed-aperture camera can make a capable photographer of anyone with enough sense to peer through the view finder and press the shutter release. These simple cameras are available in a variety of styles, fit easily in a shirt pocket and offer both manual film advances and wind-up, spring-driven types which will give that second chance to catch a dappled deer taking an early morning drink or freeze the image of a running rabbit just before it dives into its burrow.

Film for these simple cameras is available in any drug store in several black-and-white and color emulsions, and comes preloaded in handy, drop in, close and shoot cassettes for most models. Those who anticipate making or ordering enlargements and extra prints will want to get the camera that uses the 126-size film as opposed to the 110-size used by the so-called Pocket Instamatic. The smaller film size will limit enlargement of a favored image, while the 126 cartridge will allow enlargement of good negatives all the way up to poster size if such is desired.

Mass production and the popularity of these lightweight and easy-to-use cameras has held their purchase price to the point where the family budget will not go down the drain when the camera is first purchased, and has lessened the extent of catastrophe if the camera should slip from a sweaty hand and go bouncing into an inaccessible canyon, or a youngster's moment of clumsiness should get it dropped into that cheery camp blaze.

A telephoto lens will bring that skittish rabbit closer to the photographer's stand.

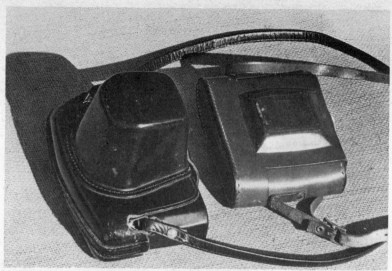

A leather case attatched to the camera body and a neck or wrist strap will help keep moisture and dust off that $500 camera.

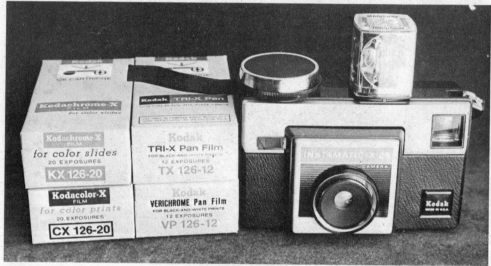

An inexpensive Instamatic camera, with fixed focus and fixed shutter speed, is the ideal choice for trip record pictures.

A bulkier variety of the simpler camera offers the advantage of being able to view the results a few seconds after the picture is snapped. Polaroid, the company which manufactures these cameras, offers a standard 3½x4½-inch picture size and the option of black-and-white or color films. Most of their models also give the student photographer a limited control of the aperture setting, which governs the amount of light to which the film will be exposed, and include simple instructions for adjusting a picture that turns out too light or too dark. The shutter speed, which controls the duration of an exposure, is preset on most of these cameras at one-sixtieth of a second — a happy medium in the range available on more expensive cameras that will handle the standard bright, cloudy or shady light situations that the family photographer is likely to meet. The one-sixtieth shutter speed also allows the shutter to synchronize with the amount of time that a flash cube or flash unit will give off its brightest light. The drawback to making use of these advantages is that most Polaroid film packets do not make negatives, so no enlargements or extra prints of pictures taken with these films are possible.

The slightly more experienced photography buff may want more control over his exposures and the extra latitude needed to deal with the fading light of dusk or the brilliance of sunlight reflected from water, sand or snow. An inexpensive camera by Olympus or Honeywell's Visimatic might be the answer. The 35mm negative film used in this type of camera is big enough for good enlargements and the photographer is able to adjust aperture and shutter speed without breaking his bankroll for the privilege.

Some of these cameras offer the packability of a retractible lens and most can be purchased in any discount store's photo or music department for under $100. Their disadvantages include a limited focusing length on a permanently attached, 35mm lens and an offset viewfinder that may cause part of the desired picture to be cut off at close ranges. This is called a parallax problem and is present because the viewfinder does not have the same point of view as does the lens. It does not affect pictures taken at between seven and fifteen feet — the distance at which most snapshots are posed — but could interfere with framing at closer distances, so that the photographer does not get the picture he thought he did. Also, in order to use the cheaper 35mm cameras to their fullest potential, it is necessary to purchase and make room in a pack for a light meter,

A medium-priced, 35mm camera, such as this Rollei 35, might be good compromise for beginning shutter bug.

Using the light body of the average 35mm camera in high winds or in low light situations requires using a tripod.

which is used to measure the amount of light, so that the photographer knows whether or not he can get a good picture and at what aperture and shutter speed he will get the best picture with his type of film.

For between $150 and $200, the picture taker can buy a slightly better 35mm camera that will give him finer aperture and shutter speed controls, and which will eliminate the parallax problem by allowing the photographer to view his subject directly through the lens. This type of camera is called an SLR, or single lens reflex, camera because, as with the cheaper models, the image is focused on the film surface through a single lens. The difference is that the image is also reflected into the viewfinder from a mirror that moves up out of the way to expose the film surface when the shutter release is pressed. This system gives the photographer an accurate image of what will be recorded on the film at the instant he presses the shutter release.

The best SLR cameras offer as complete control over how much light reaches the film as is available with the present technology of the camera industry. Their cost is in the $250 to $350 range for the picture-taking body and a standard 50mm lens.

The lenses on these more expensive models can be interchanged for any of a wide range of lens sizes that focus a smaller or larger image on the film surface at a set distance. Lens sizes vary from a 21mm super wide-angle format, which gives a ninety-degree field of view, through 28, 50 and 55mm lenses which are wide-angle and normal, respectively, on up to 135, 200, 500 and 1000mm short-to-super telephoto lenses that will allow a photographer to get a shot of the most nervous gnat from up to one hundred feet away. The different manufacturers' lenses can even, with the additional purchase of the appropriate adaptors, be interchanged with different makes of camera bodies, so that the expensive purchase of one type of body does not limit the owner to that company's range of lens sizes.

Having shelled out the extra bucks for the finer control of the more expensive camera, the dedicated photographer can peel off a few more leaves from his rapidly thinning roll for the option of electronic control over aperture and shutter speed, so his new camera body will then function in much the same fashion as the $10 Instamatic. His money might be better spent in exercising one of the better options offered by Nikon, Yashica, Minolta, Canon or Mamiya-Sekor, which is the installation of a through-the-lens metering system. This will mean one less item to be tucked into the bulging knapsack and will give the photographer an accurate measurement of available light with just the press of a button while he is focusing.

The nature photographer who wants to catch that bounding buck as he races across the plain may want to invest in a motor drive, which is fitted to the bottom of the camera body. This device automatically advances the film and trips the shutter, burning up film as fast as five hundred frames a minute for as long as the shooter holds down the shutter release and the film supply holds out. It is here, and in the fact that loading any 35mm camera is somewhat more complicated for the beginner than simply dropping in a preloaded cassette, that the commercially offered thirty-six-exposure rolls of film — and the option open to any good darkroom technician of hand loading up to five hundred frames in a single film cannister — become a strong selling point for the weight and bulk-conscious backpacking photographer.

Bulk loading means fewer bulky yellow cardboard boxes and the longer rolls mean fewer reloading hassles. This holds true even without the added cost of installing the motor drive and both the snapshot collector and the back-

packing photographer who makes a living selling his nature pictures will probably be able to get on nicely with just the commercially loaded film lengths.

The deciding factor for anyone considering the purchase of a high-quality camera and the appropriate number and type of lenses is what kind of pictures he will be taking and to what use they will be put. The family-album or trip-record photographer will probably find the majority of his photo needs met admirably by the $10 Instamatic. Three to five of the twelve-exposure cassettes should be an ample film supply. The amateur who wants slightly more equipment may find his heart's desire in a Honeywell Pentax that gives him the option of interchangeable lenses without bankrupting his travel fund. The professional will want the best optics and the smoothest, most durable mechanism he can afford, and he will most likely find it among the offerings of Nikon, Mamiya-Sekor or others of their ilk.

Here again, the room-versus-need equation comes into play for the backpacker who wants to limit his supply load to something considerably less than a twenty-mule train. Like the professional, the serious amateur who is building a collection of scenic views probably will have made the heavier investment in a Nikon or have compromised his desire for a durable, 35mm SLR with the thinness of his bankroll and settled for a Pentax or similarly priced make. Both he and the professional will have to decide first what kinds of photos they are looking for on this particular trip and what equipment can stay behind until next time.

The photographer who specializes in panoramic views, that is, a picture of, say, a vivid purple mountain range taken in three or four frames, will need a tripod to hold his camera in the same position as he moves it through a horizontal arc from left to right. This technique enables the scenic photographer to work around the limited arc of view of his long-range lens by overlapping his views. Back in the darkroom, he will either overlap his negatives and print the whole view at once, or print separate negatives and tape the overlapped prints together for his final picture.

Tripods are available at any photo supply store and range in price from $20 to $120, depending on how many camera position controls the purchaser feels he is likely to need. In areas where high winds are predominately present, a heavy tripod will be needed to hold the light body of the average 35mm camera steady while the picture is being focused and snapped. A good compromise can be reached in the $50 range, but the heavier tripod will have to be added to the backpacker's already bulging load. An adequate tripod that collapses to a length of approximately thirty inches and weighs about three pounds can be had for about $20, and its simple position controls should meet most outdoor tripod needs.

An almost mandatory accessory for the serious photographer, who may have as much as $1000 invested in his equipment, is a leather case that fits over the camera body to protect it from being scratched or dented if the backpacker should accidentally bang it against a rock or drop it while climbing. Other protective necessities would include a lens cover to keep dust or sand from getting rubbed against the lens surface and a neck or wrist strap to prevent the camera from slipping out of the backpacker's sweaty-

Good close-ups of animals can be taken if backpacking photographer wants to lug along a telephoto lens.

handed grasp. The gadget bag which will hold the extra camera body carried by the wary photographer, lenses, film and cleaning gear, with the tripod strapped to its side, is another necessity unless the backpacker finds sufficient room for all this equipment in his living pack. As this would reduce the amount of room available for edibles and extra clothes, the gadget bag is probably the best approach. It can, with the attachable strap, be slung from the back-packer's shoulder or strapped to the outside of his pack.

In order to cover all bases with the minimum amount of equipment, the backpacking photographer probably will limit himself to three lenses; a 28mm wide-angle, possibly a 135mm short telephoto and, if he knows it will be needed, one as large as the 500mm long telephoto. As he reviews the bulk of his load, he may decide to leave the wide-angle lens behind and simply use the 135mm at longer distances to get almost the same picture area. If he decides to take only one lens, it may be one of the zoom lenses, such as the 43 to 86mm offered by Nikon, which can be adjusted from a slightly wide-angle format to a short telephoto view.

Still another option available would be the use of mag-nifiers, called doublers, which fit between the lens and the body face, and increase a lens' magnifying abilities by two or three times. These doublers are designated as either a 2X or 3X doubler, according to their magnifying abilities. The photographer could then take one lens, say the 55mm normal, and use the compact doublers to increase magnifi-cation to 110mm and 165mm, respectively. This would give him the options of both the wider area of view of the 55mm and the longer range of the 165mm telephoto. When using doublers, the photographer should be careful to open his aperture slightly wider to allow more light to penetrate the extra glass.

The variables in photography are almost limitless, and the amateur will find new ways to use his equipment as he becomes more familiar with what accessories are available. A basic photography class taken at a local college might be a good move before investing heavily in expensive optical gear. The darkroom techniques learned in such a class would help pay for more film by saving the photographer the cost of commercial film processing.

Even if the backpacker has no interest in photography or does not want to make even the nominal investment in an Instamatic, he can still preserve an accurately detailed record of his trip that he can use to plan his next outing or to smugly tell his city-bound friends how unlucky they were not to be along.

A pocket-size, wire-bound notebook, costing about twenty cents in any drug or department store, or the more elaborate arrangement of a loose-leaf binder will enable the outdoorsman to remember that tricky bit of cliff face or how he got caught out in rough weather without one of those pocket-size raincoats. The backpacker might make a few notes to himself by the light of his campfire or while on the trail, and transfer the information thus recorded to a larger binder when he returns home.

Such a record, possibly illustrated with a few snapshots of favored trail companions, the backpacker's family or even a picture of all his equipment laid out on a tarp would be invaluable when planning the next trip or remembering

Binoculars offer wide-angle field of view and a choice of three focusing methods give a better, clearer view.

the minute details of last summer's hike, which the back-packer may be shocked to remember took place three years ago. Time has a way of slipping by unnoticed, and a well-kept record of the pleasurable experiences that the back-packer enjoyed in his youth would be an invaluable memento to review in later years.

If a simple binder does not seem to be enough, there are commercial record books available at camping and sporting goods stores which will serve admirably. These are divided into separate sections, with blank pages already headed "Equipment Checklist," "Trail Conditions," "Weather," etc. These records and the maps and permits used on a given trip will give the backpacker a good idea of how much prior planning a trip to the same region will involve.

One item of optical gear that might be considered a frill by some backpackers could be extremely handy should the backpacker decide he wants it along.

A good pair of binoculars, or its first and second cousins, the monocular and telescope, would give the backpacker a means to check out any potentially hazardous trail condi-tions before he climbs all the way up that hill to find his way blocked by a rockslide. The hunter who has backpack-ed into where the more abundant game roams would be able to search the hillside on the far slope of the rock-strewn canyon. The pleasure shooter who wants to sight in that new camp rifle or handgun would be able to spot his groups without having to trudge back and forth fifty or a hundred yards from target to shooting spot.

Of the three types, the monocular is probably the least bulky, but it offers a very narrow field of view, which could mean a bit of difficulty in locating the object that the backpacker wants a closer look at. The telescope shares this field of view defect, but some of the more expensive models offer a selection of interchangeable lenses that would allow the user to change its power of magnification to meet changing situations. This advantage would have to

be balanced against the telescope's weight and bulk. Also, while some telescopes can be held steady by hand, many must be mounted on a tripod to be used most effectively. This would mean still another piece of equipment to carry.

The handiest form of field glasses is probably a good pair of binoculars. Available in a variety of magnifications, this type of field glass offers the backpacker the steadiness of a two-handed grip, a good field of view — which can be even better if a pair offering wide-angle viewing is selected — and a variety of focusing methods to suit differing tastes.

Binoculars are classified by their power of magnification and the size of the objective lens, the lens farthest from the users eyes. The larger the objective lens, the more light that will be able to penetrate to the eyes, and the brighter the image will appear. A large objective lens means that the binoculars will be useful even at night, should such a use be anticipated when the backpacker goes shopping for a pair of field glasses.

The backpacker would know which pair of binoculars would best suit his needs by checking the designation stamped on each pair. A designation such as 7x35 would mean that the binoculars are capable of magnifying an image seven times the size it would appear at the standard 1000-yard range used to calibrate most field glasses. The diameter of the objective lens of these binoculars would have been measured at thirty-five millimeters. A pair of binoculars designated 7x50 would have the same seven-power magnification, but the larger objective lens would make these more suitable for night use.

The backpacker who wishes to be able to support his field glasses by hand should not purchase binoculars more powerful than seven times in magnifying ability. Beyond this limit, the image will be blurred by any hand movement, and using more powerful binoculars without some sort of additional support, such as a rock or tree trunk, will cause severe headaches from eye strain. If the backpacker feels a

Some binocular field glasses offer a separate focus for each eyepiece, which can be awkward and time-consuming.

Field glasses are labeled according to their magnifying power and the diameter of the objective lens. These binoculars magnify eight times with 30mm objective lens.

Another option is a combination of center-knob focusing and a separate focusing control knob on one exit lens.

sure the objective lens is of adequate size to handle the extra magnification.

Proper focusing of field glasses can be very important, not only in terms of a clear image, but in terms of preserving the user's sight. Eye strain caused by improper focusing of a field glass or by using a too-powerful glass without adequate support can cause a trip-spoiling headache. Continued abuse in this manner could begin to affect the user's normal eyesight.

There are three types of focusing systems offered on most binoculars. The most familiar is a center focusing knob, located between the exit lenses, which focuses both lenses at the same turn of the knob. Another features the center focusing knob with the added refinement of a left or right exit lens focus.

To adjust a pair of binoculars to his individual eye differences, the user would close his left eye, if the exit lens adjustment was on the left lens, and focus the right lens using the center focus knob. He would then close his right eye and bring the image into focus with the exit lens adjustment. The procedure is simply reversed for a field glass equipped with this focus on the right exit lens.

The third focusing system employs a separate focusing knob for each eyepiece, which can be awkward unless the user always uses the glasses at the same distance. Otherwise the focus must be adjusted each time the glasses are used and this can be a time-consuming project. Imagine a hunter frantically thumbing the separate eye adjustments while that deer he's been tracking for two days bolts into the next stand of trees at all that excess movement.

Binoculars are available in a variety of sizes and frame styles, with prices varying according to brand, style and the number of goodies built into them. The backpacker will probably want to compromise between bulkiness and quality to meet his demands of a good glass that won't weigh too heavily in his pack or around his neck. As with the more expensive cameras, the purchase of a protective leather case would be a good investment to prevent having to pack out the pieces in a brown paper sack.

The primary purpose in packing the living necessities into a knapsack and heading up-country is to get away from the crowds and the noises of city living. There are times, however, when contact with others can help fill in the

need for very powerful binoculars, he might make the additional investment in one of the models which offer a zoom lens effect from, for instance, seven to twelve-power magnification. The stronger the magnification, the thicker the objective lens through which light will have to penetrate. Anyone purchasing a powerful pair of binoculars should be

The center focus knob, featured on this pair, focuses both lenses at once.

Most telescopes are powerful, require a tripod or must be braced against a tree to avoid damage to eyesight.

A portable transceiver in the three to five-watt range is an ideal tool. The backpacker can easily call help.

silences of open-country living or bring aid to a stranded or injured camper. In this area, the inclusion of one of the transistorized walkie-talkies that have spun off from military use into the civilian marketplace could add a comforting touch to that cheery campsite atmosphere or be the means of getting help in a hurry. Such a unit would be useful for the backpacker to notify another member of his party that he is moving the campsite farther upstream, or to meet him at another point on the trail. It would allow individual members of a hiking party to break off and check out an obscure trail on their own, without losing at least vocal contact with the main group.

These radios come in many different styles and use different power levels. Their price is usually determined by how many channels they are set for and by the number of transmitting and receiving crystals used. The range or distance over which any unit will transmit is determined by its power level, the terrain in which it is used and the time of day or night, as well as certain weather conditions.

A one-hundred-milliwatt unit, often sold as a children's toy, would be inexpensive, lightweight and compact — all virtues in the eyes of the backpacker. Its small power level, however, would limit its range to about a quarter of a mile during daytime and only slightly more than that at night, when solar radiation causes less interference with radio waves. These units usually are equipped with only one channel, which would eliminate the operator's option to switch to another channel if one is being used by other operators. It might preclude his using the unit for any but

an emergency transmission if his unit has only Channel Nine — the emergency channel for all citizens' band radio users.

A more effective compromise of weight, power and expense might be one of the three-watt units. These offer a choice of how many of the twenty-three channels which comprise the citizens' radio network the buyer feels he needs and can afford, and have a range of between twenty-five miles during the day to one hundred miles at night.

The minimum power that the backpacker would need to transmit effectively over all types of terrain and under most weather conditions would be a one-watt unit. These range in cost from $25 to $60, are also lightweight and compact, and offer a selection of up to six different channels in each unit.

The maximum wattage for a unit, be it portable, mobile or base station, such as a citizens' band radio in a private home, that is allowed for use on the CB net is five watts. These units are the most expensive, but offer the full range of twenty-three channels to give the user his best chance of getting a message through.

In order to transmit over the citizens' band network on any unit of more than three hundred milliwatts in power, the backpacker will have to apply to the Federal Communications Commission for a five-year license, costing $20. Many radio shops have the necessary application forms. After a sixty to ninety-day waiting period, the applicant will receive his license and a set of call letters which he must use to begin and end any transmission. Until he has the proper license, the backpacker must refrain from transmitting over his CB radio, except in the case of an emergency when anyone — licensed or not — may use the unit to summon help.

Some groups use the portable radios in conjunction with mobile units, which are monitored by a safety man who can get a rescue party into the area as soon as trouble is reported. The emergency wavelength, Channel Nine, is constantly monitored and any call for aid over this channel will bring quick results. The injured backpacker may not know his call was heard until the rescue party finds him, but if he called over Channel Nine, somebody heard him.

This situation could come about as result of a

This five-watt mobile transceiver can be monitored by a safety man while the group is out on a new trail.

The two-way radio fits handily in the top or side pocket of any style backpack.

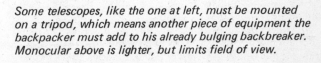

Some telescopes, like the one at left, must be mounted on a tripod, which means another piece of equipment the backpacker must add to his already bulging backbreaker. Monocular above is lighter, but limits field of view.

phenomenon known as skip. As an alternative to a detailed course in atmospherics, the backpacker who decides to get into citizens' band radio can simply anticipate times when he will hear a caller, but his signal will not reach them and vice-versa. Basically, this is caused by the signal being intercepted and diverted. The backpacker, especially in mountainous country, may not be able to talk to a friend on the adjacent slope, but will be heard by a base station two hundred miles away. The FCC has ruled that no citizens' band radio operator may deliberately send a signal more than 150 miles, except, of course, in an emergency situation when all bets are off. Even they, however, have not been able to figure out a way to regulate the vagaries of skipping signals, so an accidental transmission outside the 150-mile radius is on safe ground.

Mountainous terrain also presents another problem for the backpacker who wants to use a two-way radio in that type of country. Radio signals travel in straight lines and can be stopped or deflected by solid objects, such as a mountainside. Roadside communities, with their clusters of buildings and the attendant, glittering array of private and commercial television and radio antennas, are another good place to lose or garble a voice transmission. The backpacker who plans to have a safety man standing by at a mobile or base station transceiver should keep this in mind when deciding where the safety man should be waiting.

The easiest way to surmount this obstacle is for the backpacker to get to the highest point he can to transmit. Since the walkie-talkie is a line-of-sight unit, the user should be able to reach any point he can see and, because of the skip phenomenon, probably beyond.

When buying a multi-channel unit, the backpacker should make certain that Channel Nine is included in his range. If buying the one-watt, six-channel set, the backpacker might select a combination such as 2-7-9-11-14-22. These are the most popular channels monitored by many CB operators and having them will increase the backpacker's chances of being heard. Channel Twenty-two is the one most often used and monitored by the bandit radio set.

A bandit is a citizens' band user who has not been licensed by the FCC. Most such operators own a mobile unit and depend on its mobility, as well as the use of color-

The Skatchet, a recently introduced innovation, offers the three tools of knife, hammer and hatchet in one compact head. A green tree limb makes a good handle, and the Skatchet can be hand-held for use as a knife.

ful call names, to help them evade the FCC monitors. The FCC has the power to enforce its regulations and the fines they hand out when they do catch an unlicensed radio operator should make anyone who may one day have to justify his equipment think twice about not taking the simple step of obtaining a license.

The backpacker who leaves home with the idea of living off the land uppermost in his mind wants to do so with the least amount of heavy gear possible. He does not, however, want to leave behind any item that could be crucial to his comfort and survival.

A nifty little gadget now being marketed by the Charter Arms Company combines the necessary edges and blades of a knife, a hammer and a hatchet into one tool called a Skatchet. Originally manufactured by the Follins Corporation, the Skatchet is advertised as being capable of performing all the around-camp chores of these three necessities, being converted to a hatchet with the addition of a green tree limb. The Skatchet retails for about $15 and is available through the current national and international network of Charter Arms factory representatives, jobbers and dealers.

A handy item to keep knives sharp on the trail or to touch up that skinning blade before tackling that tough moose or elk might be the Crock Stick recently introduced by Arkansas Abrasives, Incorporated. Employing two alumina ceramic rods in a wooden base, the Crock Stick is used with the familiar slicing motions, alternating from one rod to the other. The rods rotate to expose unused surfaces and can be cleaned of metal deposits with any common kitchen cleanser.

Keeping his load to a minimum is always uppermost in the backpacker's mind but, with a little consideration and careful packing, there is no reason for the hardy trail wanderer to sacrifice many of the little items that can make his trip into the wilderness a bit more comfortable, and his memories of the highlights of his vacation a little more vivid.

Some knives are constructed with a heavy hilt to protect the user's hand if the tool should slip while in use.

The outdoorsman's basic tool, his knife, is available with a wide variety of blade and hilt sizes and styles.

(As an expert on the development and present-day manufacture of edged and pointed weapons, and the regular author of GUN WORLD Magazine's "Knife News," Jack Lewis is probably the best source of information on the backpacker's basic tool for survival, the knife. As such, he consented to pick up the tale at this point for the benefit of novice outdoorsmen whose acquaintance with knives does not exceed beyond carving a Christmas turkey.)

TODAY WE READ about all those absolutely fantastic custom-made knives which, after slicing their way through hanks of deer hair, separating curds from whey and whittling out an ebony gunstock, still split a hair and shave the owner without pulling. But not all of us own enough stock in a Las Vegas night club to be able to afford one of those super-duper blades. Most of us are affluent enough that paying $25 to $50 for a knife requires no hocking of family heirlooms. It is an unfortunate fact that hunting knives which cost in the neighborhood of $10 when I was a youngster now cost $35.

There are better steels available to today's cutler than there were forty years ago, but when one seriously looks at $250 hunting knives, he has more money than some of us. Still, I know one custom knifemaker who is about fifteen months behind in filling orders for his superb gems of the knifemaker's art. The commercial cutler also has access to better steels today than he had in what many of us refer to as the "good ol' days." Today we can buy superb commer-

cially made knives that rival the custom products in many ways. These knives feature new, modern steels, heat treatments not even heard of several years ago, handle and hilt materials that up until now were reserved to the custom cutler and even sheath designs that reflect a growing trend to better, more useful products. One commercial knife manufacturer even guarantees his product against everything, including loss for one year from purchase. That is a guarantee that is going to be difficult to beat.

Not only are the old line knifemakers such as Marble, Camillus, Case, Gerber and Olson still turning out fine knives, but there are now cutlers and new knife distributers galore. For instance, fine knives are being imported from overseas and sold in almost all sporting goods outlets. Some of the oldest knife names in the world are Henckel, Bokar and Puma from Germany, for instance. Names we associate more closely with firearms also are becoming known for their knives; included are Smith & Wesson, Ithaca and Browning.

Ithacagun is distributing the line of Track knives. These are being sold throughout the United States by franchised dealers at prices up to $67.50. Actually, these knives are custom quality but readily available.

Smith & Wesson offers fewer blade styles from which to choose but again the custom quality is there. Firearms International offers knives imported from the Scandinavian countries and Browning sells knives made here in the U.S.

You may have your choice of different priced quality knives from several manufacturers. Gerber introduced their

Prestige line of custom quality designs several years ago. Last year they brought out a new line of knives in the medium price range. Olson also is producing a line of less expensive knives for the retail trade.

There are some new names in the knife field. An old name with a new product is Sid Bell, the Alaskan silversmith. Bell's knives are made by the well-known gun engraver Bill Mains, who not only makes the knives for Sid but also offers a complete line of custom knives through his franchised dealers. Mains uses gravers steel with a hardness of 65 on the Rockwell C scale.

Western has their standard hunting knife design plus their Westmark. The Schrade brands of Uncle Henry and Old Timer offer competition to such names as Camillus, Kabar and Case. The original custom-quality knife-maker-to-the-masses Buck has added several newer knives to his line and made them even better.

I have a custom knife made for me by Ted Dowell and there is no denying that the selection of good steel, properly heat-treated and made into a good blade is hard to beat. I have dressed out eight deer with this little knife and never sharpened it. It will still shave hair from my forearm. I do nothing harder than disjoint legs and cut through the brisket with the knife. It is about the size of a paring knife and gets no abuse at all.

This same custom maker has a knife made from one piece of steel with the handles fitted between the cap and the hilt. But so does the old firm J.A. Henckels Twinworks in Germany.

The handle selection of the commercial offering may not be as extensive or as well-fitted as the custom knife, but it is different. It also is a lot less expensive. Admittedly, the commercial knife is not in the same quality class as the Dowell knife but I use it to show that good knife design is not the exclusive province of the custom cutler. The dropped point blade is the latest rage and several commercial cutlers offer this blade design in their lines of knives.

Not too many years ago, the would-be hunting knife purchaser was somewhat limited designwise, in what he could purchase. The average knife had a raised point blade with a skinning sweep. There usually was a small brass hilt, an aluminum cap, and leather or plastic washers for the handle. Some of the fancier knives had real stag handles and there even were some — usually imported — which had natural wood for handle material. On many of today's knives, plastics have become the handle material. Even the custom cutler uses plastics to a great degree.

One of the greatest advances has been the better designed leather sheath. Old knives had two pieces of leather sewn together with a safety or restraining strip to hold the knife handle at the cap or top. These old sheath designs had several things wrong with them. The knife blade eventually would cut through the threads with which the leather was sewn or the top restraining strap would allow the knife to work upwards, then cut through the side or back of the sheath. Either could be calamitous.

Another endearing feature was the proclivity of the blade to cut the restraining strap as the knife was being drawn from the sheath without unsnapping the strap which became loose with use and age.

Today's sheaths are available in many different designs. Some foreign imports have a safety guard of metal at the bottom of the sheath with the intention of retaining the blade within the two leather sides at all costs.

Probably the most common sheath design, used by both custom and commercial knifemakers, is the pouch style sheath. This design, which I saw first on an implement of Finnish origin, allows the knife to drop into a stiff leather pouch and be retained there by the knife's shape and by

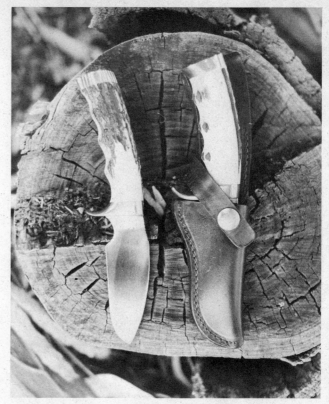

A leather sheath holds the backpacker's knife on his belt where it is handy if needed and not easily lost.

friction. Since there is little showing above the top of the sheath, it is hard for the knife to be snagged out and lost.

Variations on this design have thongs or other methods of fastening the knife more securely in the pouch. This design is used in some degree by Browning; Gerber, in their Armorhide line; many custom makers, and some imported designs. Buck's variation on the pouch design is to put a flap over the top to make it even more secure.

Many modern sheath designs have the safety strap placed at the bottom of the handle near the hilt. Usually the strap will come around and across the front of the handle to fasten by either a snap or doll's head to the front of the sheath. Better sheaths will have welts or spacers between the two thicknesses of leather, especially at the side of the knife's cutting edge. This usually is held in place by several brass rivets which, to some extent, constitute a safety factor. The safety strap described above will hold the knife in the sheath without allowing it to creep upward and either cut through the side of the sheath or be lost.

The sheaths Puma offers with their straight blades not only have the low positioned safety strap but a rawhide thong affixed at the top of the belt loop. This may be drawn through a hole in the top of the knife handle near the cap and slid back over the handle, thus holding the top of the knife in place also.

Precise Imports' sheath has two retaining straps, one around the handle near the cap, another around the hilt. Case, Buck and others utilize a wraparound design with the edge side of the sheath being closed by rivets and the handle either enclosed or almost enclosed by the top fold of the leather. Usually there is some style of fastener at the top to preclude losing the knife from the sheath. The most important thing is that knife sheaths have become better, safer and more loss-proof than ever before. Some will even fit into a hip pocket if you wish and may be worn upside down, if you are feeling lucky.

Smaller knives make in-camp cutting chores easy, a larger model gives a better grip for taking hides.

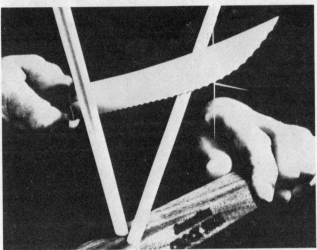

The Crock Stick, a new product, is useful for keeping knife blades sharp at home or on the trail and packs easily.

Years ago hunting knives were made from regular cutlery steel. Many still are. With the metallurgical advances of the past several years we have had increasing use of newer steels. At one time, stainless steels had a deserved name for being a poor steel for any type of knife upon which one needed to have and keep a keen edge. Today's 440 series of stainless steels have to take a back seat to no blade steel used by many of the commercial cutlers. The 440 steel can be given a high Rockwell test by proper heat treating and many of our best and most famous knives are made from this formula of corrosion resistant steel.

Another steel that has attained great favor among knife-makers of the country is the so-called "tool steel." This steel may be any of a number of high carbon, different alloyed tool steels. Heat treatment may be different from one maker to another, but the steels all are good. Bill Mains claims that the steel he uses is the same type used in gravers to engrave metal on firearms. Needless to say, it should be a good steel to use in a good knife.

High-speed tool steel is another favored by some manufacturers. Most makers will divulge the "C" scale Rockwell hardness they attain in their blades. Mains claims a hardness factor of 65. Puma makes sure you know, as they leave the diamond point imprint in each blade. They don't feel that your knowing the metal's formula will help, but scientific things like special hardness tests are what sell knives today and all the manufacturers use some form of such tests.

Not all manufacturers will state the Rockwell hardness of their steels; neither will they always state the formula of the steel from which they make their blades. In fact, it sometimes is difficult to even find out from some of them how they make their product. There is one thing which the prospective knife purchaser can remember, though: if it is not a good product, it will not have been around long. Old line merchandise can usually be counted upon to also be quality. Some new manufacturers are making good merchandise. A look at the product, judging the quality of the work evident, is often a good way to start. Check with friends, ask people who have some knowledge of knives and makers. One of the most important things is whether you like it. If you do, it will be a good knife until you find one you like better.

Blade styles vary from one maker to another. Some manufacturers offer more than one blade style. Gerber, for instance, has five new knives on the market with three different blade shapes on that new line of knives. Case has offered different blade shapes for years and Buck has several sizes and shapes available.

Knife designs also will vary, although in many instances, one maker will offer one type of knife. Track knives all are made with a half or hidden hilt. The Olson Knife Company offers a full, one-piece blade-hilt design. As mentioned, Henckel offers a one-piece blade-hilt-cap design. Gerber has the metal handle cast onto a blade, with G-96 using a similar type. Others use epoxy or rivet or both. You have to look at several different styles and decide which you like best. After all, you are the one who has to be pleased.

No matter what kind of knife you want, there undoubtedly is one made by some commercial maker to meet your demands. Look before you buy. The more knives you inspect and the more knowledgeable people to whom you talk about knives, the more you will know about knives yourself.

Just because your sheath knife is not made by one of the custom cutlers does not mean that it is not a fine knife. It may even be outstanding.

Outdoor campsite scenes such as this may soon be museum exhibits if the strictly-nature-only buffs have their way.

BACKPACKING AT YOUR LOCAL MUSEUM

CHAPTER 12

Careful family planning could flounder on the shoals of the question, "Do You Have Your Reservation?"

WHEN THE SUMMER'S first weekend backpacker drives up the gravel road to his favorite wilderness area, full of anticipation at getting away from it all, he might be a bit startled to be stopped by a freshly painted barricade and have the ranger on duty ask for his reservation. He would be even more startled to be denied access to the designated public lands if he doesn't have one.

If he manages to get in, the camping enthusiast might find he has failed to take a few things into consideration when he laid out the gear and supplies he decided were needed. He might not have included a fuel-type stove, thinking to use what dead wood came to hand for his cooking, lighting and heating needs. He might be carrying some kind of small caliber side arm for protection as a useful survival tool should an accident delay his scheduled return. He might want to do a little fishing to supplement his freeze-dried food supply and, since he plans to follow a familiar watercourse, he isn't carrying much water. He has probably failed to allow room in his pack to fit in that thirteen-foot-long list of things he is no longer allowed to

Preserving The Wilderness Is A Desirable Goal, But How Much Protection Do You Need?

This hiker would easily fit into the proposed new order, but what about the father who wants to bring his kids?

do in the wilderness that is handed to him as he sits in a daze. And he has no idea how this mess came about.

When the bewildered, would-be outdoorsman asks why, he is referred to a large, white book about 2½ inches thick entitled something like "Approved Master Plan for Reserving the Wilderness for Only Those Who Got in on the Ground Floor when We Put Our Idea of the Perfect Outdoor Area Together and Railroaded It through Congress While the Rest of the World Wasn't Looking."

On the title page, the intrepid backpacker would find a brief list of the various no-nos that gives him a rough idea of what went wrong before it degenerates into seventeen-syllable gibberish. Phrases would leap out to poke him in the eye. No hunting, fishing, fire burning, plant picking, drinking from streams, loitering, smoking, hole digging, scruffing up the dust or laying on the grass. Emergencies no exception.

On a prominent roadside sign would be a poster-size picture of a door with a half-moon carved thereon, bearing the legend "Did You Bring Your Little Plastic Bag?"

The fellow behind him in the elaborate camper outfit he was finally able to afford is in for an even bigger shock. Having paid out good cash for indoor plumbing, hot and cold-running water, range, refrigerator and cozy sleeping accommodations on wheels, he will be told there is no way he will be allowed to bring that circus wagon into what has been declared a primitive camping only area, for a radius of forty miles around. If he wants to risk his 10-year-old son's and 6-year-old daughter's health and safety by force-marching them ten miles into the wilds, without weapons of any sort to protect them, that is his affair. But no Winnebago, no. And his irate attentions will be blandly directed to still another large signpost which reads "We are not responsible

for any vehicles abandoned in the vicinity of this sentry box."

Weekends thoroughly sabotaged, the disappointed citizens turn themselves around and disappear in an indignant cloud of dust. The sentry adjusts the shoulder strap of his automatic rifle and slouches back down in his canvas camp chair, shaking his head at the nerve of some stupid people. Where the hell have they been? he wonders.

When someone gets the urge to put a pack on his back and head out for the densest stretch of trees he can find, the last thing he wants to come across after a two-day hike is some garish aluminum bandwagon, complete with air-conditioning and color stereo-vision. On the other hand, the fellow who has put his bucks aside and come up with the financing to purchase $60,000 worth of rolling luxury has every right to enjoy his new outdoor play-pretty in whatever manner and location strikes his wandering fancy.

Most of those who find pleasure in outdoor activities, in whatever primitive or portably civilized fashion, have one basic premise in common. They want to keep the outdoors in a condition that will make continued enjoyment of its many splendors possible.

There are those in the camping fraternity who sometimes lose sight of their future vacation potential, sacrificing it to the crass god of momentary convenience as they stride through the forest or dune-buggy across the desert, leaving empty cans, broken glass and tinfoil wrappers gleaming in the sun to spoil the view for the next group of intrepid adventurers who follow that trail.

It is this minority of misguided, the I-don't-give-a-damn fraternity, who have aroused the ire of a strong group of outdoor worshipers and, in the process, have threatened every backpacker's freedom to wander the trails, camp with

Politics could force the woodsman to surrender his right to roam public lands.

a small-but-cheery fire or even be allowed to enter their favorite area at all.

As in most cases where rules evolve because of the misdeeds of the one-percenters in a group, some zealots of the environmentalist set have gone overboard in what they consider to be necessary restrictions to protect the nation's wilderness areas.

Political pressure from the strict, nature-only enthusiasts has reached the point where the government agencies concerned with protecting wilderness areas for those who appreciate them are having to spend time and tax money devising new master plans for, and complex environmental impact statements on, the use to which public wilderness lands will be put.

Such proposals have ranged from limiting further commercial development of wilderness areas under the control of the National Parks and U.S. Forestry Services to eliminating all forms of travel except by foot and tearing out all present buildings, including lodges, restaurants and other such commercial facilities. All that would then be needed to complete an area's restoration to a totally natural state would be the elimination of animal and plant population control programs and the construction of a Great Wall of Yellowstone, or some such around all wilderness areas, prohibiting anyone to enter. Outdoors enthusiasts could then kick back in specially prepared bleachers and watch the bloody antics of the starving, over-produced animal populations of the wilderness through the mediums of telescope and satellite television from a safe, nature-preserving distance.

That couldn't be done, of course; except that there already are some primitive areas that have been closed to the public and can only be entered by archeologists and others with special permits and a specific, justifiable reason for going into one of these areas. Having failed to adequately police their one-percenters, the camping, hunting, hiking and backpacking outdoorsmen now find that the responsi-

ble government agencies have been forced through political pressure to step in and do the necessary policing.

The result, if the completely back-to-nature buffs have their way, would be a living contradiction of their espoused doctrine and would, of course, eliminate the possibility of enjoying the outdoors for all but a small minority of the camping public. Among these would be the man who now brings his family, including small children, into a place like Yosemite or Yellowstone, where they can breathe clean air, watch wild animals at play and sniff wild flowers instead of the paler blooms that wither in every city windowbox. People of all ages who now can condition their bodies and learn the self-reliance of doing their own cooking and cleaning, and the independence of making up their own games and entertainment in the wilderness could easily find themselves and their families facing the same strictures there that now apply on any crowded city street.

Because of the carelessness of a few shortsighted, and in some cases downright blind, abusers, those who would restrict the enjoyment of nature to only what they consider as nature's creatures have steadily gained more and more effective ammunition in their fight to bring man's rules to the wilderness.

If they were to completely succeed, they would be in the ridiculous position of forbidding one of nature's creations access to areas reserved for the use of nature's creations. Man is as much a part of the natural ecological scenario as the dandelion and the ant. He may be more elaborate in his food-gathering and housing needs, and a bit more merciful in his social organization – if more brutal in his personal relationships – but he is necessarily a natural part of the evolution of his environment.

He has learned by small, hesitant steps that, while he has developed the technology to obliterate in an eyeblink any of nature's works, as part of the living cycle of his only planet he must take steps to insure that that cycle is not disrupted. When the cycle is disturbed by the excessive

If in later years this young lady wanted to share the outdoors with her kids, new rules would stop her.

dumping of any raw refuse that will not fit in with nature's redistribution cycle, the repair work that man must then undertake becomes more than a simple preservation of esthetic pleasure. It is a matter of race survival.

Any experienced backpacker knows that he must plan his trip carefully, taking into account possible hazards, what equipment he will take for survival and comfort, and what type of terrain he will be traveling through. The backpacker decides which kind of country he likes best, be it mountain, open plain or desert, and makes his packing decisions to live within the limits of that situation.

When he takes the extra effort to clean his fire-blackened rocks, to make sure his fire is out, and to pack out any trash that cannot be assimilated by the elements, he is performing a simple courtesy for himself as well as other campers who will use that spot after he is gone. And, it is hoped, they will perform the same cleaning chores, so he will have a clean campsite when he returns that way.

The concerned camper will leave a campsite in as close to the same condition as he found it, but he will hardly be able to erase all sign of his passage. He cannot, for instance, restore the dead limbs that fueled his cooking and warming blaze, and as he has eliminated at least a small part of the potential fire hazard by consuming potentially dangerous materia[1] under controlled conditions, it would be pointless and possibly harmful if he could.

He could take the trouble, as certain purists have proposed, of packing out his body waste in little plastic bags. But why bother when the soil in which he buries it will make good use of what would be a poison to his body? The process is somewhat like that of a bee drawing honey from

a blossom, thereby helping that plant species to regenerate itself by providing it a way to fertilize and reproduce. Would the same purist perform this clean-up chore for his packhorse? That is a lot of plastic bags.

The natural food genus of the backpacker species is a viable alternative to the control of excessive growth by plants left unattended in remote regions. Perhaps it would be better to keep him out and send planes over the area to spray it down with insecticides, or allow the plants to choke themselves out, creating a fire hazard of dead, dry brambles that any stroke of lightning could turn into a devastating holocaust.

Man, who has used his superior mental abilities to fight off many of nature's population control measures and, thereby disrupted the natural life-and-death cycle of his planet, must also use these talents for extended survival and his knowledge of the world he inhabits to fit himself into the life cycles of the earth's other natural organisms. Having evolved past the point of dependency on nature's whims, man is still a part of nature and he must conduct himself according to nature's laws. He cannot isolate any part of his environment and still expect it to function as part of the whole.

People can work to maintain the balance of power between the natural wilderness and those who find themselves fit to survive in it. This has been accomplished in part by the establishment of wildlife parks and forestry districts in one of the few truly efficient moves ever made by a growing bureaucracy.

Those who have advocated that it is time to begin taking corrective action against the advancement of population centers into all wilderness areas might be a bit startled to find themselves over a hundred years behind the times.

The first move to keep some part of the wilderness open for the enjoyment of all was taken by the U.S. Congress on June 30, 1864. This legislation granted to the state of California two tracts of public land, known as Yosemite Valley and Mariposa Big Tree Grove, to be held for public resort and recreation use, being inalienable, for all time.

On October 1, 1890, Congress established what is now Yosemite National Park under the jurisdiction of the Secretary of the Interior, with protective powers to retain all timber, mineral deposits, natural curiosities and wonders in their natural condition.

A series of California and federal legislative acts from 1905 to 1919 enlarged the Yosemite Park boundaries, guaranteed voting rights at the county level for residents of the park, and granted certain lands to the city and county of San Francisco for the purpose of creating municipal water supply and power and electric plants in the Hetch Hetchy Valley and Lake Eleanor Basin, with provisions to ensure an adequate water supply for the Modesto and Turlock Irrigation Districts. A 1913 act included provisions to prevent pollution of those reservoirs. The act of February 7, 1905, established the area now known as the Sierra National Forest.

In 1914, Congress authorized the Secretary of the Interior to grant twenty-year leases to businessmen who would establish hotels, restaurants and "buildings for the protection of motor cars, stages, stock and equipment and so forth" for the comfort and convenience of visitors to the park. At that time, the special survival techniques practiced by many backpackers today were a matter of daily living conditions for many people.

Those construction projects were limited to certain areas of the park, and the procedures used by park businesses were and are under constant review. Man had begun to integrate his civilized comforts into the natural system, with built-in protections for that system, a century before people started marching in the streets, waving placards or buttonholing their congressmen.

The June 2, 1920 act of Congress accepted exclusive jurisdiction over Yosemite National Park in response to an April 15, 1919 state of California act with California reserving the rights to serve civil and criminal processes, tax persons and corporations and fix and collect fees for fishing within the park. The same act forbade hunting in the park and gave the Secretary of the Interior the right to determine fishing methods and seasons. It reiterated the preservation statement of 1890 and added animals to the list of park resources to be protected.

On March 1, 1872, Congress established Yellowstone National Park, the first area officially designated a national park, and created a new policy for public land management and use.

The National Park Service was created on August 25, 1916, to administer all national parks and monuments. The service was charged with conserving the scenery, natural and historic objects and wildlife, and providing for the enjoyment of these in such manner as would leave them unimpaired for future generations to enjoy.

In other words, the current broo-ha-hah being kicked up has compelled the Park Service into reiterating the same policies they have developed through years of experience in balancing park visitors' needs and desires with their responsibilities to keep things green. Perhaps these are the same people who complain a lot about high taxes and duplication of government projects. A large number of them are certainly the type who heads for the remotest reachable area to get away from the strictures of a governed society.

The strictly back-to-nature advocates have demanded the

By cleaning up after herself, this camper takes a small step toward protecting her right of access to the public wilderness lands. A careless act can hurt this.

removal of all concessions, facilities and accommodations from the public wilderness areas. They would limit access to foot travelers only. They apparently wish the exclusive right to wander the remote reaches and exclude those who favor combining at least a few of the amenities with the wonders of open land. What they fail to consider is that, while there are certainly ample acres in which the solitary wilderness worshiper can find quiet and relaxation, there are no longer any open frontiers where they can roam totally unmolested in search of conquest.

There are, in fact, only two kinds of land in the United States: privately owned and publicly owned. No matter what type of terrain the outdoorsman favors, mountain or desert, he must have someone's permission to go there. On private land, the backpacker must speak with the owner and abide by his restrictions. He does, however, have an immediate and binding interest in public land. His permission to enter is by virtue of his own interest in the ownership of that beckoning slope or arid sand dune. His right to restrict others from enjoying the same land in the manner they choose is denied by the fact that they have an equal ownership interest in that same tract.

Like any landowner, the backpacker and the Winnebago wanderer will want to preserve the value of their property, in this case by keeping it in the clean and green condition they all seek to enjoy. While this necessarily entails some restriction for the benefit of the one-percenters, these restrictions can hardly serve their purpose of encouraging and promoting the public's enjoyment of a region by excluding a portion of that public from the privilege of enjoying it.

There is, and always has been, room enough in the publicly owned land tracts for both. If the walking backpacker does not want to mix with the civilized camper, he can always accomplish this by using his survival skills and camping lore to stay clear of the well-traveled trails and, if he is truly competent, can accomplish a de facto isolation by hiking into country that is inaccessible by jeep or camper truck. That is, of course, the ultimate goal of the live-off-the-land backpacker.

RARELY, IF EVER, will you see a trophy-size four-legged creature sauntering down the street or through the park of a large metropolitan city. If you do, your best move would be to saunter (rapidly) in the opposite direction to the nearest telephone booth and call the animal control department.

Many serious hunters are joining the rapidly swelling ranks of backpacking enthusiasts. If the game won't come to you, then it is obvious that you must go to it and what better way is there than by backpacking into the more remote game areas?

Fishermen comprise another group who can benefit greatly from learning the principles of good backpacking. Most streams, lakes and other popular fishing spots that are

FISH & GAME
CHAPTER 13

Whether its for hunting small game for food or scaring away larger animals, the .22 is popular with many backpackers. One that is convertible to magnum is an excellent choice.

Whether You Fish And Hunt For Food While Backpacking Or Pack As A Means To Reach The Best Areas, The Sports Fit Beautifully!

Backpacking allows the bowhunter to reach the remote game areas where trophy-size game is plentiful. It then becomes a matter of tracking your prize down.

For the ardent fisherman, backpacking is the answer to the overcrowded and overfished lakes and streams. The backpacker can reach spots rarely fished by others.

reached easily have long ago been overfished, or if they are regularly stocked, are overcrowded.

In these locations you will either spend hours with nary a nibble or spend the majority of your time vying for a clear spot where you can cast your line. Wouldn't it be better to be far from the crowds and have a stream literally jumping with trout all to yourself? You can by backpacking.

The hunting phase of backpacking can be divided into two sections: those who hunt with the rifle, shotgun or black powder weapons and those who use the bow and arrow. Naturally, the techniques utilized and the problems encountered vary tremendously. In this section we have attempted to provide pertinent information for both groups.

RIFLE AND BLACK POWDER HUNTING

The rifle hunter who is looking for that trophy worthy

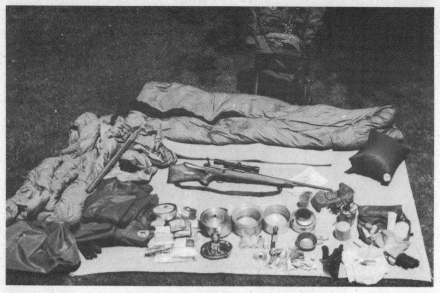

Above and right: A hunting pack trip requires additional gear, but with proper planning and eliminating of unnecessary items, the load is not too big. Below: Backpacking aids game bird hunters, as well as those seeking larger game.

of mention in a Boone & Crockett book must get away from the frequently hunted areas that are easily accessible by roads. To do this he must hike in or go by horseback. Many hunters prefer to pack in by horseback, which is handy and to many, most enjoyable; but there is the disadvantage of caring for the horses. Plus, many do not own horses or do not feel they can afford renting them for an extended trip. In this situation, backpacking is the solution.

One rule that has been stressed before, but bears repetition is that you should never backpack alone. The primary reason, of course, is safety; however, when hunting there is another practical reason. You may need help in packing out the game should you bag a good size elk or deer. In addi-

For the really big trophy, many have found that backpacking gives them an advantage over other hunters.

Many hunters will combine canoeing with backpacking to reach the really remote areas where game is plentiful.

tion, the companionship of others makes a hunting trip far more pleasurable — without a buddy, who is there to swap tall tales with at night around the fire?

Most hunting rifles on the market today weigh about eight pounds, including the optics mounted on them. These can be carried right alongside the pack frame on a shoulder strap. The type of strap used here would not be the shooting strap utilized by target riflemen, but they can aid in steadying the rifle for firing. Carrying a rifle in this manner makes it easily accessible for hunting along the trail should you come upon some likely game.

Shotgunners are not normally extreme back country hunters, since the birds they seek are found more often around cultivated areas where there is better feed. This does not preclude you from packing in for high country chukar or mountain goose utilizing a shotgun. However, since the majority of the backpacking hunters use rifles, we will limit our discussion to them.

Selection of your hunting rifle depends primarily upon the type of game you seek. A general rule followed by professional guides is that you should always carry a firearm big enough to handle the largest game in the area into which you hike. For example, if you are in grizzly country, you would be wise to carry plenty of firepower. You may not be hunting this creature, but as unpredictable as they are, you may find that you are the hunted instead of the hunter. If you carry a light rifle such as a .243 for deer and happen upon a irate grizzly about all that you can do is shoot into the air to frighten him off. You may find that he doesn't scare easily and chances of your stopping him at a full charge with a .243 or other light caliber are mighty slim.

If you prefer to hunt with small caliber rifles, as many hunters do, have another member of the group carry a 7mm

The hunter's paradise is the backcountry where few hunters ever trek. Here is where the trophies roam.

Above and below: Many hunters seeking better game bird areas have taken up backpacking in order to reach remote spots where game birds, not other hunters, abound.

magnum capable of handling such an emergency as a charging or ferocious animal. A rifle this size has enough knockdown power to handle any animal that is indigenous to this country.

A backpacking hunter will require additional gear that would not be carried normally by the average backpacker. The first consideration, of course, would be ammunition. Many feel that a loaded magazine in the rifle and a few extra rounds is sufficient. However, for the more cautious, it might be wise to carry a full box of twenty additional rounds. You will be adding weight, but there may be times that you will be glad to have them along.

An emergency rifle repair kit is a must! This can be of your own choosing; however, it should include such items as a spare firing pin, small files for adjustments and other equipment of this nature. A cleaning rod with oil should be included, especially if there is a possibility of rain or a sudden squall. If there is liklihood of precipitation, carry along a few extra plastic bags to slip over the barrel of the rifle. This is a good idea even if you are not anticipating rain; there is always moisture in the air and these bags aid in keeping out the dust and dirt. As unlikely as it may seem, even twigs and pine needles can get into the barrel when hiking through timber country and these bags will help prevent this. Another method to avoid the latter is to carry the rifle with the barrel pointing down.

Mountain goats, mountain sheep and some of the bigger

Although ducks often are found in more settled areas where feed is abundant, there are times when they can be found in the more remote areas accessible only by foot.

A well equipped bowhunter need only take his bow and quiver of arrows...a much lighter load than his counterpart, the rifle hunter.

The popular quivers attach very easily to the side of the pack, whether carrying one or two.

trophy animals are found only in the high country where there is little chance of being disturbed by the average hunter. One consideration that is often overlooked when going into high country after these animals is that at these high altitudes there is less oxygen available and a hiker is inclined to tire faster. You should always keep this in mind when planning the equipment that you will be taking. It should be kept to a bare minimum, since the weight will seem magnified many times at high altitudes where oxygen is thin.

When you do pack in for trophies, you should not add much to the regular backpacking basics, but should limit yourself to the rifle, its components, and a compact emergency repair kit. Choice of caliber and the amount of ammunition is primarily a personal matter and your own decision.

Black powder hunting popularity continues to grow each day. For the most part, these hunters use a modern version of the old muzzleloading rifles that were used by mountain men in the early 1800s. Like the rifle hunter, they too can take advantage of the backpack to get them to where the game is plentiful.

Not unlike the rifle hunter, a black powder hunter also should be prepared for emergency repairs on the trail and carry a repair kit. This would include any tools that you may feel necessary for minor repairs, spare powder in a water tight container, bullets, patches and perhaps a spare ramrod. In the event you are using a flintlock, a spare flint always is a handy item to have along. With a percussion, you would be wise to take along a spare nipple or two and a nipple wrench.

BOWHUNTING

Hunting with a bow and arrow does have one advantage over the rifle hunting and this is in the weight department: It is considerably lighter. However, it does have a dis-

advantage, which is the size of the tackle and its lack of compactness. Most hunting bows are in the sixty-inch length and the arrows are in the thirty-inch range. Stowing a rifle alongside the pack frame is relatively simple, but the longer bow, with arrows, presents a unique situation.

To a certain extent, this problem has been overcome by the modern three-piece take-down bows now on the market. The method of disassembly varies with each manufacturer, but most are taken apart easily and can be stowed in the Ensolite bag or alongside the pack frame. A disadvantage is that, should you come upon game along the trail, your bow is not in shooting form and by the time it is

Although long and awkward, a bowhunter's arrows will strap easily to the pack.

A quiver or two of arrows adds very little weight to a bowhunter's load.

With the arrows previously packed in a quiver, the hunter is ready to go.

assembled, if you are foolish enough to even try, the game is long gone.

Many bowhunters will brace the bow before leaving their car and actually start hunting as they move through the terrain. This alleviates the aforementioned problem of having a disassembled weapon when an elusive creature pokes his nose out from behind a nearby bush. The problem of the awkwardness of carrying the long arrows can be solved by using the popular bow quiver that will hold from four to eighteen arrows, depending upon its design. These

Various styles of quivers are available from those carrying four arrows to those that will carry a maximum of 18 arrows. The most popular seem about six to eight arrows, which is quite sufficient.

quivers will fit nicely on the frame alongside the pack for extra arrows if you desire more than what can be carried in the one quiver.

Conceivably, you could carry the one quiver on the bow with two more strapped onto each side of the pack and this would give you at least twenty-four arrows; more than enough for almost any situation.

An advantage of bowhunting over rifle hunting is that when you shoot a bullet, all you have left is an empty shell, whereas with a bow your arrow may be shot over and over again with little damage other than to the point. This is a good argument for carrying fewer arrows.

With the length of the arrows, it is easy to snag or catch them on overhanging tree limbs or branches. Not only can this bring you to a rather abrupt halt, but you could also

The big advantage to a bow is that it is very silent and will not spook the game as will a rifle or sidearm. However, the bow and arrow will not stop a large animal with impact as does the rifle or larger magnum pistol.

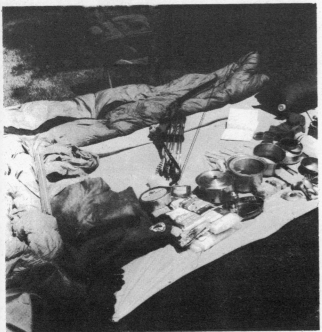

As with the rifle hunter, the bowhunter also has additional weight to pack on a hunting trip. The best way to eliminate extra weight is to lay out everything and discard anything not essential.

damage the arrows, if not careful when traveling through timber or forest areas.

Always carry extra bowstrings; spare nocks for the arrow in case one whips off or breaks on impact; and extra broadheads, if big game hunting. The broadheads should be pre-sharpened and ready for installation on the arrow. This should be about all the expendable and extra items that one would have to take along.

Some newer type arrows on the market allow changing the tip merely by unscrewing the tip from the arrow and replacing it. These have a threaded insert that remains in the arrow and you can easily replace a broken or dull broadhead. This type of arrow also allows you to change to another style of point entirely, if you switch to hunting smaller game.

Most individuals who take up bowhunting are familar with their tackle and its capabilities. For example, most know that it is a silent weapon and one often can take several shots without spooking the game. However, an arrow does not have the knock-down power of a rifle. Conceivably, you could shoot a bear with a bullseye shot through the heart and he still could get to you before he was downed. A rifle knocks game down with impact,

whereas a bowhunter kills with the razor sharp broadhead that kills by bleeding, not impact.

No matter how silent the bow is, if your pack has a banging cup or other such item, this silence is going to be of little avail. The game will be spooked by the rattling cup and all that you will see will be the white of their tails as they disappear into the underbrush. Check your pack insuring that everything is securely fastened.

CARRYING SIDEARMS

Many hunters will carry a sidearm in the back country. This not only gives them a feeling of security, but could save the day should their rifle jam. However, in the case of the bowhunter, you should always check with the local game warden to ascertain that it is legal to carry a firearm while bowhunting in that particular state. Many state game laws do not allow carrying a firearm while bowhunting. A rifle hunter can and often will carry a pistol for extra protection and, in some cases, for shooting small game as food.

As a bowhunter, if you feel you need to carry a pistol, you can always have a member of the party who is not bowhunting carry the sidearm for the group. However, most bowhunters shun the use of firearms on a bow hunt,

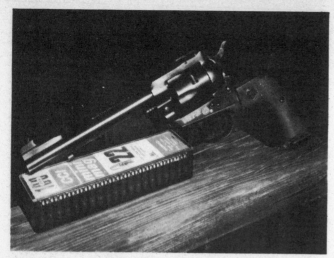

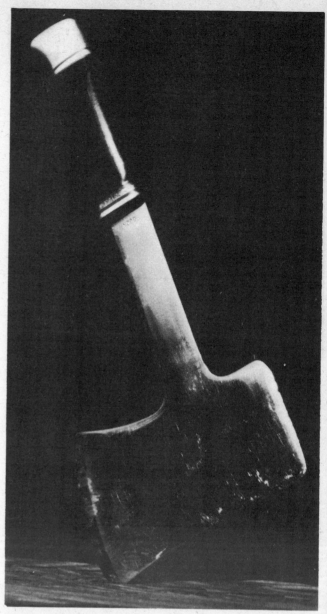

Above: The single action .22 Ruger six pistol is a very popular sidearm with backpackers. Right: A Buck Ax is a very handy item to have on a trip.

not because they are particularly purists, but because of the noise factor. While shooting a rabbit for dinner, you may well scare off every deer or other game within miles and the whole day could be a total loss.

Another problem presented by sidearms is the method of carrying them. If it's carried in a open holster strapped to the waist there is no problem, but that same pistol packed in a packbag becomes a concealed weapon, which is illegal unless you have a license. This is a point to keep in mind.

A small pistol is handy to signal for help if you are a bowhunter. Three shots of an arrow into the air will hardly bring anyone running to your rescue, whereas three shots of a rifle or pistol in rapid succession is a standard signal for distress.

Opinions as to the size of pistol to carry differ considerably. Some hunters propose carrying a pistol big enough to stop any game they are after. For bear hunting you would need at least a .357 magnum as a minimum and could possibly carry a .44 magnum. However, for the average person, a .22 is adequate. With this you can frighten off almost any large animal, even though you might not be able to stop him with a pistol this small. You can also frighten off many large animals by shouting, but the report of a pistol is far more effective for this task. Other advocates of carrying

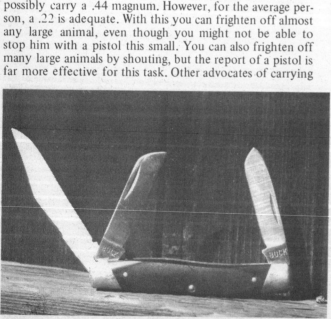

A popular knife with backpackers is the Buck Stockman which has three blades and is light, rugged and sharp.

A handy lightweight knife is the smaller two bladed pocket knife; sometimes called a pen knife.

A variety of camping knives are available, from the small pen knife to the Swiss Army knife.

a pistol along on a hunting trip feel that it is ideal for shooting small game for meals.

KNIVES

One of the most useful items that you can take along on a backpacking trip is a good knife. There are many types on the market and many are excellent for the backpacker.

The many-bladed knife such as a Boy Scout knife has numerous obvious advantages; the biggest being that you have a variety of tools in one unit. One example of a multi-bladed knife would be the Swizz Army knife, which has cutting blades, a fork, scissors, tweezers and even a hidden toothpick. The gadgetry on these knives is not only a conversation piece, but it also makes the knife extremely versatile. Many feel it has too much gadgetry and is impractical, but it bears consideration.

The folding knife, such as the common pocket knife, is an excellent choice for the backpacker. These are available in many sizes, from the small pen knife to the bigger utility knife. Normally a quality knife of this style will have better

steel in the blades than do the gadget variety. This blade will cut better and last much longer. Prices for this style of knife will range from one dollar to ten dollars, depending upon its quality.

If neither of these styles appeal to you, another type to consider would be the hunter style folding knife. These usually have one blade, which is larger and stronger than any found on the other two designs. It is intended to be used by the hunter in skinning his game, but it is also very adaptable for backpacking use. Its biggest advantage is that it is a heavier knife and can be used for tasks that require a stonger blade than those offered by the multi-bladed and simple folding knife. This type of knife is more expensive and will normally run from $20 upwards.

A knife that serves many purposes, from dressing game to opening tin cans, is the popular sheath style knife. This knife is also suitable for cutting limbs and caping a trophy animal. Normally found in sporting goods stores, this style has a variety of sizes; from under three inches to practically

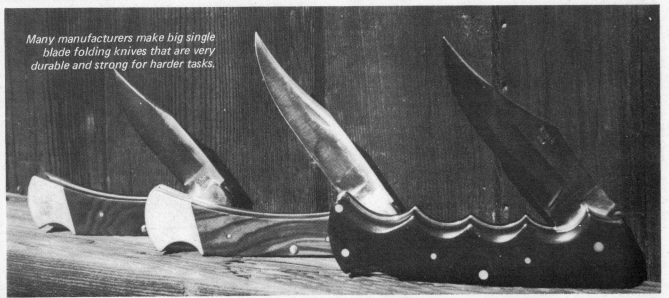

Many manufacturers make big single blade folding knives that are very durable and strong for harder tasks.

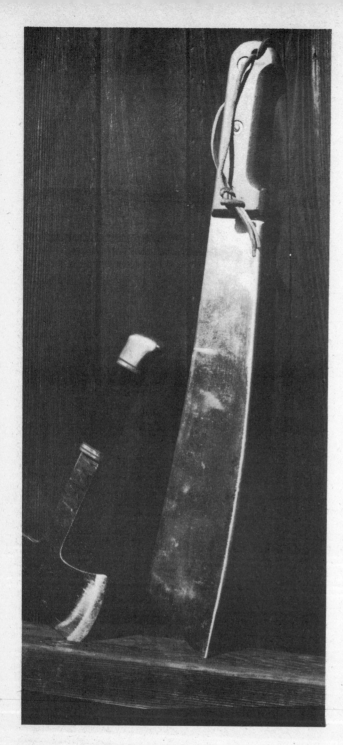

Above: A Swiss Army knife is multi-bladed and even has scissors and tweezers. Below: By far the most popular knife with backpackers is the single bladed sheath knife.

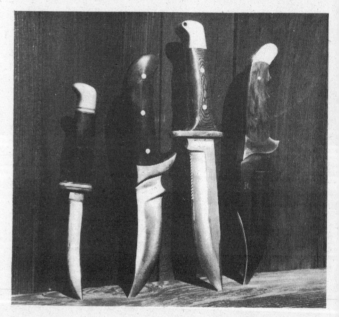

any length that you desire. These are definitely more expensive and will run from under five dollars to over fifty dollars for a custom made or quality name brand.

The sheath knife, as its name implies, comes in a heavy leather sheath. This can be either taped or tied to the webbing of the carrying straps of the pack so that it is easily accessible, but not in the way.

Larger knives will of course add a little weight to your pack, but this is balanced by the fact that a knife with a four or five-inch blade will perform almost any task that you ask of it.

One disadvantage of a knife which does not fold into its handle is that there is a possibility that you could injure yourself should you fall. However, this danger is minimized

by the leather sheath to the point where it is almost non-existent.

If hiking in an extremely dense and heavily foliaged area, you might desire to carry a machete or brush knife for cutting a pathway. These knives have a very limited use, however, and you should only carry them when anticipating heavy brush. Most of these knives will have a heavy canvas sheath and will fit in the back of the frame between the bag and the frame section of the pack. The best source for this type of knife would be an Army surplus store, where they can be picked up for a very reasonable price.

Each method of hunting has its own unique problems, but one that is seemingly universal is the tendency to carry too much gear. A backpack hunting trip is far from a hunt-

Right: The fisherman who packs into the less frequented lakes will find fishing as he may have never found before.

ing base camp or guided hunt! You will be the one carrying everything you need on your own back.

The best check for preventing too heavy of a load is to lay all your gear out before packing and eliminate everything not absolutely necessary. Remember that you will not only have your normal amounts of food, clothing, equipment and water, but you also will have the special items needed for hunting. Keep it as light as possible and carry only those things that are essential.

If you have packed three days into an excellent remote elk area and are fortunate enough to down a six-hundred pound elk, how are you going to get that monster out?

The first reaction would be to say that you would pack it out and chances are you could...for the next week to ten days. Even if you quarter an animal this size, one quarter will weigh a hundred pounds-plus. On top of this you will have the rack and hide also, a load in itself. Unless you are prepared, you may find that you might regret getting an animal this size that far away.

The best and simplest solution is to have arranged previously for a packer to meet you at your camp and help pack the game back. This can be done by making arrangements with a local rancher, if he is willing, or a professional packer to meet you at your camp on a designated day. If you have been lucky and you are a good shot, chances are that his trip will not be wasted and he'll have something to pack out. Also, sometimes there will be a sheepherder or resident in the area, who will happen by and will help you get your prize back to civilization.

A full grown elk is more than one horse can pack out in one trip, so either plan for more horses or more than one trip. If you have no prior arrangements, one member of the group can pack out and bring the horses back. Here again, you always should have enough people in the party so that there are always at least two together. For example, if it is a party of four, two can pack out for the horses and two remain at camp to protect the meat from wild animals.

Deer naturally are not as large as elk and present less of a problem. If there are at least two of you in the party, chances are that you will be able to pack it out without the aid of a packer or horses. If you plan to do this and in all cases when you pack out game, it is a good idea to bone the meat before attempting to pack it out. By removing all the bones, you can reduce the weight of the load drastically.

If you must leave your meat unprotected in the kill area or in camp, insure that you always have enough nylon rope to hang it high enough in a tree to prevent bears, coyotes and other such varmints from helping themselves to dinner on your deer.

A word of warning: There have been cases where hunters have been attacked by bear and similar varmints while packing out fresh game. Normally the smell of a human being is enough to frighten any animal off, but sometimes the smell of freshly killed game can be too tempting to resist.

Should a bear or such creature show undue interest in the game strapped to your back, give him a piece or, if he is really selfish, the whole thing. By giving him a piece, you can be long gone down the trail before he is finished with his meal. Normally, wild animals are more afraid of man, than man is of them, but since they are wild, they are also unpredictable and it behooves you to not take any chances.

FISHING

The truly ardent fisherman will allow nothing to come between him and his favorite fishing spot...even if it is miles of rugged terrain that is navigable only on foot. Conse-

The popular telescope style fishing rod disassembles and fits easily in the pack.

Above and below: The telescope style fishing rod easily assembles into a normal size rod.

quently, many have taken to backpacking, whether with a day bag for a short distance or a full pack for an extended trip into the boonies. Many hunters will also take along fishing equipment in order to be able to supplement their diet with fresh fish.

For these reasons many manufacturers are now making rods and other tackle for use by the backpacker. The most popular rods used by packers are the telescoping variety that will reduce to a unit that is only about fifteen inches in length. The choice of reel can vary from the bulkier (although not overly bulky) spinning reel to the more compact simple fly fishing reel. The spin casting reel is larger due to its unique construction, but many find that it is much simpler to use, especially for large bodies of water. However, if you are fishing a small stream, perhaps the simple fly style will be more to your liking.

Another type of pole often used by backpackers are the split bamboo poles that can be disassembled into sections of about three feet and when reassembled will be eight feet long. Disassembled these will strap very nicely on the back of the pack.

The choice of bait can sometimes be a problem. Flies are quite popular since they take up very little space and are exceedingly lightweight, however, practically any type of

standard bait can be used with the exception perhaps of fresh bait. The type you choose will depend primarily upon your own personal preference, the time of year, location, and the type of fish that you are seeking.

Normally backpacking is associated with fly fishing for trout, however, there is nothing that says you cannot backpack to out of the way lakes for larger muskies, pike or panfishes. Another type of fishing that is becoming more and more popular is where you load your pack aboard a canoe or other small boat and float down a river for fishing like you may never have had in your life. These floating fishing trips are not new and hundreds are joining the ranks of its enthusiasts daily.

Certain areas in the high country are noted for their fantastic fishing and it is the backpacker who is enjoying them. An example would be the golden trout found in the high lakes of the Sierra Nevadas in California and the only way you can get to them is on your own two feet.

Taking along fishing tackle may not always be very feasible on some of your packing trips because of the area and the fact that you know that there is no water. However, if you are not certain about the availability of fish in the area where you are packing, it is always a good idea to take along some monofilament line, a fly line, a few hooks

and a couple of flies just in case you do happen upon a likely looking fishing hole. Your fishing pole can be a cut willow and your outfit is complete. Fresh fish for dinner or breakfast can be a welcomed change in your diet of dried or canned foods!

You might note that bear also find fish a rather welcome change to their diet and if you are lucky enough to catch fish don't leave them lying around camp or you are liable to have an univited visitor for supper. Also, along

Some of the back stream game fish give the backpacking fisherman quite a battle.

these lines, if you have wiped your hands on your clothes while fishing, you should not leave these lying around the camp either, as their fishy smell may also attract bears.

Whether you are a hunter who likes to supplement his diet or an avid fisherman, the best fishing is not going to be found along the well traveled roads and paths...you are going to have to hike for it and backpacking is the key to your success.

The choice of a reel is an individual matter. Many use the simple fly reel, while others use the spinning reel.

CHAPTER 14
THE THRALL OF THE WILD

Wildlife Weaves A Magic Spell And Here Are Notes On How To Keep It From Causing Unwanted Trouble For You!

Although this grizzly is little more than a cub, he already is sufficiently large to show potential size and danger.

ONE OF THE biggest delights of backpacking is observing the wildlife you encounter when you pack into the backcountry. If you take the time and keep a sharp eye out, a trip into the wilderness can be a complete course in nature. In fact, animal watching, like people watching, can be a fascinating pastime.

Fortunately, in the United States there are relatively few animals that can be considered really dangerous, but as mentioned earlier, all wild animals are unpredictable and potentially dangerous.

Perhaps the most notorious of all animals indigenous to this country is the bear and, for the most part, this bad reputation is unjustified. Granted, he is big and ferocious looking, but in general his nature is rather easygoing. An exception would be the grizzly.

There are four species of bears that are indigenous to North America: the common black bear, the grizzly, the big brown bear and the polar bear. The big brown and polar bears are rarely encountered by the average backpacker, since they inhabit the arctic zones and the extremely remote areas of Alaska.

The black bear, which ranges in color from light cinnamon to jet-black, can be found in almost all parts of the country, from the southern states to the Rockies and western mountain ranges. As a general rule he is easygoing and prefers fish, berries and grubs found under logs and rocks as food. If it is a particularly lean time and he is unable to find this subsistence, he may upon occasion substitute this diet with meat. He will eat carrion anytime.

Normally his meat source will be deer and small animals, but if the times are really bad, he may turn to sheep and cattle. This is rare.

The black bear is more of a nuisance than a danger, for he loves to raid the food locker of an unprotected camp site. If you have come across a marauding bear, you know the mess that he will leave behind. Even if the food is kept in a tight container or out of reach, they have been known to almost completely demolish a camp in search of food.

Black bears have become even more of a nuisance and, in some cases, a danger in national park areas where they have overcome their innate fear of man. In fact, in most of the cases where you hear of a bear attacking or injuring a person, it has been in a park area. Any wild animal that has lost his natural fear of humans can be dangerous.

When camping in a park area, avoid setting up camp near a dump or trash receptacle area. Many of these "tame" park bears subsist by rummaging through the trash cans of the parks. If your camp is nearby, he is liable to look for his dessert in your food locker.

A black bear, like any animal, is extremely protective of its young. A playful bear cub is a joy to watch and an excellent subject for photographing. However, should you come upon one, be extremely careful, for the mother is not far off and looks with jaundiced eye upon anyone who comes too close to her offspring. Photograph and observe to your heart's content from a respectful distance. Bears can move at an incredible speed and a mother black can be upon you in a flash, if she feels her cub is in danger.

The domain of the really big one — the grizzly — is the northwestern states like Idaho, Montana and Wyoming. These fellows have a personality that is far from easygoing. In fact, it is not unusual for them to attack with no provocation.

The main difference in appearance between the black and the grizzly bear is that the latter has a hump across the shoulders and is usually larger than the black. However, if you have any doubt, don't hang around to find out. Chances of your coming across a grizzly are slim, unless you are really into the back country, but if you do happen upon one you would be well advised to give him the right of way!

A black bear often can be stopped or turned by merely shouting and waving or making loud noises with a pan, but it isn't advisable to try this on a grizzly. Once he has started to charge, there is almost nothing that will stop him. Even a black will not always be stopped by loud noises, so be prepared to take other steps.

You cannot outrun a bear, whatever species, so you should not even attempt it. This is not to advocate that you just stand there, but don't try to outrun him for any distance. Your best bet is to find a tree and do some fast scaling. This is a good escape and evasion procedure for a grizzly, but black bears are noted for their tree climbing abilities, so you would not be entirely home free by climbing a tree. However, you would have a vantage position where you might be able to fend the bear off with a stick, until it becomes tired and wanders off in search of less elusive prey. A grizzly will not try to climb a tree, unless it is slanted so there is not too steep an angle.

Bears are known for their very poor eyesight, but have excellent hearing and smell. You may be able to stand still and allow the bear to amble by, but few people remain calm with an animal this size in close proximity. The best protection is to avoid the creature, whenever possible. They are large enough that they can be seen for quite a distance and it is purely a matter of changing your course of direction to avoid them.

Many campers will carry along a cow bell and this has been known to work in scaring off bears. However, again, you should be prepared to take other measures.

If you keep a clean camp and don't leave any food around, chances are you will not be bothered by bears looking for food. In fact, you could spend an entire lifetime camping and never even see a bear, although they abound in the forest and mountain country of North America.

Many articles have been written and stories told about the king of the western mountain ranges — the mountain lion. This sleek, tawny cat is found in the southern, southwestern and central Rockies and some far west areas. It is a beautiful creature to observe, but here again, many outdoorsmen have gone an entire lifetime without ever sighting one. They are extremely shy and will stay away from the human smell. Should one be in the area where you hike, chances are he will be long gone before you would ever see him. Their main diet is deer; if this game is scarce, they have been known to attack livestock, but normally the smell of man is strong enough in the area where livestock graze that it keeps them away. There have been rare cases in which a mountain lion has attacked a person, but this has almost

Black bear, although color may run to brown or cinnamon, is a species that is found throughout the U.S. today.

The lynx, although found in most of our states, is shy and operates at night. As a result, he is rarely seen by the casual backpacking buff.

The so-called bobcat is a member of the lynx family and has many of the same characteristics of conduct.

With his mammoth size, the bull elk can be dangerous in rutting season. Flies also can make him irritable.

always been when they have been injured or are sick. They are not animals you need to be afraid of and, if lucky enough to see one, you are fortunate for they are beautiful creatures to behold. However, like any wild animal, you should never corner or tease a mountain lion. Under these circumstances, he will attack purely for self-protection.

A smaller member of the North American cat family is the short-tailed lynx, which can be found in nearly all portions of the continent north of Mexico. There are two types, the Canada lynx and the bay lynx (often called the red lynx, wildcat or bobcat). Here again, these cats are shy and, except when cornered, will not voluntarily attack a man.

Any wild animal can be dangerous and the larger, the more dangerous. Elk, moose and even deer have been known to attack people, but normally only during the rutting or mating season, unless frightened or cornered. Elk and moose especially become antagonistic during mating season and should be avoided. Flies also will often irritate moose and elk making them meaner than normal. Avoid them, since they can be seen easily. Don't try to outrun them for any distance, but head for the nearest tree. Campers have been treed by these animals, but they will normally tire after awhile and move off.

One animal not often considered dangerous, which you may encounter is the common range cow. Little can compare to a mad range cow that thinks her calf is endangered. A young calf is about as cute as any baby animal and one is always tempted to pet it, but don't. The mother is big, fast and often equipped with some mighty sharp horns!

Perhaps the only animal in America which is deliberately malicious and mean is the wolverine. About the size of a full-grown bulldog, this animal is found in the northern Cascades, the Rocky Mountain region, the Arctic region and many parts of Alaska. The wolverine has a voracious appetite, a fierce temper and great strength. It is one of the few animals that will kill for pleasure, even when it is not hungry or protecting itself. It has been known to raid cabins and camps, leaving total destruction behind. Should you come across this creature, don't even pause to observe it.

Some areas of the country have wild hogs, which are in many cases, from domesticated stock that has returned to a wild state. With very little fear of man, these animals will attack. Normally they will travel in groups and are often called sounders. They are equipped with sharp tusks and

Top: Wild or feral boar are found primarily in Southern and Western states; they can be dangerous if cornered.
Left: The pronghorn antelope, once nearly extinct, has made a great comeback as a result of conservation effort, but average backpacker doesn't get near this fleetfoot.
Below: Fawns are interesting to watch and at this age often appear to be totally unafraid of human beings.

they know how to use them! These hogs may be found in almost any locale, but most are in the southern states and some of the more remote western areas.

Many of the animals that you will encounter on the trails certainly cannot be considered dangerous, but they can most definitely be a nuisance.

It is amazing how much damage chipmunks can do to a camp. Considered cute and often a welcomed guest in a camp, chipmunks get into anything that is left lying around, such as food packages, packs and similar items. The best protection is to keep your camp picked up and to hang any items from trees where they cannot be reached by these rascals. If you want to feed them, do it away from camp.

Found primarily in the Southwest and Mexico, javelina are classified as members of the peccary family. They are reported in legend to attack men on foot, but there are no such authenticated records of reports.

Raccoons are cute and considered to be harmless, yet they can create a good deal of havoc in your camp.

As frightening as they may appear, porcupines are not dangerous, although they too can be a nuisance as they will raid a camp at night in search of salt. Here again, keep items out of reach in high places and they should be no problem. If one happens to wander into camp, he can easily be guided out with a stick. Their quills give them a formidable appearance, but for the most part they are quite harmless.

One of the most beautiful animals in North America, the skunk is a bold marauder that also will raid camps in search of food. Should one wander into your camp or tent, leave it alone, until it decides on its own to amble back out. Sometimes they can be coaxed out by leaving a trail of bits of food, but don't try to frighten one out of camp. If you do, you are liable to find yourself and camp area smelling less than pleasant.

Always in search of items to build nests, birds will often carry off small items that are left lying around. Keep things picked up and put away and you should not be bothered.

The most dangerous animal that you are likely to encounter on the trail is the snake. Fortunately, here in the United States there are only four poisonous varieties: the rattlesnake (14 species), the copperhead, the water moccasin (cottonmouth), and the coral snake. Nonpoisonous snakes indigenous to the northern continent are far too numerous to discuss in this chapter.

The rattlesnake can be found in almost all of North America, from desert to forest, from mountains to plains. They come in various sizes and colors; normally a color that is harmonious to their surroundings.

For example, the timber rattlesnake is the color of dead leaves and damp earth, which hides it from its natural enemies when it is in its natural environment of the forests and timberlands.

Although rattlesnakes are difficult to see because of their coloration, they are equipped with rattles that give off a warning whirring or buzzing sound when they are frightened or disturbed. If you have ever heard this sound, you know the chills it can send down your spine.

A beautiful but deadly snake, the copperhead is found in the woods and rocky regions of the eastern area from Indiana to the Atlantic coast and southwestward to Texas. On the Atlantic coast they can be found as far north as the New England states, but in the middle west, they are not normally found north of Indiana. They are a small, short snake, easily recognized by patches of dark and light copper coloring.

The ugliest and perhaps the meanest of all North American snakes is the water moccasin or cottonmouth found in the damp grassy swamps and water areas of the south. These snakes are found most often along the banks of water partially submerged or on logs or overhanging limbs around water. The water moccasin is the only poisonous snake in the northern continent that is pugnacious and will not retreat when approached. Most snakes will slither off when encountered, but a moccasin will hold its ground and prepare for battle. They are totally devoid of bright colors and their skin has the appearance of dried mud. The most distinguishing feature is when it opens its mouth, it appears as if it is filled with cotton, which is why it has been given the nickname of cottonmouth.

The coral or harlequin snake is found from South Carolina, southward to the Gulf and southwestward to Texas. Instantly recognized by the alternation of brilliant red, yellow and jet-black rings which encircle its body, this snake is quite small and delicately formed. It is often mistaken for the king snake, which is harmless, but is very similar in color. An old children's rhyme: "Yellow and black, friend of Jack; yellow and red, kills you dead," is a good way to remember how to distinquish between the dangerous coral and the harmless king snake.

The moose is one of this country's largest animals and even the cow, a seemingly lethargic creature, is deserving of anyone's respect.

The coral has a red stripe immediately next to a yellow stripe, whereas the king has a yellow stripe next to a black stripe. The coral is an extremely timid serpent and chances of your running across one are very slim.

The best protection from snake bites is always to be on the alert whenever hiking. The majority of them are timid and will move off, given the chance, with the water moccasin as an exception. The primary danger with snakes is that often a hiker will not see the snake and will step upon it or, in climbing, grab a rock or limb where the snake is lying. This is how most people are bitten and the problem can greatly be alleviated by taking care where you step or place your hand.

A rattler normally will give you a warning shake of his tail, but don't depend on this warning. You may come upon him by surprise and he will not have time to issue his warning.

Never walk where you cannot see the ground ahead of you and never place your hand anyplace where you cannot see. If you hear the buzzing sound of a rattler, immediately freeze and look around for the source. If it is a rattlesnake, look again for his mate, since many times they travel in pairs, especially during mating season.

you are most likely to run across them and you should be extra careful during these hours.

In their quest for relief from the heat of the sun during the day, snakes will seek shady, damp areas such as under rocks and logs. Always be careful when moving any of these objects. Many times they will seek the coolness of stream and river banks, so be wary when hiking in such an area.

Since snakes do their hunting at night and sometimes will seek a warm area, they have been known to crawl into sleeping bags. The best protection is to not leave your sleeping bag, or other items like clothing or boots, lying around on the ground. If one decides to crawl into the bag with you when you are sleeping on the ground there is really not much you can do, other than lie deadly still until it decides to crawl out. A rather frightening thought, but there is little else you can do. You certainly can't get out of the bag fast enough to prevent it from striking you as you move. Chances of such a happening, however, are exceedingly slim.

The venom of a baby snake, even one that has just been born, is just as poisonous as an adult snake. A baby snake may not have as much venom, but what he does have is certainly enough to make you quite sick and, if not

Pound for pound, the wolverine can be the most fierce fighter in the forest and is one animal that is reputed to kill for sheer joy of it.

When you run across what is known as a snake bed, which is a large group of snakes that have gathered, get out fast!

Most snake bites occur on the legs, arms or hands. For the best protection of the leg area you should always wear thick leather, preferably high boots and when in a known snake country, wear your pant cuffs on the outside of the boots. The fangs are not too long and with the protection of boots and the pant cuffs, they may not be able to penetrate into the flesh. For bites on the hands and arms, about the only protection is to be careful where you place your hands when hiking or climbing.

Carry a walking staff whenever you hike. With this instrument, you can kill a snake without having to get too close. However, most snakes, even the poisonous kind, have an important role in our ecosystem...they control rodents and other harmful varmints. They will not bother you, if you do not bother them, and the best philosophy is to just leave them alone.

Most snakes are extremely sensitive to heat and, during the day will seek cooler, shady areas. However, at night, especially during early evening, they come out and warm themselves on the rocks and warm soil. This is the time that

immediately taken care of, it could result in death.

Be just as wary of the more common variety of harmless snakes. Their bite is not poisonous, but any snake bite can become infected, if not properly treated.

A reptile that fits in the dangerous category is the gila monster. This large, rather colorful lizard resides in the desert regions of Arizona and other southwestern states. It is easily distinguished by the Navajo blanket pattern of jet-black and orange-yellow beads that cover its body.

The gila monster (pronounced he'la) is slow and clumsy. The danger is that it is such a fascinating creature that often people will be tempted to pick it up for a closer look. This is when they are bitten and even then, the lizard is so slow that he has trouble getting hold of a finger or a hand. However, once he does, it is almost impossible to get it to open its mouth again. It is debated whether or not its bite is poisonous, but it is known that a bite from a gila monster has made people quite sick. It could be caused by a natural poison in the venom or else by infection, since the mouth of the lizard is extremely dirty.

The best philosophy to adopt concerning animals when backpacking is to enjoy observing them from a distance, but always respect them and they, in turn, will respect you.

The cottonmouth moccasin is reputed to be the only poisonous snake that actually will launch an attack and follow what is considers its enemy.

Coral snake is confined to a small area of the United States, but is one of most poisonous types known.

The copperhead is named for color of its body. It abounds in Eastern part of U.S., south as far as Texas.

There are several types of rattlers in this country, but all have the familiar feature that is supposed to help warn one. Don't count on it.

CHAPTER 15

This summer tent features netting over the entrance to keep out flying insects, a rain cover and built-in ground cloth. It won't keep out cold.

PROTECTING YOURSELF AND YOUR GEAR

That Surprise Rain Shower Can Mean A Ruined Trip If The Backpacker Is Sleeping Under The Stars

NIGHT IS APPROACHING and the tired hunter has located a nice little clearing in which to set up the base camp from where he will move into the surrounding brush to find that elusive record elk. A fisherman has topped the final rise to see the reflective smoothness of that isolated lake his buddies told him about, and prepares to settle in for a week of casting and wading, unbothered by wake-throwing ski boats or the prospect of elbow-dueling other fishermen. The nature photographer has discovered a likely place to find a few patterns of hoarfrost and is anxious to get his living pack and the gadget bag that holds perhaps $1000 worth of camera body and lenses under cover from the cold and snow.

As the beneficiaries of synthetic fibers and lightweight alloys, these outdoor appreciators have a long list of advantages over that original backpacker; the dogface who has

The extra layer of material in the sides and top of this three-season model will trap a second layer of warming air.

The grommet and seams of this tie-off point will need to be bar tacked to stand up to the added stress put on it.

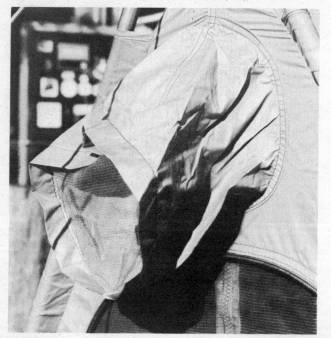

carried the living necessities on his back into almost every recorded disagreement between strangers. To shelter the men and weapons of their fighting forces, commanders have depended on some form of collapsible and reasonably portable dwelling that attempts to keep people and gear dry in the rain, warm in the cold and shaded in extremes of heat.

During the Civil War, the Army developed a two-piece shelter dubbed the pup tent. Designed to accommodate two men, each of whom carried one-half of the canvas tent wrapped around his bedroll, the tent was set up by buttoning these two halves together and supporting them with two poles, one at each end. The resulting shelter had no ground cloth, but was considered sufficient to meet the basic field living conditions of the infantryman.

Shortly after that, some ragged doughboy decided that a blanket was warmer to sleep on than dew-dampened grass or a lumpy puddle of mud and the ground cloth helped every outdoor sleeper rest easier.

The arrival of synthetic fabrics in the 1950s gave tent manufacturers an alternative to the clumsy canvas material used up until then, and the development of lighter metals provided a replacement for the breakable wood poles that were prone to swell in rainy weather and dry rot in sunnier climes.

Instead of the single sheet of cloth draped over a tree branch to make a simple lean-to, a modern backpacker's so-called crude shelter may be anything from a two-man summer tent to a five-man expedition model constructed to withstand winds in excess of thirty-five miles per hour and insulated against sub-zero temperatures. Supporting them might be anything from fiberglass poles or inter-fitting metal ones to the recently introduced shock poles, which have an elastic cord in the center to allow quick assembly and reduce the possibility of losing one or more of the three pole sections. Some tent manufacturers will laugh themselves silly at a camper's frantic efforts to purchase just the one pole section he lost, without having to buy an entire new pole. Others may view such a request with a bit

The three-season tent is designed to bridge the unpredictable weather patterns of Spring, Summer and Fall. It will need insect netting, like the summer tent, and the added features of cookhole and air vent for Winter.

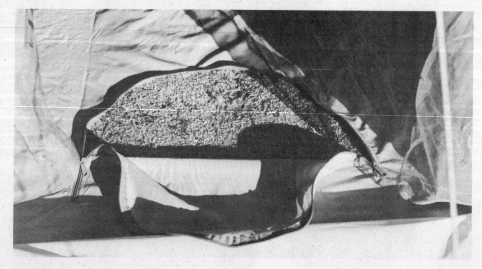

A tent that will fulfill the backpacker's needs must be large enough so that all members of the camping party can sleep comfortably. This model obviously qualifies.

This dome-style tent offers the added feature of a special extension that will protect the cross-country traveller's means of transportation.

With just a piece of plastic tarp and a roll of strong twine, the backpacker can construct a makeshift shelter.

With the corners tied off at each end, and part of the tarp folded under to make a ground cloth, camper is snug.

This summer tent would provide good protection from insects, but needs a rain cover to be adequate against wind, rain.

This year-round model has anti-bug netting, would provide shade in hot weather and has addition extension to provide more leg room to sleepers.

A modified wedge, such as this type, has the added support of extra poles in the center.

This three-season model has the option of a flip-top for access to cool breezes, rain protection.

more courtesy, but the unlucky woodsman is still going to have a long wait while his order is filled.

As in other areas of modern life, tent manufacturing has become a bit more specialized since the pup tent days. There are basically three types of tents now being marketed: summer tents, winter tents and one which is used during the unpredictable weather patterns that span these two extremes, called a three-season tent.

The summer tent should be capable of withstanding winds of at least twenty-five mph from any direction. A winter tent should bear up under considerably more without the snug backpacker inside being annoyed by flapping sides or goosed by a stray breath of chilly breeze because the edges of the tent have pulled loose or because a poorly constructed vent or door is letting the cold leak in.

A summer tent is used primarily as protection against that seasonal afternoon shower or the rare flash storm. It will have netting over the openings to keep out flying or crawling bugs. The backpacker may even use the tent simply to protect his equipment from forming dew and roll up in his sleeping bag outside if the night is mild enough. He certainly won't be forced to cook his meals inside a summer tent, so the added cost of a cooking vent is not necessary. The weight of a summer tent may range from

The traditional pyramid-shaped design usually has over-lapping entrance flaps, tie-down flaps over screened vents.

This year-round tent has tunnel entrance and rain cover, but might be too heavily constructed for convenient summer use. This would be a good tent for fall winds.

just over two pounds to as much as seven pounds. Their purchase price might be anywhere from $40 to $125.

The three-season type is designed for use in Spring, Summer and Fall, combining the bug protection of a summer tent with the heavy-duty construction to withstand an unexpected snowstorm. This means it will be able to stand up under the weight of fallen snow, have a cookhole that allows culinary combustion inside the tent and adequate ventilation for an extended stay. A number of the three-season tents are marketed by Jansport; Eureka; Sierra Designs; Mountain Equipment, Incorporated; Gerry; and others. Prices generally run from $85 to $225 and weights for the two-man model run from about four pounds to ten pounds.

Winter tents, with their special insulation and other features, are strictly a cold-weather proposition. Sometimes called the expedition model, a good winter tent will hold out against winds in excess of thirty-five mph and remain

This model has zip-up flap over net-covered entrance. Good Summer or Fall.

Similar to model above, this tent adds rain cover, which is good, but has main support pole right in front of entrance, making access clumsy.

stable in over four feet of snow. Designed for lengthy bivouacking, the winter tent will feature a cookhole and a tunnel-type entrance. A tent rated as a two, three or four-man tent should be big enough to enclose that number of campers, plus their gear. When shopping for a winter tent, visualize having to live in it for four or five days. If the idea isn't feasible with one model, look for another one to buy. Winter tents generally weigh much more than the summer or three-season variety and cost from $125 to $250 for the two-man size; more for the bigger sizes.

There are some cheapie models of all three types available, but a bargain basement tent that rips easily and is not properly insulated for the intended use will be no bargain at all if it costs the backpacker his health and the expense of replacing other equipment when that great deal of his gets blown down the side of a mountain in the middle of the night. The slightly more expensive tent made of Ripstop nylon, with a sewn-on ground covering and a rain fly that

Extra-long sides on rain cover of this model insure that water will not gather at seams, provide shade, anti-rain protection for net-covered windows. Pole by door is bad.

The door of this model is also blocked by support poles. Exotic shape might make user stand out in the crowd and in breeze. Check with old-timers.

The lower profile of this model will help it resist gusting winds, though the low walls will cramp the amount of available headroom. Poles, again.

This dome-style model has separate rain cover, sleeps two campers and protects their gear without cramp.

drapes over the top may be a wiser and healthier investment.

Most tents are made by backpack or clothing manufacturers and the difference in scale in sewing the larger item can often cause workmanship problems. When shopping for a tent, look closely at the seams to make sure they interlock correctly. Points of stress, such as the door flap and the pole sleeves should be bar tacked. The best way to get a good look at where all that money is going is to set the tent up in the store. This may bug the sales force a bit, but it is the buyer's best bet for getting a good product.

Check for good ventilation. Two campers will exhale about a pint of moisture during a night's sleep and that moisture, and the exhaled carbon dioxide, must have someplace to go unless the user wants to live in a terrarium. The shape of a tent, be it a dome, wedge or out-sized tetrahedron, will help determine its stability in high winds. This is a hard thing to be sure of until the camper finds — after his tent has blown over, leaving him open to the elements — that he misjudged the one he bought. A word with more experienced backpackers might help the newcomer to make a good choice the first time around.

When checking the seams, make sure the stitches are straight and that there are at least six or seven stitches per inch. Look for broken threads. These may be a weak spot in an otherwise satisfactory shelter. Put the poles in place to make sure they fit properly and work the zippers to see if they operate smoothly.

'Note the amount of time it takes to complete setting up the tent. Nobody will be happy with a model so complicated that it takes a construction engineer forty-five minutes to figure it out. A good tent should go together in a short time, even when put up by the least experienced member of a group.

Be sure the tent material has been treated to be fire-retardant, especially if the situation may require the backpacker to do his cooking indoors. Several family outings have ended in disaster when a fuel lantern or cook stove was placed too close to the tent wall or got knocked over by a sleepy youngster. Some of the Oriental fabrics of which many imported tents are made will go up like a bomb when heated to their flash point.

To combat this problem, the tent-making industry has developed what is known as the CPA-84. This is a set of

This is a winter-only tent. Note heavily insulated walls, raised sill across entrance, ground cloth.

This two-man, half-dome style tent employs tension center-lock poles for low silhouette, weighs 5¼ lbs.

This full dome shelter has added rain cover, offers good headroom.

This all-weather tent is lightweight, has cookhole, air vent, tunnel entrance, regular entrance with zip-up closing flap. Good winter tent.

Dome tent such as type pictured above would sleep two campers or could be used on mild night to cover gear.

specifications that are an industry standard for measuring the susceptibility of tent fabrics to flame. To meet these standards, fabrics are subjected to an open flame for twelve seconds and the extent of the burn is measured. To be considered flame-resistant, the fabric sample must not burn in an area larger than ten inches during the twelve-second test. The fabric must also be self-extinguishing within two seconds after the flame is removed. This will give some leeway to the father frantically scrambling to limit the damage of youthful clumsiness.

Once that $100 to $200 investment has been made, the backpacker will want to get the best and longest service possible from his new tent. The best way to protect the tent is to use the stuff sack that comes with it or get a hardier one that will provide even more protection. No matter how it grates against any personal standards of precision and neatness, the backpacker should literally stuff his tent into the stuff sack each time. This puts random wrinkles in different places each time, so that no particular point of the tent is creased again and again, preventing the weak spots that will form if the tent is folded neatly at the same places over and over. A commercial sealer applied to

This one-man half-dome is six feet, ten inches long, forty-two inches high. Weight is 3¾ pounds complete with tension center-lock poles.

the major seams of the tent will help improve its effectiveness in rainy weather.

Take care with the use and storage of the tent poles. Replacements are hard to come by and the tent is useless without something to hold it up. When the campsite has been decided on, clear the ground where the tent will be set up of any sticks, branches or sharp rocks. Nobody needs any extraneous holes in a brand-new tent. Check the trees above the area for any dead limbs that may be ready to fall on and tear the rain cover or tent roof.

On returning home, hose off the tent and hang it out to dry. Make sure it is completely dry before storing it. Synthetic materials deteriorate quickly in the damp coldness of the family garage. A hall closet is a much better storage place.

A tent is probably the most expensive piece of equipment in the backpacker's list of necessities, but it will be well worth the heavy investment to keep from having a weekend spoiled by rain or that snowstorm the television weatherman swore was headed the other way. With proper maintenance and careful use, a good tent will serve the backpacker through many years of trips in the wilderness.

This low-profile model has plenty of staking points to aid in resisting mountain winds. Poles are out of door.

IN THE EVENT OF AN EMERGENCY...

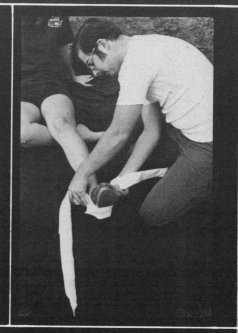

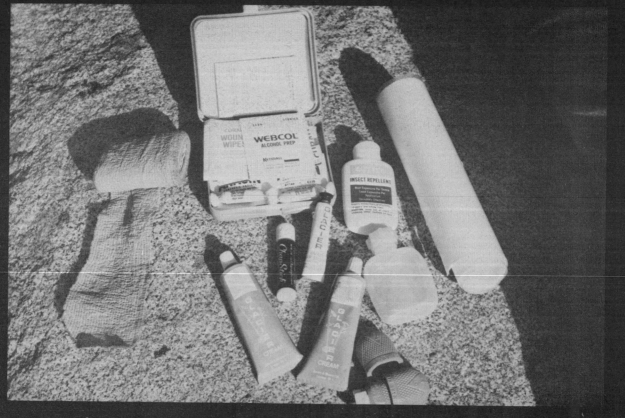

CHAPTER 16

THE MANY MILLIONS of campers who take to the forests and parks each year rarely, if ever, have need of first aid skills. This will also apply to the backpacker. But in isolated cases, the knowledge of first aid will be more than handy — it can save a life.

The matter of first aid, both in concept and application, continually changes as new developments appear in the medical field. Therefore, some of the methods mentioned in this chapter, while they are correct and usable, may be outmoded or outdated when you purchase BACKPACKER'S DIGEST. In such cases, follow the newer practice — providing it comes from a reputable source and has the blessings of such groups as the American National Red Cross.

Basically, first aid means exactly what it says — the first type of aid to be administered to an accident victim until professional help can be obtained. Naturally, in the smaller, more usual cases of insect bites, abrasions and the like, first aid may be all that is required. In the more serious cases, however, trained authorities should be sought posthaste.

This chapter will not go into a great amount of detail, nor will it cover every facet of first aid training that an individual should possess. Rather, it is recommended that each prospective backpacker attend a free first aid course offered by local chapters of the American National Red Cross. Students that have completed the course have saved many lives throughout the years.

There are three emergency situations with which everyone, backpackers included, should be familiar: Severe bleeding, cessation of respiration and poisoning. These will be discussed at some length later in this chapter. However, there are a few basic steps that should be taken with any serious or seemingly serious injury.

First, keep the victim lying down to protect him from unnecessary manipulation and disturbance. Often an injured person will cause further damage by moving about. Heat, in the form of blankets, should be applied only to keep his body temperature from dropping, following investigation for injuries.

Checking for injuries can be difficult. The victim may have some ideas of the extent or location of his injuries, if he is conscious, and they can be added to your findings upon examination. The extent of examination should be determined by the type of accident.

It is easier to note and diagnose external injuries than those affecting internal organs for the simple reason that there often are no visible signs of internal damage, using internal bleeding as an example. You can only speculate, based on the seriousness of the accident.

Many first aiders, upon finding an injury of major proportions, tend to abandon the search for further injuries. This is a mistake as a second serious injury that passes unnoticed can negate all of your efforts on the one initially discovered.

If a person is in a swimsuit, it is much easier to check all anatomical areas than if he is fully dressed. Care must be taken when removing any clothing articles, for the injury

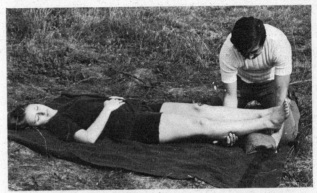

Above: Unless head or chest injury is present, or the shock victim has difficulty in breathing, feet should be elevated. Below: If the outside temperature is cold, the shock victim should be covered to prevent heat loss.

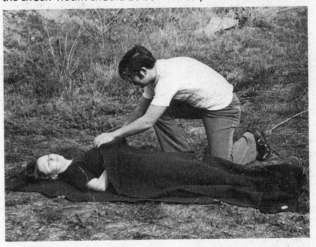

may be made worse. Even if there is no visible sign of injury to a specific location, yet you have reason to believe it may have been harmed, avoid bending, twisting and shaking that spot. Don't jackknife the patient.

Naturally, attend to the serious injuries first, but don't overlook those of lesser magnitude. Don't give fluids of any type to an unconscious or semi-conscious victim, for the fluid may enter the windpipe. Don't attempt to rouse an unconscious or semi-conscious individual by shaking, striking, talking or shouting at him. Instead, loosen the clothing around his neck and, if there is no fracture on one side of the body, turn the patient on that side. This allows any secretion to drain freely, preventing drowning. Place a pillow of some sort under his head.

Moving the victim depends largely upon the site of the accident and the seriousness of his injuries. We are not qualified in detailing procedures for moving the victim, and suggest this be obtained from ANRC. In many cases additional injury has been induced by such action. In no case should an injured person be lifted by grasping his belt, as this often aggravates injuries of the back or internal organs.

In a backpacking situation, when a member of the party is seriously injured and obviously unable to walk out on his own accord, moving him or getting professional medical help is not simply a matter going to the nearest telephone. Here is the time when having a citizens band radio could save a life. However, if you are not so equipped, someone is going to have to be sent for help. Here again, we cannot overstress the importance of always having at least a minimum of two people in the party!

In the event that the person is injured this seriously, under no circumstances should you attempt to move him on your own. The local forestry service and sheriff's department are trained and equipped to handle such an emergency evacuation and they should be contacted immediately by whatever methods you have available.

If the victim is conscious, reassure him by explaining the first aid steps you are undertaking and their effect. Never insinuate that the person is going to die, or be horrified by his injuries, as this sometimes will send the victim into shock. Don't discuss his condition with bystanders; however, helpers can be given necessary information.

If at all possible, seek medical advice of qualified personnel. Here again, obtaining this advice is not a matter of finding the nearest telephone...someone is going to have to pack out for help, if the injury is severe enough that it cannot be handled by simple first aid procedures.

SEVERE BLEEDING

If the victim is bleeding profusely, there are several techniques that can be used to stop the blood flow. The most effective is the use of direct pressure on the wound. Using either the bare hand or a handkerchief, press firmly on the wound until the flow of blood lessens and stops. This does not happen instantly, so the pressure must be applied until it does.

The second method used for controlling blood flow is by applying pressure to the supply blood vessel. There are only two points on both sides of the body where pressure against the supplying vessel occasionally can be used: On the inner half of the arm, between the elbow and armpit, and just below the groin on the front. In the former, pressure forces the main vessel against the bone and diminishes bleeding below the point of pressure. In the latter, the main vessel is forced against the pelvic bone, diminishing the flow of blood to the lower extremity.

SHOCK

Shock is a depressed condition of many of the bodily functions due to failure of enough blood to circulate through the body following serious injury. If a person develops and remains in shock, death may result even though the injury causing the shock would not be fatal otherwise.

Shock sometimes is difficult to diagnose, as all of the symptoms and signs may not be present. The most important evidence is the victim's weakness coupled with a skin that is pale and moist and cooler than it should be. The eyes often will be vacant and lackluster, with the pupils dilated. Breathing is shallow and irregular, and the pulse is weak or absent. He may be nauseous. His mental reactions may appear normal at first. Later, he may be restless or lose alterness and interest in his surroundings. He may be thirsty.

As it sometimes is difficult to diagnose, all seriously injured individuals should be given first aid for shock, according to the First Aid Textbook of the ANRC. The patient should be kept lying down, preferably on a blanket, and covered only sparingly, according to the outside temperature. On warm days, leave the victim uncovered, as

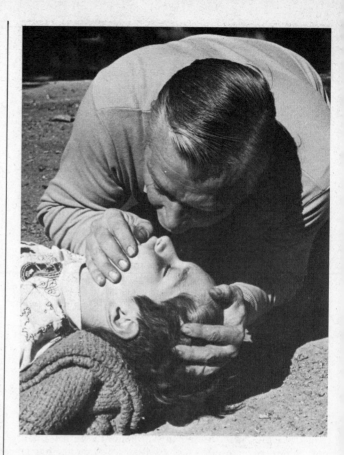

When giving artificial respiration to children cover victim's mouth, nose totally with your own. Blow in and let the victim exhale about 20 times per minute.

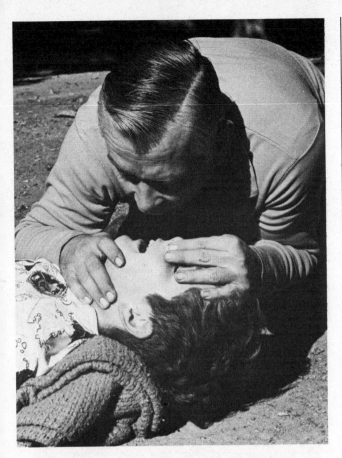

In giving artificial respiration pinch the nostrils
closed while grabbing the jaw and opening the mouth
with the other hand. Then place mouth around victim's.

There are plastic tubes on the market that can
be used in giving artificial respiration. Many
prefer this method to the mouth to mouth style.

the main objective is not to heat the body, but to prevent a
large loss of body heat.

Once down, elevate the feet eight to twelve inches, if the
injury is severe or loss of blood a great amount. Do not
elevate the feet if there is a head injury, difficulty in breathing increases, or the patient complains of pain when it is
attempted. The reason for elevation of the feet is so that
more blood will flow to the head and chest areas, where it
is more needed than in the legs. If there is a head or chest
injury or the patient encounters breathing difficulty,
elevate the head.

Often a patient in shock will become thirsty, and there is
value in the administration of fluids. They must not be
given to individuals suffering from an abdominal wound; a
victim who is nauseous; one who faces an early operation;
an unconscious or semi-conscious victim, or one that can be
treated by medical authorities in an hour or less.

As there may be a delay with the backpacker, it may be
advisable to issue small amounts of plain water, neither hot
nor cold, intially. If the delay in procuring medical help
may be substantial, a half-glass of water mixed with a one-
half level teaspoon of salt and the same amount of baking
soda may be administered about every fifteen minutes.
However, if the victim becomes nauseous, forego any future
administrations of water.

ARTIFICIAL RESPIRATION

The prompt usage of artificial respiration has saved
many lives throughout the years, and the backpaker should
be informed of the practice. According to the ANRC First
Aid Textbook, the objective of artificial respiration is "To

maintain an alternating decrease and increase in the
expansion of the chest and to maintain an open airway
through the mouth and nose."

A person can stop breathing for a variety of reasons. If
you were not present when the accident took place but
rather came upon the victim shortly after its occurrence,
you must take steps that could save the person's life. We'll
not discuss the procedures required for removing the cause
of the breath stoppage, as the causes are wide and varied.

The first move you should make is to clear the victim's
airway of any debris that may be blocking the passage of
air, which can be done by sweeping a finger through the
mouth and throat area. At the same time, press the tongue
forward.

Next, lay the victim on his back and place an object
beneath the shoulder blades and neck, which will cause the
head to tilt downwards, with the lower jaw jutting out.
With one hand, pinch the nostrils closed while grabbing the
jaw and opening the mouth with the other hand. Now place
your mouth completely around the victim's, forming an
air-tight seal and blow into the victim's mouth. Remove
your mouth and, applying pressure on the chest — providing he has no chest injury — let the victim exhale. This
should be repeated about sixteen times per minutes for
adults until he is revived.

If the mouth is damaged or otherwise prohibits the use
of artificial respiration through the mouth-to-mouth
method, it is possible to use mouth-to-nose resuscitation to
revive a victim. With this process, the mouth is closed as
tightly as possible and the first aider blows through an air-
tight seal around the nose. Again, after each breath the

chest is allowed to exhale, with help from a pressing hand, providing there is no chest injury.

With children a combination of the mouth-to-mouth and mouth-to-nose methods is utilized. The resuscitator covers both the nose and mouth of the child victim and goes through the motions described for adults, although repeating the practice some twenty times per minute.

For those individuals who don't hanker to performing mouth-to-mouth, there is a plastic tube marketed and used by many agencies who specialize in saving lives. One end of the tube is placed in the victim's mouth, which then is closed tightly around it, and the first aider blows in another portion of the tube and never contacts the victim's mouth with his own.

The ANRC First Aid Textbook claims that artificial respiration will not help if heart action has ceased completely, because oxygen then is not carried from the lungs to the body cells. However, if the heart is beating and the victim is not breathing, waste no time, for the normal person will die approximately six minutes after cessation of normal breathing. Every second can count.

POISONING BY MOUTH

The train of thought associated with poisons and the treatment of victims has undergone serious examination during the last ten years, and some previous theories have been thrown out the window, especially in the area of antidotes.

According to the ANRC First Aid Textbook the first step is to quickly administer fluid in large amounts — four glasses or more with adults. As water will usually be the handiest item, use it.

Sometimes it is important to induce vomiting by inserting a finger or spoon in the mouth. Make sure that the assumed position of the victim is such that he will not re-swallow the poison after it is regurgiated. Then administer commercially produced universal antidote according to package instructions.

Vomiting should not be induced, if the poison taken has strong acids like carbolic acid or alkalis like lye, strychnine, kerosene or when the victim already is in a coma or is exhibiting symptoms.

In the case of acid poisoning, do not induce vomiting for, just as the acid damaged the body going down, so it will on its way back up.

In the case of strychnine poisoning, like that from rat poison, try to keep the victim from moving. The slightest movement could send the victim into convulsions. However, if only a few minutes have passed since the poison was taken, give fluids and induce vomiting. Don't keep it up long, and get medical help quickly.

PLANT POISONING

The possibility of contacting a poisonous plant is somewhat more realistic for the backpacker than the previously mentioned mishaps. Depending upon the locale of the campsite, there is a goodly chance that a species of poison ivy, poison oak or poison sumac — the most common types in the U.S. — will be growing. There are a few individuals each year that contact and are poisoned by primrose, smartweed, nettle and cowhage, but they are in the minority when compared with the total that brush against the previously mentioned three types.

The active substance that causes the itching and irritation is an oleoresin called urushiol, which is contained in the sap, leaves, fruit, flowers, roots and bark. The plants are sometimes difficult to identify, simply because there often is variation of the leaf structure on the same bush.

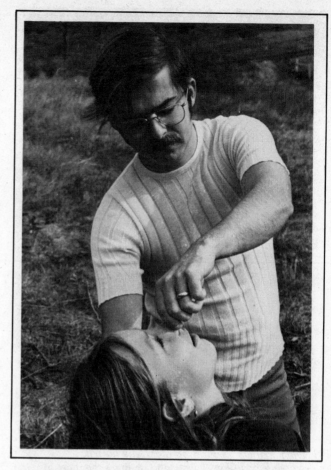

Above: For a nose bleed have victim throw his head back and lightly pinch the nostrils together. Below: Applying cold, wet towels will often also help.

However, most of the poison ivy species can be identified by the fact that they have three leaves per sprout. The upper surface is a glossy, waxy dark green, with the underside being lighter green in color with fine hairs upon occasion.

196

The poison oak plant derives its name because the leaf structure much resembles that of an oak tree. The western poison oak species may appear as a bundle or clump of plants, with many stems rising from one root system.

Poison sumac in a woody shrub or small tree, never a vine, which is found especially in swampy areas. There are seven to thirteen leaflets, each about three inches long and an inch wide or so. It is bright orange in the spring, changing to dark green in the summer months.

All three species change color in the fall months. Poison ivy and oak changes to orange or red in the fall. The poison sumac turns to orange-red or russet in the fall.

Should you be unlucky enough to brush up against one of them, this is what to expect: Within a few hours to several days afterwards, the skin becomes red and small blisters appear. It itches like hell. The area may increase in size, with marked swelling and numerous large blisters. Fever may rise and discomfort become great.

About the only thing you can do to rid yourself of the problem is to wash the affected area as quickly a possible with soap and water. Sponge the area next with rubbing alcohol, and follow up with a liberal application of calamine lotion. This will usually relieve the itching and eventually will dispose of the infection. If it doesn't, apply wet compresses of Burow's solution diluted one part to about twenty-five parts of water. This usually will relieve the discomfort and the itching.

BLISTERS

In this instance, we will speak specifically of water blisters, those unwelcome sore spots that develop when the skin is chafed continually or rubbed by ill-fitting clothings, shoes, et al.

The proper way to attend to them follows: The fluid gradually will be absorbed by the body if the source of irritation is removed. If this is impractical, the blister may be punctured. First wash the area thoroughly with soap and water. Then, using a sterilized needle — usually one passed through a flame several times — the blister is punctured at its edge. A sterile bandage should be used to apply pressure on the edge of the blister, to force the water out of the pin-sized hole. It then should be covered with a sterile bandage. If the blister already has burst, simply wash the area thoroughly and apply a sterile dressing.

The water blister is the most common injury associated with backpacking and, for the most part, there is no need for them to occur, if the proper preventive first aid is taken.

Prevention of blisters begins when you buy your first pair of backpacking boots. Always buy them strong enough to support your weight and the weight of the pack; insure that they are a proper fit; and break them in prior to starting your trip. If you take these steps and use the two sock system mentioned in the chapter on clothing, you should experience little difficulty with blisters.

However, should they occur anyway, much of the pain and further injury can be prevented by applying a piece of Dr. Scholl's moleskin to the tender area. The best method is to cut a hole the size of the blister in a piece of moleskin that is about an inch wider than the blistered area, allowing the blister to stick out through the hole. Apply a second patch of moleskin over the first and replace your socks. You should never apply the moleskin directly on the blister.

EYE INJURIES

The ANRC First Aid Textbook separates eye injuries into three categories: Injuries to the soft tissue surrounding the eye or the eyelid, injuries to the surface of the eyeball

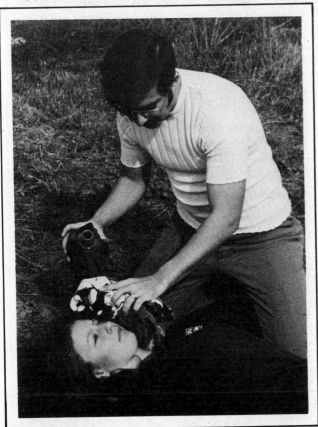

For heat stroke have the victim lie down and bring the body temperature down by sponging with lukewarm water. If severe, remove clothing and sponge the entire body.

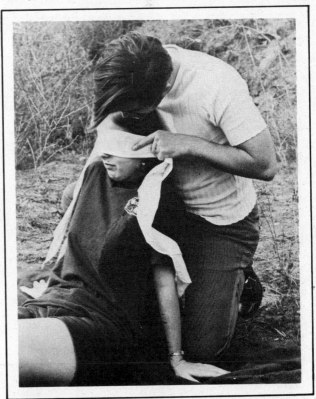

By applying covering over both injured and uninjured eyes, unnecessary eye movement is prevented. This can prevent further injury to the already injured eye.

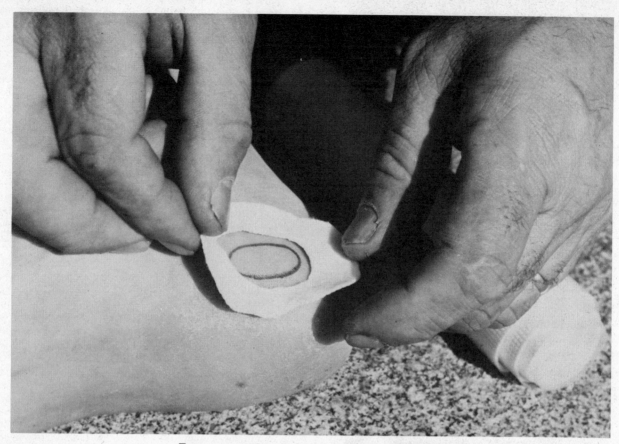

To prevent a blister from becoming worse, cut a hole in a piece of moleskin slightly larger than the blister and apply to the wounded area. Cover this with another piece.

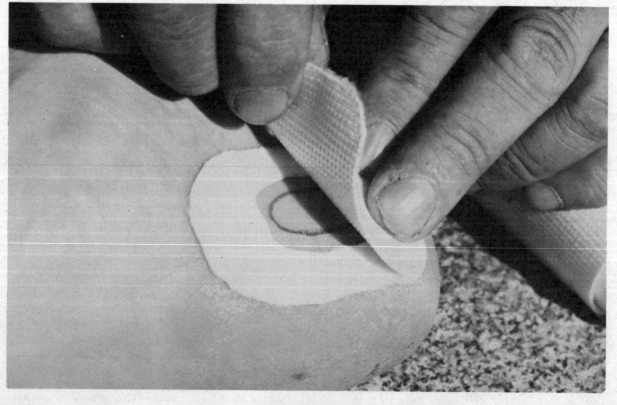

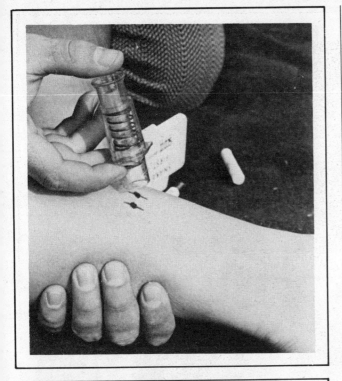

and injuries beyond the surface of the eyeball.

Naturally, the first is the least serious of the bunch, and a black eye falls into this category. There really isn't much you can do except apply a sterile dressing on the affected part and secure it with a bandage that encircles the head.

The second category of eye injury definitely is serious. When most individuals have something in their eye, they pull the upper lid down over the lower lid to see if this dislodges the foreign matter. Often it will. If the foreign matter is under the lower lid, pull the lid away gently and remove the substance with a handkerchief or the like. If cotton is used, dampen it before attempting to remove the object.

If the object is a chemical like salt from the roadway, the best method of obtaining relief is to flood the eye with water. This may be done with a canteen or at a drinking fountain, or from a hose.

There are important don'ts that the first aider should not attempt, including rubbing the eye, for this drives the matter deeper into the eyeball. Don't check the eye until the hands have been washed, or you may introduce more objects than you initially had. Don't attempt to remove the object with a toothpick, match, pine needle or the like. Make sure that the individual sees a physician if the injury involves an imbedded piece of material in the eyeball.

The third category involves objects imbedded in the eyeball. The first aider should not attempt to remove the foreign matter, as his actions may lead to loss of sight in the eye. Instead, both eyes should be covered and the individual placed in the care of a physician at the earliest possible opportunity. The reason for taping both eyes is simply so the individual will not move his one good eye, which generally is followed in direction by the injured eye, perhaps causing more injury.

SNAKE BITE

In actuality, few individuals are bitten by poisonous snakes during the year, but there is the chance that this could happen. There only are four families of poisonous

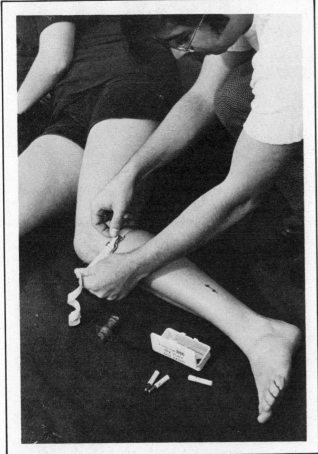

If bite appears perpendicular to bone structure, twin cuts are made just beneath the skin and poison extracted with suction cup (top). If bite occurs parallel to the bone, single cut is made. Constricting band goes above. Right: A rattlesnake being "milked" for its venom.

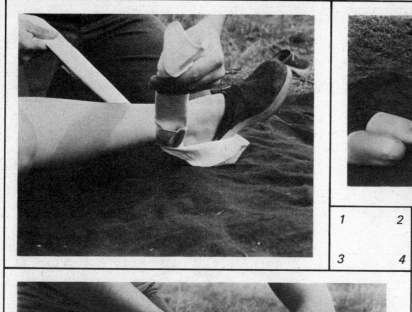

1 2

3 4

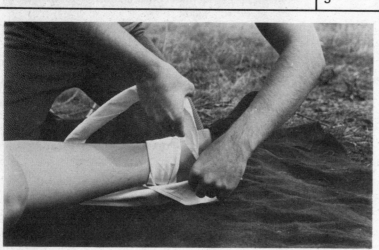
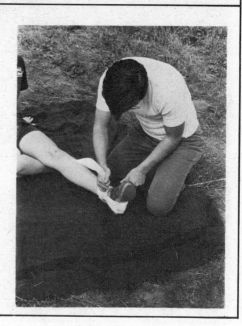

For ankle sprain, cloth is wrapped around shoe heel and crossed behind (1). Points are then crossed over top of shin (2) and pulled through on both sides (3). Tighten and tie (4).

snakes in the U.S., the rattlesnakes, copperhead and water moccasin of the pit viper variety, and the coral snake in a category by itself.

If bitten by a pit viper, which derives its qualification by having pits between the eyes and nostrils, this is what to expect: Immediate pain followed by swelling and discoloration. As the poison circulates through the system, the victim becomes weak, short of breath, nauseous with vomiting, weak, rapid pulse and sometimes dimness of vision. He may become unconscious and, if untreated, can die if enough venom has been injected by the snake.

Symptoms of a coral snake bite are identical, except that instead of immediate pain upon being bitten, there generally is only a slight burning sensation and mild swelling at the bite location.

Once determining that the snake was of the poisonous variety, quickly break out the snake bite kit that you should have taken along. Place a constricting band above the bite site, but not too tight. If the two holes are parallel or appear as a : on the skin, then make one incision just under the skin through both marks with a sterile razor blade. If the bite appears .. on the skin, make two top-to-bottom incisions just under the skin, one through each fang

mark. No longer are the X cuts prescribed for each fang mark — often this cuts ligaments or blood vessels and causes no end of problems, including getting the poison into the bloodstream faster.

The next move is to apply suction to remove as much of the poison as possible. There are some disputed theories about mouth suction for this purpose, as some claim that recent tests indicate that the venom will penetrate the lining of the mouth and be induced into the first aider's system. Others claim that it won't hurt the first aider at all, even if it is swallowed.

If suction cups are provided with the kit, as they most generally are, use them. Continue the suction for an hour or so, then get the victim to the care of a physician as soon as possible. The best way is to secure help at the site, thereby eliminating the hazard of speeding the poison's spread through the system by muscular activity.

In event of snake bite, the individual should never attempt to walk out by himself, but should be carried out by other members of the party. If by chance, you have wandered away from the party and are by yourself, the first thing is not to panic.

If possible kill the snake or at least get out of striking

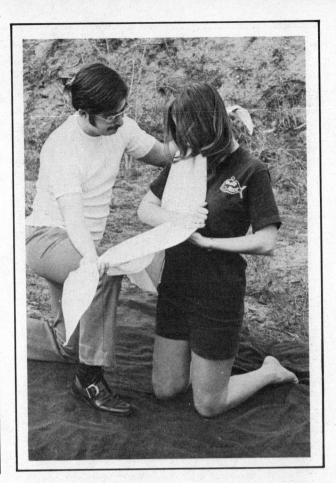

Left to right, top to bottom: 1). For arm sling, cloth is folded into triangle. 2). It then is slipped under arm and one end laid on shoulder. 3). Lower corner is brought

around opposite side of neck with ends tied on the side of neck. 4). Final step is knotting points at victim's elbow.

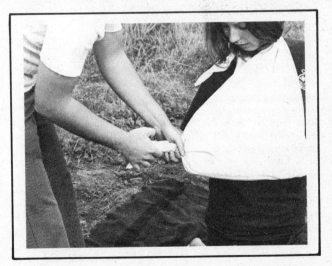

distance. However, don't run...you can easily outwalk a snake and running will only speed the venom through your blood stream. Proceed with the above steps, then calmly walk to camp where you can get further assistance. Few individuals have ever died from a snake bite, but many have died from heart attacks caused by fear and panic.

ANIMAL BITES

Should you be bitten while camping, whether by domestic or wild animal, do all you can to restrain the animal and, if necessary, kill it only as a last resort. Both types are susceptible to rabies. If you are bitten and the animal escapes, prepare to undergo a series of excruciatingly painful inoculations in the stomach, the only defense currently known to man for rabies. However, if you can capture or kill the offending animal (do not damage its head!), authorities can determine its rabidity or lack of same and perhaps prevent your ordeal.

Skunks, opossums, coyotes and foxes are the usual carriers you may encounter on your excursion, and it would behoove you to avoid any contact with them. Remember also that squirrels and chipmunks — those cute

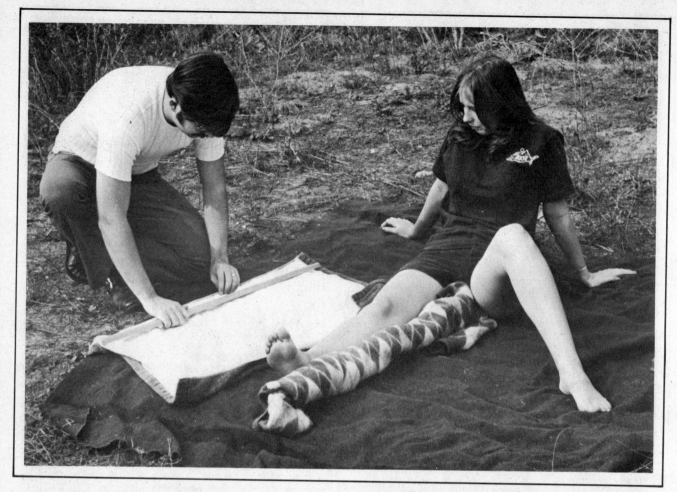

Improvised splints for a broken leg can be wood, branches, rolled inside towels, sweaters or any other piece of material readily available that will keep leg immobile.

critters that eat bread from your fingertips, that you're not supposed to feed — sometimes are infected. Leave them alone, no matter how harmless they appear.

While on the subject of skunks, should one have the misfortune of encountering the wrong end of one, about the only thing that will remove the odor from your epidermis is tomato juice. Rub it over the skin, don't drink it. Your clothes will have to either be buried or burned, as there is nothing to remove the odor from them.

INSECT BITES

The best way to treat insect bites is to avoid them through the use of the many types of commercially-produced repellents. After the bite has taken place, everything that can be done is limited. In most cases, a paste of cold cream and baking soda will relieve the itching, as will calamine lotion. For bee and wasp stings, ice or cold water lessens the pain.

TICK BITES

Ticks are frequently encountered while backpacking and are pesky critters that cling tenaciously to the skin. They often transmit diseases, including Rocky Mountain spotted fever. For this reason, it is best to get the tick out as soon as possible — the longer he remains in place, the greater the chance of contracting the disease.

Although heat from cigarettes frequently has been used to dislodge a tick, the best method is by covering his

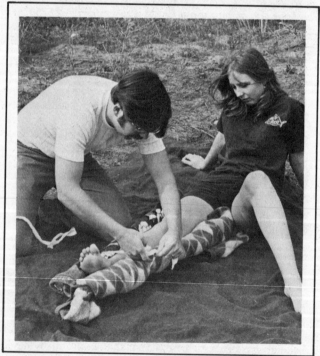

Splints are then bound together with cloth, twine, rope, etc. These should be firmly tied, but not to the point where they will cut off circulation.

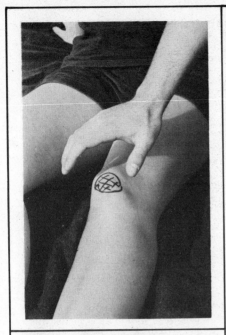

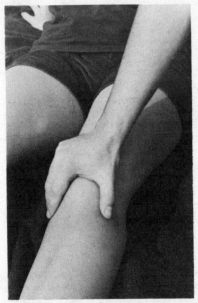

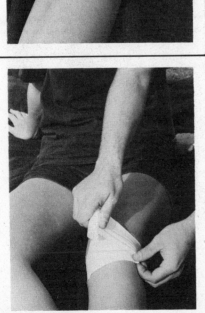

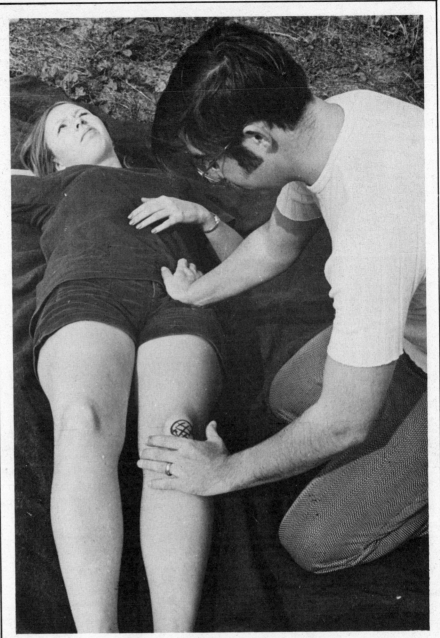

Left and Above: First aider prepares to administer direct pressure to simulated wound. Often this pressure must be continued for long periods. When blood flow stops, bandage with clean cloth. Pressure can also be applied to the groin.

breathing pores with a coating of heavy oil, be it mineral, salad or motor. This often will have the tick backing out lickety-split. If it doesn't, leave the oil on the skin for a half-hour, then remove the insect with a pair of tweezers. Make sure that all of him is removed, for a small chunk left inside may result in an infected camper. Once out, scrub the area with soap and water to remove any disease germs prevalent on the skin.

BLACK WIDOW BITES

Contrary to popular belief, the black widow spider is not found only under old stacks of boards or within the abandoned house suspected of housing eerie residents. Rather, it is quite commonly found in hollow stumps, under rocks or any place that offers some shelter, primarily

— but not exclusively — in the southern half of the nation.

It is one of the most easily recognizable spiders of the arachnid family, and the female almost always has a shiny black body with red hourglass on the underside of the abdomen. The male of the species has a variety of white stripes in addition to the hourglass on the abdomen, a red stripe down the back, and shiny black coloration. The young often have a series of red dots on the back.

If bitten, this is what to expect: Immediate, severe pain, little redness or swelling at the bite site, with the pain spreading rapidly throughout the body. The victim becomes nauseous, sweats profusely and may encounter difficulty in breathing. He may experience painful abdominal cramps or other muscular pains, but in a day or so will usually recover.

If bitten on the finger or toe, put a tight, narrow constricting band near the base of the extremity immediately. If the bite is higher, use a wider band above the bite on the heart side. Remove the band after five minutes. Next, apply cold water on the area for two hours, keeping the site lower than the rest of the body, and cover the victim to keep him warm. If the bite is not on an arm or leg, the only remedy is to apply cold water locally. Seek the aid of a physician as soon as possible. If medical attention is some hours away, hot wet applications or hot baths may relieve some of the muscular pains.

TARANTULA BITES

Unfortunately, science fiction movies have portrayed the tarantula, a normally calm, inoffensive creature, as an ogre that spreads death and destruction with his mammoth, powerful jaws. This is the farthest thing from the truth. In actuality, deaths from tarantula bites are extremely rare, and usually occur in the aged or infirm persons who suffer allergic reactions to the injected material.

By and large, the tarantulas that reside in the Southwestern regions of this country are non-poisonous. Their bite feels like nothing more than a pinprick. However, some tarantulas that sneak through customs aboard loads of fruit sometimes are poisonous, and cause marked pain, redness and mild swelling. Few die from these.

Should you be bitten, follow the first aid procedures for a black widow spider bite. Clean the area well with soap and water and apply a sterile dressing.

SCORPION STINGS

The vast majority of scorpions that reside in the American Southwest are not poisonous and their stings are no worse than a wasp sting or the like. They usually are found in cool, damp places like under houses, loose banks, in your boots. It is wise to check boots and other likely areas that may house scorpions before sticking either foot or hand into them.

A few scorpions are poisonous, and the sting can cause death, usually in infants, young children and infirm aged. Adults will have a rather uncomfortable time for a spell. In this type of sting, there is usually just a slight burning sensation rather than marked pain and discoloration. If a child is badly poisoned, he becomes restless, nauseous, has cramps in the abdomen and sometimes will go into convulsions.

The treatment procedure in this case is the same as for the black widow spider bite. There is no sense in making cuts similar to snake bite and trying to suck the poison from the area, as the amount of poison is so small.

FRACTURES

Fractures are breaks in bones and the objective of the

first aider is to keep the broken bone ends and adjacent joints quiet.

Fractures are categorized in three varieties: The simple or closed fracture, in which the broken bone is not separated, the compound or open fracture, in which the broken bone extends through the surface of the skin, and the comminuted fracture, in which the bone is broken in several places, separated, and may or may not protrude from the skin.

In the case of a closed or comminuted fracture that doesn't break the skin, there may be some doubt in the diagnosing of the fracture. In this case, it is up to this first aider to use his own judgment, coupled with reports from the victim. Sometimes there may be tenderness, swelling, deformity and pain on motion. If this is observed, generally a fracture is present. If there is a suspected fracture, always treat for one.

The best way to discover the proper method for treating fractures is to take the first aid course offered by the American National Red Cross. It is much easier to visualize the method of splinting, for example, by seeing it done first hand.

A simple splint may be all that is required in many cases. However, in the advent of a suspected neck or spine injury, the victim should not be moved by untrained personnel, because such movement may damage the spinal cord, leaving the injured person paralyzed for life.

BURNS

Burns are placed in three categories according to depth or degree. First degree burns cause slight reddening of the skin; second degree cause reddening of the skin and blisters develop and third degree, the cells that manufacture new cells below the hair follicle level are destroyed.

Much new research has gone into the area of burn treatment, and the American Medical Association advocates the usage of cool water only for lesser burns. They say that the old methods of applying pastes or greases and wrapping the affected area in gauze only hinders the doctor's efforts when the patient arrives at the hospital. They feel that the grease or pastes can add to the possibility of infection, and that covering with bandages later causes excruciating pain when the doctor has to scrape them off.

They feel that, for minor burns that can be immersed in water — those covering less than ten percent of the body — this should be done immediately. It allegedly lessens pain and perhaps promotes healing. However, in burns of greater size or seriousness, they feel the time is better spent in getting the victim to a hospital. The best way to treat burns is to avoid situations that result in them.

NOSEBLEEDS

These are common during pack trips at high altitudes, or when hot, dry winds pass through for any length of time. There are three ways to stop the bleeding: Assume a sitting position with the head thrown back, or lying with the shoulders elevated; pinching the nostrils together, sometimes after having been stuffed with gauze; and applying cool, wet towels to the face.

HEAT EXHAUSTION

Heat exhaustion is typified in two degrees: mild and severe. In the mild form, the individual is unusually tired, with headache and perhaps nausea. The severe case symptoms are profuse sweating, pale, clammy skin, weakness and he generally has a normal temperature.

The best thing the first aider can do is have the victim lie down and rest, then administer salt solutions of one-half teaspoon salt per half-glass of water every fifteen minutes

Squeezing the pressure point between the armpit and elbow will lessen the blood flow for a cut on the arm or hand.

or so for three or four doses. Get the individual to a doctor for the severe cases.

HEAT STROKE

Heat stroke usually strikes the aged, although younger individuals are not exempt. The symptoms are headache, dry skin, rapid pulse, accompanied occasionally by dizziness and nausea. In severe cases, unconsciousness may occur. Temperatures range well above normal, often to 106 or 109 degrees.

Medical attention is extremely important in the case of heat stroke. While awaiting transportation, try to bring the victim's body temperature down to the vicinity of 103 degrees by removing his clothing and sponging the body with alcohol or lukewarm water. If there is no thermometer on hand to check the temperature, count the pulse rate. A rate of 110 beats per minute usually is associated with a tolerable temperature.

Once this stage has been reached, watch the patient carefully. The temperature may continue to drop, or it may start to rise again. If the latter is the case, repeat the sponging procedure. The victim may be given salt solutions if fully conscious.

SUNBURN

Sunburn can always be a problem for the backpacker. Again, the best first aid is prevention, which basically means to keep your skin adequately covered.

The most susceptible sunburn spot for a backpacker is the back of his head and neck. By merely wearing a hat will prevent this area from burning. Many hikers will like to hike without a shirt; however, this is not advisable for any extended period of time. A light shirt, preferably with sleeves, is good protection for the upper torso and arm areas. Should you become sunburned there are many ointments on the market that will ease some of the pain and prevent blistering. Glacier Cream and zinc oxide ointments seem to be the best.

MOUNTAIN SICKNESS

If you hike to high country, you should be prepared to treat what is commonly called mountain sickness, which is caused by insufficient oxygen. The symptoms are very similar to motion sickness: headache, queasy stomach and if it becomes severe, vomiting. The best cure for this is,

upon signs of the first symptoms, stop and rest for a period; if necessary set up camp and spend the night. Primarily what you need is rest and a chance to acclimate yourself to the high altitudes.

Hiking in altitudes of 10,000 feet or above may bring on another illness that is even more serious than mountain sickness — pulmonary edema. Its symptoms are very similar to the flu or a bad cold and again, the best cure is to stop. If you feel that a member of your party has been afflicted with this illness, by placing your ear against his chest you can check to see if there is a gurgling sound; this is an indication that fluid is building up in the lungs. If you can possibly get the individual down to a lower altitude, do so immediately and send for help for it can develop into a very serious ailment. While waiting for help, have the individual sit down, but never lie down since this might cause him to drown in the fluids.

SNOWBLINDNESS

Backpackers often will be afflicted with snowblindness, which is caused by the glare of the sun, whether off of the snow, water or ground. Prevention is the only cure for this ailment. A good pair of sunglasses will solve this problem.

WATER PURIFICATION

Although water purification is not considered a first aid subject, it is a preventative.

The best method to purify water is to use Halazone tablets, which can be found in almost all sporting goods stores. However, these are dated and are not good after a certain period of time, so check before using them.

Another method used is to add four drops of Purex to every pint of water. The Purex solution is almost all chlorine and will kill any bacteria that may be in the water. Boiling the water first also is another good method for purifying water and has been used with good results for centuries.

As mentioned at the beginning of this chapter, the area of first aid is changing constantly. The subject alone can — and has — covered complete volumes and many thousands of printed pages. We have neither the space nor the desire to produce a first aid handbook in this book, and therefore have touched only lightly on the overall subject. For more information on the area of first aid, contact your local chapter of the American National Red Cross.

CHAPTER 17

IF YOU FIND YOURSELF LOST

It's A Chilling Experience To Lose Track Of Your Whereabouts But Here's How To Get Back On Course!

THE THOUGHT OF becoming lost may appear somewhat ridiculous to many backpackers, but it can and does happen; with far more frequency than most would like to admit. When it does happen, it is far from a laughing matter!

How not to get lost through the use of a compass and topographic maps was covered in some depth in a previous chapter. However, little was said about what to do in the event you did. It is a subject we feel should be covered in some detail since your life well may depend upon how you react to this type of emergency.

For the normal individual, realizing that he is indeed lost, the first reaction is something close to panic. Later, when safely back at the campsite, it may be rather humorous, but for the moment the fear is very real and it is an emotion that almost everyone will experience.

This fear often will cause an individual to strike out blindly in an attempt to find a familar landmark or a path that is known. He usually will do this without thinking and in haste: trying to find his direction as fast as he can. If it's a group, often the members will angrily argue as to which is the correct direction. Both situations only can lead to trouble.

When you have determined that you are really lost or if you prefer the term, "turned around," the first thing to do is to sit down and think it through rationally. This accomplishes two things: first, it takes the mind off the fear of being lost, and second, it allows time for clear thinking to develop. The best step to take at this point is take out your topographic map and look for landmarks on that map that coincide with those in the immediate area. By doing this, you often can find your exact location. Then with your compass you will be able to get on course.

Whatever you do, never split the group and send individuals off to find landmarks or the proper trail. Stay together and work the problem out as a group, endeavoring to reassure those in the party who are overly nervous. What you don't need is a nervous or panic-stricken hiker on your hands!

If one member of the group is overly nervous or frightened, often a bit of humor will help alleviate some of his fear. Of course there is little that is funny about the situation, but a little levity might cause him to overcome his nervousness. If not, many times kidding might become irritating enough to cause the nervous hiker to become angry; again an emotion that will help him get over his fright. Once he is over his fear he will begin to think ration-

Hunter looks as though he has ventured into the wilds with no means of survival should he become lost. This can happen even on a casual hunting trek into forest.

The seeming lack of equipment affords hunter freedom
to swing his rifle should game show itself in area.

Unseen from front, needs for a day
can be carried in compact fanny pack.

ally and in terms of solutions rather than the consequences of being lost.

There are times and conditions that cause one to become disoriented more easily. One is during the late evening hours when the light begins to dim and landmarks or check points are harder to recognize. Overcast, rain and snow also will make it easier to take the wrong turn, especially if you are hiking over unfamiliar terrain. If you do run into a storm, your wisest move would be to find a natural shelter or build a hasty shelter and sit it out. Many hikers have been known to become even more lost and some have even lost their lives trying to continue on during a storm.

Never travel at night unless you are highly familiar with the terrain and have traveled over the area many times. There is really no reason to do so and those who try are foolish. Plan your day so that you will arrive at your desired destination before dark. It is not an easy matter to

set up camp after dark either, so there is another reason for doing your hiking during daylight hours.

When you do lose your way, look for a ridge or high ground where you can get a good vantage point for checking landmarks. If you are hiking in flatlands, even a tree will give you some height and you will be able to see farther. In doing this don't wander too far from the spot where you first realized that you were lost. Many times you will find that from this first spot you are not really too far off course. Here again, don't split the group and allow individuals to wander off on their own. Once you have found familiar landmarks that coincide with your topographic maps, it is then often an easy matter to plot a route back to your original trail, a new trail that will lead to the desired destination, or if your enthusiasm has waned at this point, a trail that will take you back home.

Getting lost is no joke, nor is it a thing about which to

An advantage of the fanny pack is that it can be swung about the waist to the front in order to obtain gear. (Upper right) Police whistle, seldom heard in back country, is good for signal. (Right) A spent rifle cartridge case can serve as a whistle for strictly limited range due to its low tones.

become embarrassed. It happens to the best as well as the beginner. A backpacker normally is self-contained with everything he needs for survival on his back, so there is no real reason to panic. Relax, think it out and even do a little fishing if there is a likely stream. After awhile, chances are you will find a route out or someone will happen along who can help.

It seems as though the hunter becomes lost more frequently than other outdoorsmen. Perhaps it is because he is usually not as familar with the terrain over which he is

Emergency pack — sans food and water — contains compass, map, mirror, snake bite kit, matches, fire starters, first aid kit, whistle, spare ammo for rifle in box and knife. Some prefer folding hunter in case over sheath type.

hiking. Many times he also is not prepared to cope as well as the backpacker in the event he does become lost. Whenever you are out in the wilderness, whether on a one-day hunting trip or have hiked just a few miles from camp for some fishing, you always should carry along certain survival items. These would include a knife, matches or perhaps several methods to start a fire, a compass, a few items of freeze dried foods, first aid items, a lightweight trail tarp or space blanket, water, and a signaling device.

Many backpackers carry a sidearm that can be used as a signaling device, however, there are others who never think of taking such an item along. With a sidearm or a rifle, anyone lost or needing help can fire three shots into the air in rapid succession, which is the standard signal for help.

For those who feel they do not want to take along a gun, there are other signaling devices that can be used. One that is very handy and lightweight is a whistle; a police whistle being the best. The sound of a whistle carries for many miles, plus it is a sound that is not normal for the back country and anyone hearing it will more than likely investigate. Here again, you should use the standard distress signal of three short blasts in rapid succession.

Visual signs also are quite helpful. One of the best is a simple stainless steel mirror. It should be small, about the size of a pack of cigarettes, and should have a hole in its

center for an aiming system. Naturally this item should be carried in your pocket or somewhere where it always will be with you. There are several smoke signaling devices on the market that can be carried also. These are good, but often will weigh slightly more than the simple mirror.

Whatever type of signaling device you select is up to you, but you should never be in the wilderness without one. Should there be an emergency or if you become lost, you can yell to your heart's content and still there is a good chance that no one will hear you.

As mentioned, there seems to be a greater possibility for a hunter to become lost more readily than the trail hiker. There is a good reason for this. The hunter often uses backpacking to get back into remote areas where there are fewer hunters and more game. These areas are normally quite rough and for the most part are not charted or marked. In addition, the hunter who gets a hit on game and starts tracking is so intent in his tracking that he neglects to look for landmarks. When he finds the animal or eventually gives up the day, he sometimes finds that he is in an area that is totally unfamiliar to him and he has not thought of looking for landmarks to find his way back. Here again, like any other outdoorsman the hunter should not panic, but sit down and take a moment to think it through. If it is about dark, the best thing to do is set up a temporary camp and

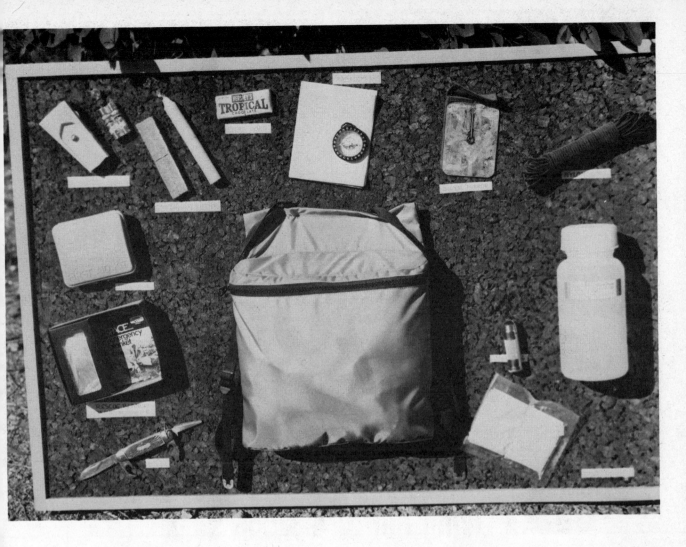

Ten essentials carried by backpackers and hunters can be packed into a small bag as shown or carried in the fanny pack. The plastic bottle is meant to hold water.

wait for morning. Many times the next morning after reviewing your previous day's route, you can easily get back on trail. If you are the type of hunter who carries his entire pack with him as he hunts, there is no problem setting up a temporary camp. On the other hand if you have left most of your belongings back at the main camp and have hiked out for a day's hunting, planning to return that night, you may have a problem. For this reason, we stress always carrying the essential survival items mentioned earlier in this chapter. With matches along you can always start a fire, not only to keep you warm, but also to signal anyone who may come looking for you.

If you find the next day that you are still hopelessly lost, it is better to stay put. Set up a more permanent camp and if you are short of food, look for small game. Normally you can survive until the search party finds you. If you try to find your way back you may find yourself walking in circles and all that you will do is become more confused or wear yourself out. Stay put and place signals on the ground for air recognition. Help will eventually come.

If you are in mountainous terrain and become lost, the basic rule of thumb is to go downhill. Sooner or later you will come to a fence, a road or a stream. When you find one of these, follow it. They normally will lead to help eventually. The man-made roads and fences will certainly lead

to something since they are built for a purpose and have to end somewhere. You may follow a road the wrong direction and it leads to a deadend, but then it is just a matter of turning around and following it in the opposite direction... it also has to start somewhere.

If you have hiked the hills and valleys for any length of time and have never become lost or turned around, then you are indeed fortunate. Most of us at one time or the other have been at least temporarily lost, although we may not like to admit it. However, if you don't panic and if you keep your senses, you soon will be back at camp laughing at how ridiculous it was that you thought you were ever lost in the first place.

CHAPTER 18:
TO MEET THE ULTIMATE CHALLENGE

The Art Of Outdoor Survival Is Not Limited To Living Out Of A Nylon Sack

The lighter and softer-soled friction boots require considerable experience on the part of the rock climber in order to get the most effective use.

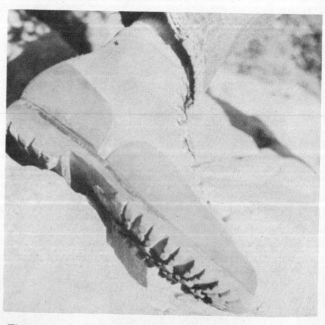

The more heavily constructed boot is generally best for the beginning climber as it can be worn on many different types of climbs. The lugged sole grips well.

This climber is making a traverse of a canted rock face, using risers, ropes, and either pitons or wedges.

WHILE THE BACKPACK purist may not be willing to admit it loudly, rock climbing and similar efforts are becoming allied with hiking into the wilderness. However, many backpackers tend to fancy themselves mountain experts without really knowing much about proper gear or techniques.

To get some of the answers, we went to Richard M. Baron of La Jolla, California, who manages to combine both interests, backpacking and climbing.

Within the past few years the gain in popularity of rock climbing has been evident with the numbers of new climbers doing their thing throughout the many climbing areas in the country. New climbers learn quickly that being properly equipped for a rock-climbing experience is an absolute must, if the climb is to be a safe one and the climber is to arrive at his destination in one piece.

Climbing equipment does not come cheap. Most equipment is made from very high grade materials and is tested time and again well beyond the tolerances which it will be expected to withstand during its normal lifetime. Manufacturers of climbing equipment are subject to the scrutinization of the UIAA – the Union Internationale des Associations d'Alpinisme – an organization of climbers principally concerned with the quality and integrity of climbing equipment used throughout the world.

Equipment bearing the seal of approval from the UIAA is regarded as being the best available in the world. When purchasing equipment, one must remember that his life can depend on that equipment. With this thought in mind, price should only be a secondary thought.

"Goldline" and "Kernmantle" ropes are the two types most widely used by climbers as a safety device.

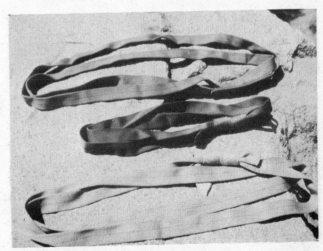

Risers are employed by climbers in the construction of belay seats, slings and to hold a sleeper.

The most basic piece of equipment a climber uses is his boots. Climbing boots come in a wide variety, but basically the boots are lightweight and have a fairly soft sole for adhesion to the rock. They are made with canvas or leather uppers and have an inner sewn welt, so the sole of the boot will be next to the uppers for edge control when on the rock. When fitting boots one should remember that climbing boots are an extension of the foot. A boot should not be clumsy, but should be controllable. Therefore, a tight fit is essential. The boots should fit as snug as is possible without cutting the blood circulation to the foot. Remember also that climbing boots are made for climbing, not walking; walking anything more than a very short distance in them can be a painful experience.

There are different types of climbing boots made for different types of climbing. For climbing where the rock is relatively rough and there are a pretty fair amount of footholds available, a boot with a lugged sole is used commonly. This boot is among the heaviest and most rugged of rock-climbing boots. For climbing where the rock is rather smooth and there are relatively few footholds available, a so-called friction boot is used. A friction boot is extremely lightweight — it almost looks like a sneaker — and has a flat sole made of extremely soft rubber, so it can grip the rock

A carabiner hooked through the eye of a piton gives the rock climber a place to tie off his safety rope on a face.

Several different types of carabiners: (from left to right) a standard oval by Eiger, a Bonaiti Blue Gate "D," an Eiger color-coded blue "D," an Eiger locking "D," a Choinard modified "D," a Bonaiti modified "D."

*With pitons holding his pivot points,
this climber can make what would
otherwise be an extremely tricky traverse.*

by friction where there are no footholds to speak of — thus the name friction boot.

There are many variations of these types of boots and selection of the proper boot will depend on the type of climbing one will be doing. Generally, a beginning climber should start with a lugged boot as this boot is adaptable to many different situations. It usually takes a lot of practice and experience for climbs where friction boots can be used to their fullest extent.

Basically, climbing equipment is divided into two categories: softwares and hardwares. The softwares include such items as ropes; webbing which is used to make climbing slings, belay seats, et al.; gloves; packs and other miscellaneous items. Hardwares include carabiners, chocks, pitons, hammers and other specialty equipment.

It is difficult to say which piece of equipment is most important. The equipment used the most is important. It must be the most reliable, having to constantly withstand the stresses and strains put on it. The climbing rope is the one piece of equipment the climber owns which is used most often, and therefore comprises a very important part of the climber's equipment.

A rope is a critical item to the climber. He must depend on his rope to help absorb the impact in case of a fall and the rope must be maneuverable during the course of normal climbing. Ropes are tested for breaking strength, impact force and stretch at low loads.

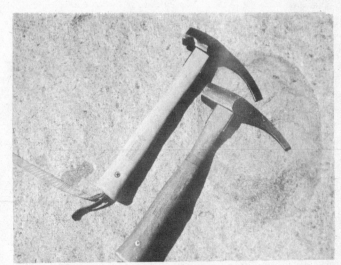

There are two basic types of hammers used by most rock climbers; a rock hammer (at left) and a crag hammer.

A chock placed in a crevice will help save the climber the trouble of prying out the piton he might otherwise use.

Some wedges and chocks used by rock climbers to avoid damaging the rock: (from left to right) a bong, a large angle, a small angle, a bugaboo and a knifeblade. These terms are climber slang.

A clean climb is the ultimate challenge for a rockface climber — to avoid leaving piton scars or chalk marks.

Most ropes sold meet or exceed the standards set for these tests. The most widely used ropes are made of a "kernmantle" construction. These ropes have a core (kern) with braided sheath (mantle) for protection. The unique construction of the core determines the shock-absorbing characteristics of the rope. The recommended size of rope for normal climbing is 11mm in diameter. Some climbers use two 9mm ropes together, but one 9mm rope alone never should be used.

Goldline is an inexpensive rope compared to the kernmantle ropes and is made with three-strand, hard lay construction. Goldline is not as maneuverable as kernmantle rope and the stretching qualities of the rope are not as great as those of kernmantle ropes. For this reason, Goldline is not as widely used as are the kernmantle ropes.

One should take good care of a rope, storing it away from excessive dampness or heat and keeping an accurate record of what the rope has been through. After a serious fall on the rope, one should examine the rope carefully and possibly retire the length, as internal damage to the kern is not always visible. As a rope absorbs more and more falls, it loses its elastic qualities and the danger of breakage becomes more and more real.

The most common piece of equipment used in climbing is the carabiner. The basic shape of a carabiner is oval and it resembles a link in a chain. But instead of being solid all the way around, it has a hinged gate which enables the climber to insert slings, chocks, pitons and other safeguard paraphernalia into the carabiner. Most carabiners are composed of aluminum alloys for strength and light weight. Some are

formed in a modified "D" shape for added strength and special applications.

Also available are locking carabiners which are usually the strongest made. The gate is the weakest part of a carabiner and with the locking type, the gate is locked in place with a sort of nut which keeps the gate from opening accidentally. This locked gate increases the strength tremendously.

It always is wise to carry a good supply of carabiners on any climb, because these are the most used piece of hardware on any climb.

Chocks comprise a large percentage of the equipment in the climber's rucksack. Chocks are placed in cracks between rocks, in crevices, etcetera. Chocks provide protection to the climber, support loads, save the rock — the uses are endless depending on your imagination.

Chocks come in many sizes and shapes — from small hexes to large bongs to medium wedges to small copperheads. Chocks, or nuts as they are called, are used largely in place of the piton. The latter is a steel pin that is hammered into the rock much like a nail.

In recent years, there has been a movement toward minimizing impact to the rock and therefore a move away from the use of pitons because they scar the rock and leave a reminder to following climbers that man was there once before — a most disconcerting fact when one is hanging 1500 feet in the air from his fingertips and has sweated for a day and a half to get there!

Nuts offer a more challenging climb than do pitons as it is critical as to how the nuts are placed in the rock, if they are to give the ultimate holding force of which they are capable. Nuts are becoming more and more popular with

Large angle, carabiner and riser are employed to make use of every tiny crevice that may offer a holding spot for the safety line on which the climber's life depends.

217

Cross-country ski-touring is rapidly gaining in popularity as more skiers discover this way to get away from the more strictly controlled slopes. The backpacker who adds this wrinkle to his outdoor projects must be good.

Backpacking onto snow-covered slopes in the dead of Winter takes much physical stamina to resist the cold and added exertion of high altitude.

climbers nowadays as they offer a clean and natural way to climb.

There are certain situations that may arise once in a while where a climber may not have the proper size nut or where it is simply not feasible to use a nut. In these cases, a piton often is used.

Basically, all pitons look like a nail with a hole on one end through which a carabiner is placed. Almost all pitons are made of steel, which conforms somewhat to the crack as it is being pounded into it. Pitons still are widely manufactured and distributed and probably will be for a long time to come, although their use is being limited as much as possible by most climbers today.

Climbing hammers come in a broad variety of shapes and sizes. Basically, there are rock hammers and crag hammers. Rock hammers have been used for many years to hammer in and remove pitons from the rock. Crag hammers can be used the same as rock hammers, but are more specialized for the removal of chocks because of the long, thin pick on the back of the head of the hammer.

Most climbing hammers have a steel head and an ash or hickory handle with a cord or sling attached, so the tool can be secured to the climber and not accidentally dropped. A small holster or sheath is usually carried on the side, so the hammer is readily at hand when needed.

The more climbers use their imaginations, the more new innovative equipment appears on the shelves of the climbing shop. But one should master the basic skills of climbing before using many of the specialty items available. After basic knowledge is acquired, a climber may opt to use some specialty items, but until this point one should keep to the basics. Climb with someone else who has experience, and use the most basic tool of man — common sense!

Some bare rock climbers use chalk to mark the handholds they have found for the following members of the party. It can also be used on the hands to prevent slipping during a retreat or rappel.

To the climbing purist, leaving the easily-spotted white smears of chalk for another party to follow makes traversing an otherwise difficult rock face about as challenging as painting by numbers. Such discourtesy might be compared with that of those impatient scalers who leave their pitons in place as they continue up a cliff face, impeding the possibility of a clean traverse for the next climber to follow.

As the various techniques of mountain conquering continue to evolve, the emphasis has begun to shift from domination by trail-making equipment to handhold discovery and a closer examination by feel as the free-climber finds an alternate route across the surface he has challenged.

A down or fiberfill-insulated winter sleeping bag is essential to maintaining the cold weather backpacker's health and for preserving his body heat against the freezing temperatures of a blustery mountain night.

While some of the more difficult faces may or may not yield to the hammerless climber, the alternatives offered by such replacement equipment as the various chocks or wedges give the determined climber access to routes up the Tetons, Devil's Lake and the Shawangunks.

The argument then becomes technology versus technique and, while the beginner may be compelled to rely on the rock-defacing pitons for his protection, the experienced and professionals — some of whom have never bothered to form the piton habit — probably can find a way up, over or around the obstacles that block their progress without despoiling the landscape as they go.

In looking for a place to climb, or just a quiet spot to pitch camp, backpackers are finding it harder and harder to get away from the thundering herd. As more and more

people join the swelling ranks of outdoor enthusiasts, open trails and unoccupied clearings are getting pretty scarce. By mid-June each year, the John Muir Trail is as crowded as a four-lane highway at 5 p.m. By the Fourth of July, there isn't a decent empty campsite to be found anywhere along the Appalachian Trail.

The development of lightweight gear has permitted deeper penetration of the once-isolated national wilderness areas by more and more summer backpackers. Signs of civilization are apparent in all too many places that were once pristine. For the winter ski enthusiast, the cost of lift tickets and the length of the lines to the chairs are becoming increasingly discouraging. Those who favor the solitude of the deep wilderness and yearn for the beauty of unspoiled nature are looking to the possibilities opened by taking to the hiking trails in the dead of Winter, when less enthusiastic campers are bundled snugly in their city homes.

Whether traveling on snowshoes, by snowmobile or on cross-country skis, a hearty new breed is taking to the back country to rediscover the art of cold weather survival.

The wilderness is substantially less forgiving in Winter than during the warmer months and the advantage of winter camping — fewer people — also presents the greatest danger. If the backpacker gets into trouble, his chances of getting outside assistance are greatly reduced. If planning a trip during the snow season, never consider going out alone. Travel in groups of four or more and make adequate preparations to meet food and shelter needs. The winter camper should be sure he is tuned up physically for the harsher environment of an outdoor winter trip. Be prepared for the additional rigors of high-altitude living and do not try to push a trip beyond the limits of at least two — preferably more — of the party.

The backpacker's first consideration, if he intends to take up winter camping, is the effectiveness of his personal program of physical conditioning. Daily exercise and a high-protein diet are essential to cold weather survival. When organizing the trip, plan several day hikes into the area before the first snow to test the strengths and weaknesses of all the members of the party. Each hiker should overload his pack to get a realistic sense of carrying weight in snow. The backpacker will quickly discover how many additional calories his body will burn, how much more energy he needs and what his particular limitations are in cold weather.

On such one-day hikes, the backpacker will get a chance to test his equipment and discover for himself that it's a whole new ball game. This applies whether the gear to be used is old and well-known for dependability or whether it has just been purchased. Some of the equipment used in summer excursions will be useful on a winter trip, but it will probably develop previously undiscovered idiosyncrasies. Other items will be useless or even harmful to the backpacker's health.

The winter backpacker's boots must be waterproof. There are several good sealing products on the market and several wax preparations that can be used for this purpose, as well as boots which are advertised as having been treated for waterproofing. Rubber boots may be a better answer. Whatever type the backpacker chooses, he should get a large enough size to permit him to wear two pairs of wool socks.

Thermal underwear, wool trousers, fiberfill-insulated outer trousers and parka, and a nylon wind shirt with a hood are all necessary clothing for combating freezing temperatures. Glasses to cut snow glare and insulated gloves or woolen mittens to prevent frostbite are vital to the backpacker's comfort and survival.

A sleeping bag intended for winter use should be fiberfill or down insulated and in the four to five-pound category.

A well-designed winter tent will have a cookhole cut in the ground cloth and the added measure of an air vent to prevent the winter camper from being accidentally suffocated when heavy snow blocks his entrance.

This winter mountaineer has what is probably the ideal snow weather tent, with its protected air vent, collapsible tunnel entrance and insulated top.

The synthetic bag will weigh more than the warmer down type, but if the down bag becomes wet from melting snow or sleet, it will quickly become useless while a synthetic-fill bag will hold at least part of its loft if wet. The choice then becomes a matter of how dry the backpacker can keep his sleeping bag. A down bag could be carried in the living pack and only taken out inside the tent. The tent's ground cloth would keep ground moisture from getting to the bag and it could be repacked inside the tent before moving out.

Because of the additional load of food, clothing and stove fuel, a summer backpack may not be large enough for cold weather use. The straps of a winter backpack should be adjustable to fit over the camper's additional clothing. The leather bottoms featured on some packs are fashionable enough, but leather absorbs moisture and, when wet, is considerably heavier. Don't add more poundage than needed to that already bulky load.

Accessories such as crampons, ice axes and snow shovels must be selected for their light weight and function, so the backpacker gets the most use out of the lightest load possible.

The butane cartridge stove that served well in milder weather will not work in Winter. If he doesn't already have a gas-type stove, the backpacker should get one and learn to use it proficiently before going out. If accustomed to the operation of a gas stove in Summer, try it out a few times in cold weather before setting out on an extended winter trip. The stove will perform somewhat differently and the backpacker should be aware of the differences.

The winter backpacker should be sure he has good trail directions. Trails are often less than evident in the snow. Where tree markers are present, they are often almost invisible in even a light powder fall. Normally visible horizon lines and land forms are often unrecognizable even when visible in the Winter. Carry a good compass and a topographical map, and refer to both often on the trail.

The two major health risks to watch for in winter camping are asphyxiation and hypothermia. Asphyxiation may occur while a camper snoozes inside his comfortable tent or snow cave if falling snow should block air vents or cookhole. Normal breathing or the use of a candle or stove will quickly consume all the oxygen and the camper will

If snowmobiling in isolated areas appeals to the outdoor enthusiast, he should be certain before starting out that he has all the basic maintenance gear he is likely to need. Repair and parts shops will be somewhat lacking.

first doze off, then die. Hypothermia is a more complicated problem. Hypothermia is the cooling of the body's core below its normal temperature of between ninety-eight and ninety-nine degrees. The symptom stages go from violent shivering to rigidity to coma with no reflexes to death when the body core temperature cools below eighty degrees. Exhaustion compounds the effects of exposure to cold geometrically, and hypothermia can occur at temperatures well above freezing.

Hypothermia can be combatted by being suitably clothed and sheltered from the elements, and maintaining body heat with proper nutrition. Asphyxiation, on the other hand, comes from the victim not providing a way for fresh air to get to him. A good winter tent with well-insulated walls, a tunnel-type entrance and well-designed vents is the compromise that will prevent both.

The winter camper's major enemy is moisture. Try to keep both the sleeping bag and the inside of the tent dry. Condensation caused by melted snow, perspiration or exhalations inside a tent will freeze, so plan for fresh clothing, adequate ventilation and exterior moisture protection.

Snow camping provides a wilderness experience like no other. The beauty, self-testing and grandeur of nature cannot be understood by those who haven't tried it. Variations of the basic camper, such as backpacking on snow-shoes or cross-country ski touring are also becoming more popular. Foot-traveling lovers of the wilderness compete with the mechanical approach of the snowmobilers. Dog sledding is another variation on basic winter camping that is on the rise. Several small companies have begun to market well-designed sleds. A sled dog can pull up to three times his weight, depending on conditions. That means up to a 210-pound payload for an average seventy-pound dog, which is plenty of gear for a long trek by four or five people.

Because it is a different experience than summer camping, and because of the attendant dangers, winter camping must be planned for with a view of rational caution and adequate preparation. It is not a game for fools or gamblers. Nature is the hardest teacher and is exceptionally unforgiving of stupidity in her domain. Winter camping is the most challenging and, therefore, the most unforgiving of all.

A Brief Summing Up Of Points That Have Been Touched On, But Are Important Nonetheless!

CHAPTER 19

TRAILS AND AWAY!

A FEW SPRIGS of green are beginning to struggle up through the melting snows of winter and the air around you takes on the smell of the newness of spring. Everywhere you turn nature seems to beckon with renewed vitality...the days of planning have ended and it's time for your first backpacking trip.

It could be the first for the season or possibly even the first of your lifetime...it is of little importance. What is important is that you are about to hit the trail toward an experience that will be long remembered.

If you are a beginner, chances are that you have spent many pleasurable hours poring over books similar to this one in an attempt to learn all that there is to know about backpacking. Or, even if you are a veteran backpacker, there is a likelihood that you have done some boning up, if for no other reason than not to make the same mistakes again.

However, whether a beginner or a seasoned packer, each trip is always a learning experience and you will return with new information. This chapter is to present a bit of back-

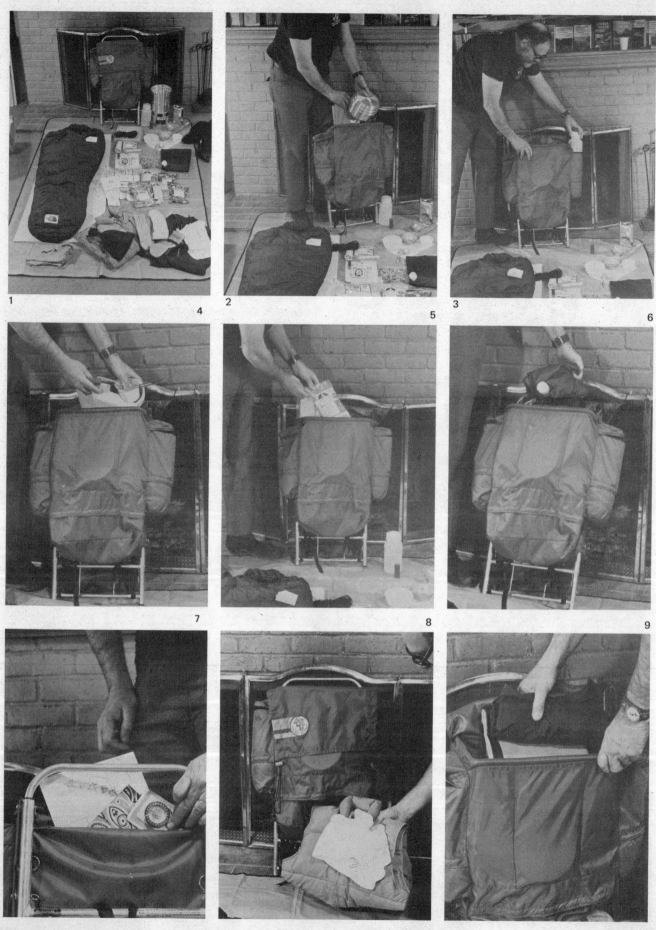

This bag contains all the necessary items needed for a summer trip, but it could still hold more if desired.

A transparent backpack shows how the items are arranged on the inside. Note sleeping bag is attached to bottom.

1) A typical layout for a backpacking trip during the warmer months. Includes all items of food, clothing and shelter that is needed. 2) Cooking gear is packed in the bottom section of the middle bag. 3) The water bottle fits easily in a sidepocket. 4) Following the cooking utensils comes the towel, water dipper and cup. 5) Next comes the food. 6) The deflated water bag is packed on top of the food items. 7) Trail map, compass and spare handkerchief fits into the map pocket. 8) Thermal underwear, down vest and extra clothing is placed in the lower pocket of the main pack. 9) Survival blanket and rain parka is packed on top of the main bag. The sleeping bag is attached to the bottom of the pack frame for easy carrying. If you carry an ensolite ground covering, it can be strapped to the top of the pack, although this is not shown. Additional items could be packed in this rig, but as always, in backpacking, you attempt to eliminate any unnecessary items.

packing potpourri that will add to this information, as well as be of interest and assistance to both the novice and the experienced. It wraps up many years of backpacking experience and offers a few tips that hopefully will make your next backpacking trip the best ever.

If you are a beginner or an experienced packer with new equipment, the best place to acquaint yourself with your pack and other related equipment for the trail is in your own backyard. However, we are not referring literally to that bit of lawn located behind your house...we mean a weekend hike close to home. On a short trip such as this you can test your equipment and learn whether it is adequate for your needs. On these short overnight trips you can also learn how to pack properly and eliminate unnecessary items. It will surprise you how many items you can eliminate after that first overnight trip.

Another advantage to short trips in a known area is that, if you are unfamiliar with the use of a compass and topographic map, here is an ideal opportunity to practice. If you learn the technique in an area that is known to you, you will have much less difficulty when you get into unfamiliar country.

Often overlooked by both the veteran and the novice are the many backpacking and hiking groups or clubs that have sprung up all over the country. If there is one in your area, it is an excellent opportunity to meet others who have similar interests and who, in many cases, have much experience and knowledge to pass on. These clubs normally have

227

regularly scheduled meetings and hiking trips that are open to anyone who is interested.

There are many advantages to joining a group such as this, one being the opportunity it gives you to learn from those who have had more experience. It also offers the chance to check various types of backpacking equipment owned by others, without having to invest in it yourself. And there is the companionship of hiking with others who have similar experience and interests. Many people will remain with a backpacking group for years, never really going off on a packing trip on their own.

If there are no local groups in your area, several national organizations offer hiking trips that are of interest to backpacking enthusiasts. Two such organizations are the Sierra Club and the Wilderness Society.

Experienced backpackers often will join one of these hiking trips because they offer a chance for them to become familar with an area on one of these trips, then they return at a later date for further exploring on their own. For the beginning backpacker, these organized trips allow him to get his feet wet under supervision before striking out on his own.

Many of these sponsored trips will have a doctor along on the trip, which often relieves the anxiety of the beginner who is concerned about what to do in the event of an emergency. Often they will even provide all necessary equipment. This allows one to get the feel of backpacking before really investing any money; it allows the beginner a chance to learn if he does not care for the sport.

Led by an experienced guide who knows the terrain, these sponsored trips usually return to the same area each year. The majority of the organizations will publish a yearly or seasonal bulletin giving the dates and the locations of the trips, which are available by writing to the organization.

Backpacking trips sponsored by national organizations such as the Sierra Club run from several days to only one or two days. If you are not interested in hiking for several

Below: Whenever hiking you should always heed the no trespassing signs. Right: For a long hike, many hikers will use a walking staff for additional support.

To pick up a heavy pack, grasp the shoulder strap and swing pack around the side and to the back, holding onto the strap. Then adjust tension on shoulder straps, using the pull keepers. You are then ready to go.

days to get to your destination, they have available hikes covering only a day or even a few hours, ending at a pre-determined campsite. One can hike in, set up camp, spend several days fishing or exploring, and hike back out in a day or a matter of a few hours.

Many find such packaged trips too calm for their taste after a few seasons. If you are this type, you will want to seek your own hiking trials. The best start is by proper planning at home. Pick the area where you want to hike and obtain a topographic map of that area. Then, before striking out, determine the terrain by the topo or, better yet, by talking with others who are familar with the area; decide upon your campsites prior to leaving home.

You should also determine how far you plan to travel each day. With this and the total number of days you plan to be out, you can decide whether you will go full circle and return to your starting point or whether you will need help in getting back. This can and should be done on paper long before you hit the trails.

By prior planning you can also lay out your meals and even test various brands of food at home before finding out that you don't like a specific brand once on the trail.

Prepackage your food according to your appetite and

(Photograph courtesy of Bill Whyte, Trailways Magazine)

the number in the party. Here again, you should plan on a minimum of three in the party. Many find that a group of five is an excellent number for a packing trip. However, when selecting your partners you should insure that all the members are compatible. Many backpacking trips have been spoiled by personality clashes on the trail!

Although we advocate estimating the approximate distance one will travel each day, we do not imply one should set any hard and fast rules. A primary purpose of backpacking is to escape clocks, time schedules and other hectic elements associated with our everyday working lives. Taking a tight schedule along on a packing trip defeats the purpose.

The name of the game is flexibility. If you happen upon a great fishing spot or a particularly interesting area that you would like to explore, be flexible enough in your schedule to stop...even to spend the night, if you desire. You may not be able to go as far as you planned, but it rarely makes that much difference.

When planning a trip, always let someone at home know where you are going, your proposed route, where your vehicle is parked, and about when you expect to return. If there is an accident or you become lost and there is a

serious delay, those so informed can send aid or a search party.

If you find that you are going to be late, you can always give a passing hiker heading back a note to drop into a mail box for you. Better yet, if you can get to a telephone, let your friends or family know that you will be late. It will save a lot of anxiety. Since it is an unwritten rule among backpackers to assist one another, you should have no problem finding someone willing to carry your note for you. However, if you don't come across one, you may have problems. This would be the time that it would be nice to have along that citizen's band rig. With this equipment you can always reach someone willing to call your friends.

Some hikers prefer to file an estimated intinerary with a local Forest Ranger or sheriff's department. However, if you do, you should also inform them when you are leaving the area as well.

We often hear of a group that has had all sorts of problems because through some sense of false pride they tried to push themselves too hard. Almost immediately members begin to develop blisters, aching muscles, heat exhaustion and other such problems. Many times this is caused by our competitive nature.

If a hiker in the group is faster or a better climber, let him go ahead and don't yourself try or allow others in the group to try to keep up with him. A packing trip is meant to be a fun, relaxing time, not an endurance contest. A good way to maintain a pace suitable for the entire group is to have an experienced packer in the lead and one bringing up the rear. This also helps in keeping track of everyone in the group. Should one wander off, the tag-along man normally will notice and stop the group.

If you need to leave the trail for a moment, whether it's the call of nature or some other reason, leave your pack alongside the trail. This will let others know that you are there and, should you fall or injure yourself, they can come to your aid. Always have complete identification on your pack, including information on whom to contact in the event of an emergency.

The more traveled trails are clearly marked, but often hikers will look for markers along the ground and cannot

Many of the new marked hiking trails offer the backpacker a variety of challenging terrain, as well as beautiful scenery.

find them. This is because many times the markers will be placed high on trees where they will not be covered by snow during winter. The Forestry Service now is numbering the trails also, which makes it easier to stay on the desired trail. It is similar to our highway system, but a little less complex. If you are, for example, on Trail No. 42 and come to a junction, you just look for a marker with a 42 on it and follow that direction.

The best method by which to mark a trail without leaving lasting signs is with small pieces of colored cloth or ribbon. By tying these around tree limbs or securing them with a rubber band, they will be visible to those following and the last man in the group can gather them for use farther down the trail. The best placement for this type of a marker at a junction is to place the first one before the trail junction, another one at the junction but still on the

For the more hardy, the ultimate in backpacking is striking off crosscountry on their own. Here you rarely see others and the scenery that awaits you is well worth the extra effort.

trail being used and still in sight of the first one, then a third one in sight of the second one, but down the trail that is to be taken. Do remember to pick up these ribbons as the last man goes by. It not only will confuse other hikers coming along, it would become unslightly after awhile if many others also forget to gather theirs.

A good example of what not to do when marking a trail involves a group that used spray paint to mark their route. As they went along they would spray a rock every now and then. After about two days a Forest Ranger caught up with them and they spent the remainder of their trip backtracking and scraping off the paint.

Although it may have been common practice for the pioneers to blaze a trail by slashing a tree with an ax or knife, this method is far from acceptable today. It not only defaces the natural surroundings, it damages the trees. Piling rocks along the trail is also no longer an acceptable procedure. If you must mark a trail, stick with the cloth ribbons and no one will be offended.

The best way for any group to stay on course is to know how to use the topographic map and look for natural markers such as rock formations, split trees and other such landmarks. These are found easily almost anywhere you hike and by following them it is a simple matter to stay on trail or to return down the same trail, if you desire.

Up to this point, we have been discussing local short trail systems. There are several larger trail systems in existence however. Many are still in the development and planning stage. They are primarily hiking trails, but you will often

also find horsemen using these same trails. Some trails are designated as either only hiking or only motorbike trails, but many will be a combination.

One of these systems, the Appalachian Trail, extends from Georgia into Maine. Many East Coast hiking groups offer trips along this trail during summer and fall months. The West Coast counterpart is the John Muir Trail, which covers 220 miles through the central Sierras that are uncut by any roads.

A new trail under development that appears to offer the backpacker a variety of terrain is the Continental Divide in the Rocky Mountains. One of the biggest and no doubt the longest system under development is the Pacific Crest Trail that runs from Tecate, Mexico, up through the Laguna Mountains in San Diego County through the Santa Rosa Mountains, the San Bernardino Mountains, the San Gabriels, the Sierras and the Cascades. It should total about 2200 miles when completed.

These larger trail systems are maintained in most cases by donations of time, labor and money from various hiking and wilderness clubs. A government agency such as the Forestry Service will mark it and lay it out, but it is primarily up to volunteer organizations to maintain the trails and keep them open for hikers. Here is an area where there seems to be no generation gap. Boy Scouts, college students, those above 30 all chip in for the benefit of all who enjoy the outdoors.

Should you desire to pack into an area where there are no designated trails and wish to gain access to private

property, you may encounter everything from complete cooperation to absolute refusal. In the latter case, chances are that the property owner has good reason. Previous hikers or campers have misused his generosity by being careless with fire, letting his livestock out or senselessly littering the area.

In order to not be guilty of such infractions, there are

Above: As a backpacker the whole outdoors awaits you. Right: A closeup of a typical packing method used by many backpackers. A well packed bag takes a little extra effort and time, but on the trail it is worth it.

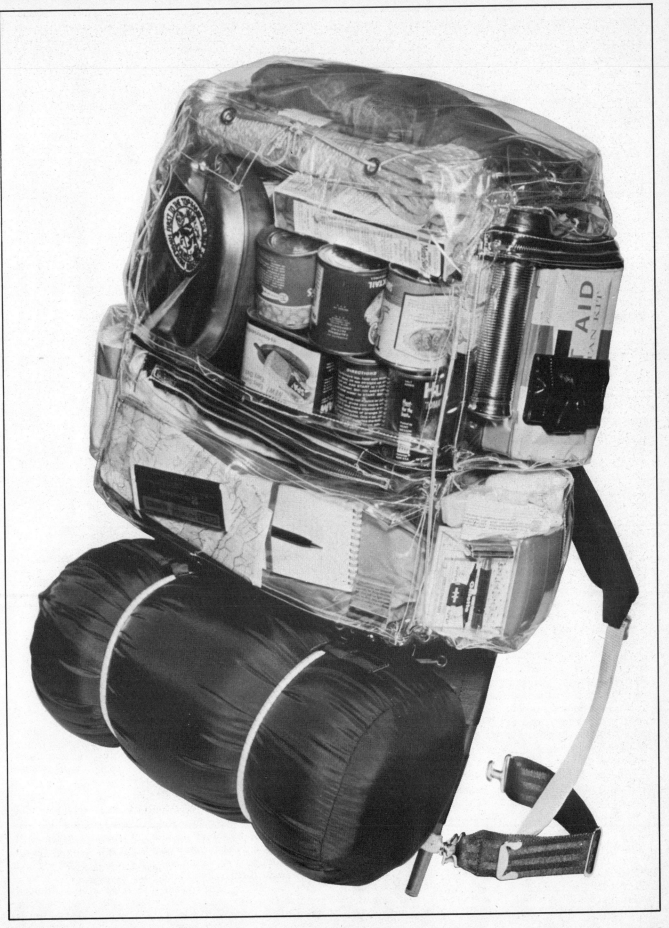

several rules that you can follow whenever traversing any private land. One of the first and cardinal rules is always to leave gates as you find them. If they are open, leave them open; and if closed, they should be closed behind you. The fences and gates are used to control livestock and by carelessly leaving one open, you can inadvertently allow the animals to escape. It may take a rancher many hours to round up his cattle after a careless hiker has neglected to close a gate behind him.

Should you encounter undue suspicion when requesting entrance to private land, you might consider a little diplomacy. Offer to assist the owner with chores in return for use of his land. Most times he will thank you and allow you entrance without holding you to your offer. However, if he doesn't and you do give a hand, that's all the better. Either way, you have made it a little easier for the next backpacker coming through his area.

One group gained access to a wonderful wooded stream area by mending fences for the owner. The area was ideal for weekend or three-day outing and, by hiking along the fence line, mending fences as they went, they not only made a lasting friend, but also had a marvelous time. Of course before starting something like this, you should know what you are doing, but most ranchers would be glad to give you a few lessons in fence mending, then leave you on your own with complete access to their property.

Use of pack animals is debated often among backpackers. For a large group hiking to a definite campsite, pack animals allow the group to carry more items. Having a pack animal along is also an advantage if someone is injured and needs to be carried out. Other than these circumstances, most backpackers feel that they are more trouble than they are worth.

The most common pack animal is the burro, however, mules and horse are also often used. The biggest problem is that the majority of hikers are inexperienced in handling animals and the common practice is to rent them for the duration of the trip. The animal is often picked up at the beginning of the trip and returned at the journey's end, which means that the hiker does not know that particular animal nor does the animal know the hiker.

Should you decide that you would like to use an equine on a packing trip, it is not a bad idea to carry a few lumps of sugar or apples to use as inducement. This will not only sometimes get them moving again when they arbitrarily decide to stop along the trail, it can also be used to help keep them around the camp at night. The usual method to keep pack animals from wandering off at night is to hobble them. However, most inexperienced hikers will be amazed at how far a hobbled horse or burro can travel in just a few hours. To be entirely safe, the best method to keep them around is to tether them to a tree or other suitable object.

If using pack animals, how are you going to feed and water them? In some hiking areas, this would not present any problem since water and grass would be available for grazing. However, in the event you are hiking into an arid area, taking a pack animal would be foolish. In addition to your own food and water, you would also have to pack the animal's subsistence.

On any trail — marked, wilderness or just a stock trail through the mountains — always observe common trail courtesy. If you meet livestock on the trail, they always have the right of way. When a herder with his livestock approaches you on the trail, either from the front or rear, you should step off the trail some distance as to not spook the stock and let them go by. A good herder will normally wait until you are off the trail a sufficient distance before moving his herd past you.

Never try to pet them or make a sudden movement around these animals or you may find yourself starting a stampede. Should the herd begin to act up, don't try to help the herder unless he asks. He is experienced in handling the animals and, being on horseback, many times can bring them back into line. Although well meaning, any assistance that you attempt may spook the herd even more.

An unwritten law of the trails and most certainly common trail courtesy, is that you will always help any hiker in trouble. If you cannot do anything personally at the time, you should offer to go for help.

Another trail courtesy often overlooked or unknown by beginning hikers is the custom of asking for, "Trail" as you approach and want to pass a group of hikers ahead who are moving slower. As you approach you simply state, "Trail," which means that you would like them to step to the side so that you can go around.

Experienced hikers will know this custom, but should you run across others who don't, it is a courtesy to explain what is meant by this expression. Almost all will be appreciative and will more than likely begin to follow the custom themselves in the future.

The utimate in backpacking is to strike off cross-country, self-contained, entirely on your own, plotting your own course as you go. Many feel that this is the goal in backpacking, while others are content to stick with the marked trails.

If you are the type who wants to take off on his own, leaving the marked trails behind, be thoroughly adept in the use of topographic map and compass.

Any group of hikers that strikes off across country on their own should always have at least one experienced packer along; preferably one familar with the particular area. Three inexperienced hikers totally unfamilar with an area are no better than one.

Moving across new terrain, one of the best methods to find your way is to find a game trail that meanders in the same direction that you wish to go. Game animals have a way of finding the easiest way to get from one place to another. The only problem is finding game trails leading in the same direction you wish to go.

When moving up a canyon, stay out of the stream bed. This may sound unimportant, but a dry stream bed can turn into a raging torrent, even when it is not raining in the immediate area. It can rain miles from you and that dry stream bed becomes the funnel for flash floods. There may be times when you have to follow a creek bed, because of hills on the sides, but only do so when absolutely necessary. Never get yourself into a low area such as a creek bed where there is no escape to higher ground. A sudden rain in the mountains may cause you to reluctantly swim your way out! If you plan to use a stream bed as a landmark to follow, you can often travel much more easily along the hillside above the stream.

If you are hiking in high country or unknown terrain and see a open grassy meadow, be wary. It might be an oozing bog. Many mountain meadows contain a great deal of water during the spring months and one extra step into one might find you waist deep in muck. If there are any doubts, skirt the meadow at the brush edge or above.

There may be times when you must cross a flooded meadow. If this happens, you should cut a staff to poke ahead of your path to determine if the ground is firm. If

the meadow is completely flooded you may or may not have a creek bed running down the center, invisible to you. In this case you could be in a few inches of water and suddenly find yourself in water over your head. Poking a staff ahead of you could prevent this.

The choice of a campsite while far from the beaten path is primarily a personal matter. It is ideal, of course, to be able to camp near water, but this is not always possible. If you camp by a running brook, pick a location that is sheltered from the elements. If it is a waterhole situation, never camp right on the waterhole. Both wild and domestic animals may also use this as their water source and your camp would frighten them off. Camp at least five hundred yards from the water source. This is close enough to be convenient and it will also not scare off the animals. Another problem you may encounter by camping too close to a water source is that you may find your camp raided by varmint type animals that are seeking the water and find your camp a bonus.

When hiking in mountainous areas, find a ridge or hilltop from which you can see for quite a distance. By this method, you should be able to find an ideal camp location, without wearing yourself out in looking.

The biggest problem that arises either with trail or cross-country hiking is that individuals or groups may try to cover too much territory in the time that is allotted. This can cause at least some members of the party to overexert themselves. Know the abilities of the members of the group and plot your hike in accordance with them.

There may be times when, even using your topographic map, you find yourself bottled up in an area bounded by rocks, cliffs or other natural barriers. Should this occur, don't try to climb your way out; backtrack and try another route. Rock climbing is an art in itself and shouldn't be tried without experience and training.

Common sense is the best item to take on any backpacking trip. Don't attempt distances that are too far or terrain that is too rough for you as an individual or for any member of your party. Try to select hiking partners equal to you in physical stamina and hiking ability. Keeping these two points in mind when you plan your trip will insure that it is a pleasant excursion and not a chore.

AND WHERE TO DO IT

CHAPTER 20

A Survey Of National Forests And Similar Areas Rates Them For Backpackers

National Forests are other areas which the backpacking enthusiast should not overlook. They have rules and regulations not unlike the national parks, so it would be wise for the camper to check with a forest ranger either beforehand or immediately upon arrival for specific regulations to follow.

Some of the national forests may not be suitable for backpacking so the addresses of the forest supervisors for each forest are listed at the beginning of each location. It is advisable to write and seek recommendations of permanently-based personnel prior to finalizing plans.

ALABAMA
WILLIAM B. BANKHEAD NATIONAL FOREST
Office of the Forest Supervisor: P. O. Box 40, Montgomery, AL 36101 This area offers much to the hunter and fisherman, should you pack along such gear. There are 21 campsites within the forest, with a total of 49 units.

Port Orford, Oregon, offers the backpacker swimming, fishing, camping and many other outdoor activities; including hiking trails.

Panning for your own gold is only one of the many activities offered to backpackers at Chugach National Forest, Alaska.

CONECUH NATIONAL FOREST

Office of the Forest Supervisor: P. O. Box 40, Montgomery, AL 36101 Close to Andalusia, this forest abounds with lakes and ponds ideal for the fisherman or nature lover. Scenery is superb. There are 11 camping units at only one campground, so it would behoove the camper to get to the forest early.

TALLADEGA NATIONAL FOREST

Office of the Forest Supervisor: P. O. Box 40, Montgomery, AL 36101 A good site for bird and game watchers, usually in the early morning and evening hours, as the forest harbors South Sandy Wildlife Management Area. There are 70 camping units at four campgrounds. Good waterfowl and upland game bird hunting, as well as impoundment fishing for bass, bream and perch.

TUSKEGEE NATIONAL FOREST

Office of the Forest Supervisor: P. O. Box 40, Montgomery, AL 36101 A small forest, used mostly for picnicking or overnight camping. There are only five camping units at one campground within the forest, and these probably are taken early.

ALASKA

CHUGACH NATIONAL FOREST

Office of the Forest Supervisor: Anchorage, AK 99501 As with most of Alaska's National Forests, this area is for the hardy and the daring with its high altitudes and cold temperatures. The scenery is unexcelled practically anywhere in the world and game abounds. It's not unusual to see moose, mountain goats, sheep and brown bear in the course of a day's hiking. There are 20 camping units in the forest. Take your winter woolies.

TONGASS NATIONAL FOREST, NORTH DIVISION

Office of the Forest Supervisor: Juneau, AK 99801 This would be a nice spot to visit. It is an immense area, Comprising more than sixteen million acres. Cold weather gear is in order.

TONGASS NATIONAL FOREST, SOUTH DIVISION

Office of the Forest Supervisor: Ketchikan, AK 99901 Really rugged yet beautiful country, with two campgrounds for overnight stayers. There is picnicking, hunting and fishing as main attractions.

Panorama of Mounts Foraker, Hunter and McKinley from Curry Ridge, north of Talkeetna, at the Mount McKinley National Monument, Alaska. One of the beautiful viewpoints in Alaska.

ARIZONA

APACHE NATIONAL FOREST

Office of the Forest Supervisor: Springerville, AZ 85938 Located close to the New Mexico border, this forest really heats up in the summertime, There are numerous scenic spots, however, especially along the Colorado Trail which cuts through the forest. Camping is permitted in 23 locations. Hunting and fishing is permitted according to state regulations.

COCONINO NATIONAL FOREST

Office of the Forest Supervisor: Flagstaff, AZ 86001 There is plenty of beautiful scenery awaiting the hiker who endeavors to hike in the up-and-down country. Camping is permitted in 22 sites throughout the forest, which is a popular spot for tourists throughout the year. This forest contains the San Francisco Peaks — 12,611 feet high — the highest point in the state.

CORONADO NATIONAL FOREST

Office of the Forest Supervisor: Tucson, AZ 85702 Varying terrain is the by-word in this forest, where snow skiing and swimming are separated by about forty miles.

Camping is allowed in 616 units in 27 locations throughout the forest, Get there early.

PRESCOTT NATIONAL FOREST

Office of the Forest Supervisor: Prescott, AZ 86301 For the individual that wants to get away from it all, this might be the site. The one million-plus acre forest has ideal year 'round climate. Be in shape. Camping is allowed in ten campgrounds.

STIGREAVES NATIONAL FOREST

Office of the Forest Supervisor: Holbrook, AZ 86025 This near 800,000 acre forest is a favorite during the winter months, when the desert clime is somewhat cooler than during the summer months. There are many trails excellently suited to hiking, but be sure you take plenty of water on any excursions away from the campground. There are three campgrounds within the forest, and they tend to fill up fast.

TONTO NATIONAL FOREST

Office of the Forest Supervisor: Phoenix, AZ 85001 Elevations in this forest range from 1,500 to 7,000-plus

A view from the mile-high overlook in the Great Smoky Mountains. For the packer who looks for ruggedness, this is ideal terrain.

feet. Water sports are big in this forest, so don't leave the swimming trunks behind. And, due to the popularity of water sports, plan to arrive at one of the 22 campgrounds early in the morning, or you may not get a spot!

ARKANSAS

OUACHITA NATIONAL FOREST

Office of the Forest Supervisor: Box 1270, Hot Springs, AR 71902 There are 305 campsites at 18 locations throughout the forest, which features numerous scenic trails. For the sportsman, there are eight lakes which have some of the top bass fishing in the nation. Hunting for squirrels, deer and quail is permitted. Beautiful countryside plus these other attractions mean full campgrounds, so get to the forest early.

OZARK NATIONAL FOREST

Office of the Forest Supervisor: Russellville, AR 72801 Some of the most beautiful scenery in the nation is found in Ozark National Forest, which has a wonderful warm climate suitable for the camper. Many scenic trails cut through the area, and camping is permitted in 284 campsites at 17 locations. Stream and lake fishing is popular, as is deer and small game hunting.

ST. FRANCIS NATIONAL FOREST

Office of the Forest Supervisor: Russellville, AR 72801 A relatively small forest of about 10,000 acres, camping is allowed in 34 units at two separate locations. Fishing, picnicking and swimming are major attractions to the forest, which has two recreational lakes.

CALIFORNIA

ANGELES NATIONAL FOREST

Office of the Forest Supervisor: 1015 North Lake Avenue, Pasadena, CA 91104 This close-to-Los Angeles forest is generally full the year 'round, as it features water sports in summer and skiing in winter. There are 1,470 campsites at 94 separate locations. Many hiking trails crisscross the forest. Get there early!

CLEVELAND NATIONAL FOREST

Office of the Forest Supervisor: 1196 Broadway, San Diego, CA 92101 Situated about midway between Los Angeles and San Diego, this forest welcomes residents from both cities to its 612-unit, 20-location campgrounds. For the hunter, there are 26 separate camps specifically established. Fishing and waterfowl hunting generally is good, the climate temperate and the sightseeing fine.

ELDORADO NATIONAL FOREST

Office of the Forest Supervisor: Placerville, CA 95667 Located partly in Nevada, this forest has 1,205 campsites at 41 locations in its nearly two million-acre expanse. It encompasses Lake Tahoe among others, which are water sport favorites. Winter sports are big in season, as is gambling on the Nevada portion of the forest. It is pretty high country, so come prepared for cool weather.

INYO NATIONAL FOREST

Office of the Forest Supervisor: Bishop, CA 93514 Bring along an oxygen tank if you expect to spend any time in this forest, especially if you plan to hike to its borders. At

Little can match the beauty of the giant sequoias during the wintertime. Heavy clothing and warm shelter is needed here.

extremely high altitude, the forest houses the oldest living things on earth. a grove of Bristlecone pine; Mt. Whitney, the highest point in the continental U.S.; Mammoth and Reversed Creek Recreational Areas, and more. There are 2,011 units at 66 campgrounds within the forest.

KLAMATH NATIONAL FOREST
Office of the Forest Supervisor: Yreka, CA 96097
Located on the Oregon-California border, this forest is one of the most beautiful in the entire country. It has 359 campsites at 26 locations. It is big for water sports, fishing, hunting and picnicking. Altitudes vary, so be prepared for some grades.

LASSEN NATIONAL FOREST
Office of Forest Supervisor: Susanville, CA 96130
Everything from desert to high mountain area await the visitor to this forest. It is warm in summer and cold in

Left: The Petrified Forest offers the hiker the unusual beauty of the dessert. No camping is permitted, but it's worth seeing.

Above: Shenandoah Mountains have year 'round appeal, but are especially breathtaking during the Fall when the leaves begin to change.

winter, with rain not unheard of during the summer months. Hunting and fishing is good, as is the hiking through the many paved roads and trails that abound in the forest. Watch for logging trucks, as it is a big industry in this neck of the woods. There are 993 campsites at 54 locations.

LOS PADRES NATIONAL FOREST

Office of the Forest Supervisor: Federal Building, Santa Barbara, CA 93101 Home of the California Condor, this forest offers practically everything a backpacker could want, from semi-desert to ocean to oak and pine forest. There are 1,056 units at 114 different locations within the forest, which has altitudes ranging from sea level to 9,000 feet. If you plan on utilizing the oceanside camping, take a good warm sleeping bag.

MENDOCINO NATIONAL FOREST

Office of the Forest Supervisor: Willows, CA 95988 Located on the coast some hundred miles north of San Francisco, this forest has beautiful ocean vistas and roads from sea level to nearly 9,000 feet. Camping is permitted in

440 campsites in 51 locations. The area is popular with local residents, so plan on arriving early.

MODOC NATIONAL FOREST

Office of the Forest Supervisor: Alturas, CA 96101 Nestled in the extreme northeastern corner of the state, this forest encompasses much heritage-rich acreage, famous especially for the exploits of the army in their pre-1900 efforts of evicting Captain Jack and his band of Modoc Indians from the lava beds. It is some mighty beautiful country, but is also rough. It tends to be cool in the late fall with plenty of snow during the winter. Camping is allowed at 285 units located in 23 different areas throughout the forest.

PLUMAS NATIONAL FOREST

Office of the Forest Supervisor: Quincy, CA 95971 One of California's best national forests for the camper, and for that reason it generally is packed yearly. Camping is permitted in 671 units at 32 different locations, and plan on arriving early in the day during the summer months. There are many trails offering unrivaled scenery.

One of the natural wonders of the world is Old Faithful Geyser at Yellowstone National Park. Viewing it at sunset is unforgettable.

SAN BERNARDINO NATIONAL FOREST

Office of the Forest Supervisor: Civic Center Building, 175 W. Fifth Street, San Bernardino, CA 94201 One of the most popular national forests for Californians, due to its close proximity to Los Angeles and San Diego, this offers camping at 42 spots in 989 units. It also is one of the few that permits reservations for groups. Main attractions include numerous lakes for water sports and the highest peaks in the southern half of the state, the San Gorgonio mountains, which reach to over 11,000 feet. There are plenty of trails suitable for hiking.

SEQUOIA NATIONAL FOREST

Office of the Forest Supervisor: 900 W. Grand Avenue, Porterville, CA 93258 The giant sequoia trees are not the only attractions that fill campgrounds the year 'round in this forest. There also are water sports on the lakes and streams, riding, scenic drives and hunting and fishing. There are 807 camping units at 53 different sites throughout the forest. Group camping is permitted on a reservation basis. Come early in the day.

SHASTA-TRINITY NATIONAL FOREST

Office of the Forest Supervisor: 1615 Continental Street, Redding, CA 96001 Actually two forests joined

together, this one mammoth recreational area comprises more than two million acres, so there is plenty of room for the camper in it. Some of the forest is located at high altitude, like Mt. Shasta, at 14,162 feet above sea level. It's difficult hiking in these areas, but the scenery is unexcelled. Water sports are popular, as is fishing and hunting. Camping is permitted in 1,426 units at 99 different locations. It's usually full early.

SIERRA NATIONAL FOREST

Office of the Forest Supervisor: Federal Building, 1130 O Street, Fresno, CA 93721 Another million-plus acre forest within California's borders offers much to the packer. The temperate climate is ideal during the fall months, for those unable to break away during the summer season. Many lakes and streams equal great water sport, and the country is rich with game and birds for the hunting enthusiast. Make sure, if hiking in the area, that you take pains not to dress in dull colors, for this is asking for trouble. Camping is permitted in 1,326 units at 87 locations.

SIX RIVERS NATIONAL FOREST

Office of the Forest Supervisor: 331 J Street, Eureka, CA 95501 Just four of those nationally-famous rivers for which this forest is named are Smith, Klamath, Eel and Mad, and they cut through some mighty mean territory. The climate is cool and mild throughout the year, and come prepared for periodic rainstorms. There is plenty to do and see, including fishing, hunting and water sports. Camping is featured in 212 units at 14 locations. Watch for logging trucks.

STANISLAUS NATIONAL FOREST

Office of the Forest Supervisor: 175 S. Fairview Lane, Sonora, CA 95370 Close to San Francisco, this forest has 978 camping units at 39 locations. It offers much to the hiker in regard to scenery. Take care when hiking on the forest roadways, for the drop-offs are deep in the canyon areas.

TAHOE NATIONAL FOREST

Office of the Forest Supervisor: Nevada City, CA 95939 This forest is best known for its skiing attraction, Squaw Valley, and for Donner Pass, which was the site of the ill-fated group of emigrants that didn't make it over the mountains and into the valleys before winter set in. The area is at a high altitude and extremely rugged, but for those who can handle it, the scenery more than makes up for the roughness. Streams and lakes also are present, including Lake Tahoe, a gin-clear impoundment that is guaranteed to refresh any bather. There are 926 camping units at 58 locations. Get there early.

COLORADO

ARAPAHO NATIONAL FOREST

Office of the Forest Supervisor: 1010 Tenth Street, Golden, CO 80401 The whole state of Colorado is rather synonymous with the Continental Divide, so be prepared for some rough hiking. For those who would be interested in the lower, more mild hiking areas, it should be noted that 24 campsites comprised of 600 units are available. Take the cold weather gear.

GRAND MESA-UNCOMPAGRE NATIONAL FORESTS

Office of the Forest Supervisor: 11th and Main Streets, Delta, CO 81416 These two joined forests result in more than 1,300,000 acres of varied terrain for the camper, cyclist, hunter, fisherman or hiker. Only 15 locations with 275 camping units are available, so plan on arriving early.

Castle Geyser at Yellowstone National Park is also a sight to behold. There are many hiking trails in the area for the packer.

GUNNISON NATIONAL FOREST

Office of the Forest Supervisor: 216 N. Colorado, Gunnison, CO 81230 This forest has twenty-seven peaks of more than 12,000 feet in altitude. The area is dotted with many high lakes, streams and prime hunting locations. There are seven winter sports areas, which is an indication of the conditions to expect late in the year. Camping is permitted in 481 units at 27 locations.

PIKE NATIONAL FOREST

Office of the Forest Supervisor: 320 W. Fillmore, Colorado Springs, CO 80907 This forest has as a major attraction Pikes Peak, and the terrain leading to the summit is rough. There are 703 camping units at 46 different locations throughout the area.

RIO GRANDE NATIONAL FOREST

Office of the Forest Supervisor: Fassett Building, 914 First Avenue, Monte Vista, CO 81144 Another high-altitude forest, with the major attractions being a primitive area, many lakes and streams that are sure to interest the piscator. There are 32 campsites with 621 units en toto.

ROOSEVELT NATIONAL FOREST

Office of the Forest Supervisor: Rocky Mountain Bank & Trust Building, 211 Canyon, Fourth Floor, Fort Collins, CO 80521 A beautiful forest, this again has many up and down grades that the hiker may find tough to traverse. There is top fishing in lakes and streams, and skiing during the winter months. Hunting also is good for deer, elk, sheep, bear, grouse and duck. Camping is allowed in 476 units at 16 locations. Take a sweater, light jacket or the like, even during the summer season.

ROUTT NATIONAL FOREST

Office of the Forest Supervisor: P. O. Box 1198, Steamboat Springs, CO 80477 Pack warm clothing if your desire is to visit this forest, for the nights get a mite chilly at the high altitudes. There are a few locations with snow and ice the year around. Fishing and hunting is superb, as is the scenery. Camping is permitted in 330 units at 20 sites.

SAN ISABEL NATIONAL FOREST

Office of the Forest Supervisor: P. O. Building, P. O. Box 753, Pueblo, CO 81002 Take along an oxygen tank if you plan to hike to this forest, for it has the highest average elevation of any national forest in the country. This means cold nights and cool days. Fishing and hunting are great. Camping is featured in 362 units at 20 locations.

SAN JUAN NATIONAL FOREST

Office of the Forest Supervisor: Oliger Building, P. O. Box 341, Durango, CO 81301 Many historical points and archeological ruins are found in San Juan National Forest, which can turn a camping spree into a history lesson. Many high peaks are found within the forest. Camping is allowed in 619 units at 31 sites throughout the forest, which usually are kept full by the visiting anglers or hunters.

WHITE RIVER NATIONAL FOREST

Office of the Forest Supervisor: P. O. Building, P. O. Box 948, Glenwood Springs, CO 81601 This forest is the area that produced the marble for the Lincoln Memorial and the Tomb of the Unknown Soldier. It has more to offer than quarries, however, including fine hunting, fishing and scenery, of which the camper can partake. Camping is permitted in 640 units at 35 locations throughout the nearly two-million-acre forest.

FLORIDA

APALACHICOLA NATIONAL FOREST

Office of the Forest Supervisor: Box 1050, Tallahassee, FL 32302 A beautiful location for the winter camper, this forest has varied terrain including swamps, hardwood forests, lakes, streams and the like. Some of the best bass fishing in the country is available in Florida, along with perch and bream. Camping is limited to 108 units at nine locations throughout the forest. Take the mosquito repellent!

OCALA NATIONAL FOREST

Office of the Forest Supervisor: Box 1050, Tallahassee, FL 32302 Hundred of lakes spell outstanding water sports in this forest, which is named for the Indian tribe that used to prevail in the area. Fishing and hunting are superb, and wildlife photography is a natural in the wildlife management area within the forest. Camping is allowed in 333 units at 9 locations.

OSCEOLA NATIONAL FOREST

Office of the Forest Supervisor: Box 1050, Tallahassee, FL 32302 Close to the fishin'-minded folks of Jacksonville, this forest has numerous lakes that are home of some hog-sized bass, bream and perch. The climate is wonderful during the winter months, and quite warm during the summer season. The forest is less trafficked during the summer, as Florida is known for its winter vacation-time visitors. A state breeding ground for wildlife is located in the forest, so some fine photos are not out of the question. During the winter, plan on arriving early in the day if you hope to camp in the 43 units at one location.

GEORGIA

CHATTAHOOCHEE NATIONAL FOREST

Office of the Forest Supervisor: Box 643, Gainesville, GA 30501 This forest houses the highest peak in the state, Brasstown Bald at 4,784 feet. Camping is permitted in 534 units at 24 locations, and plan on arriving early in the day throughout the year.

OCONEE NATIONAL FOREST

Office of the Forest Supervisor: Box 643, Gainesville GA 30501 A fine spot for camping, fishing or hunting, this forest has a temperate year 'round climate. Archeological ruins are to be found inside its boundaries, along with the Piedmont Wildlife Refuge. Only 42 camping units are established at two locations, so be an early bird.

Loxahatches Recreation Area in Southern Florida offers excellent fishing and water sports.

IDAHO

BOISE NATIONAL FOREST

Office of the Forest Supervisor: 412 Idaho Street, Boise, ID 83702 Some mighty rugged country exists within this 2.5-million-plus acre forest, and the scenery is second to none. Water sports are big on the numerous lakes, as is fishing on the many streams that originate within the forest. Hunting is a prime fall sport, and skiing takes over during the winter months. Camping is permitted in 826 units at 91 locations.

CARIBOU NATIONAL FOREST

Office of the Forest Supervisor: 427 N. Sixth Avenue,

The Everglades have little to offer the backpacker, but if in the area, it's worth a stop. Several camping sites are available in nearby towns.

Pocatello, ID 83201 This forest, located partly in Utah and Wyoming, is big for the sportsman and hiker. Many towering mountain ranges divide valleys that have fine hiking trails. Camping is permitted in 302 units at 19 locations. Be prepared for cool daytime temperatures.

CHALLIS NATIONAL FOREST

Office of the Forest Supervisor: Forest Service Building, Challis, ID 83226 There are some ultra-high peaks located in this forest, but plenty of low-land with traversible trails make for fine hiking and sightseeing. Hunting and fishing are big drawing cards, as there is plenty of rugged, little used area and fine streams and lakes. Camping is permitted at 331 units at 24 sites throughout the forest. Look closely and you might see a mountain goat, sheep or antelope.

CLEARWATER NATIONAL FOREST

Office of the Forest Supervisor: Federal Building, Orofino, ID 83544 Lumber mills are the big business in this area, which means logging trucks can be expected to be barreling down the narrow roads and high-mountain passes.

If you vacation here, take special care not to become a hood ornament for one of the big bruisers. Hunting and fishing is outstanding, as is the sightseeing. Many stands of virgin white pine exist, and it's easy to spend a few weeks here. Camping is permitted in 204 units at 15 locations in the 1.5-million-plus acre forest.

COEUR D'ALENE NATIONAL FOREST

Office of the Forest Supervisor: 218 N. 23rd, Coeur D'Alene, ID 83814 The main attraction in this forest is Coeur d'Alene Lake, which is great for water sports enthusiasts or the fisherman. Some of the best elk hunting in the nation is found in this area, so by all means don't dress in dull colors. Camping is permitted in 129 units at 12 locations.

KANIKSU NATIONAL FOREST

Office of the Forest Supervisor: Sandpoint, ID 83864 This forest, which spills over into Montana and Washington, has 264 camping units at 18 sites for the visiting campers. Boating, fishing, hunting, swimming and scenic drives headline the attractions at the forest during the summer months. There are slide presentations and movies put on by Forest Service personnel around the campfires, which can be a perfect end to a day of hiking. Don't arrive too late in the year, or snow will be on the ground to greet you!

NEZ PERCE NATIONAL FOREST

Office of the Forest Supervisor: Grangeville, ID 83530 This is one of the few forests that has an outfitter present for individuals that want to traverse the rugged Selway-Bitterroot Wilderness Area on foot. Many canyons, rivers and streams cut through the forest, which means fine fishing and hunting. Camping is permitted at 84 units at 13 locations throughout the forest.

PAYETTE NATIONAL FOREST

Office of the Forest Supervisor: Forest Service Building, McCall, ID 83638 The deepest gorge in the U.S. is found in this forest, the Hells Canyon on the Snake River. More than 150 lakes mean water sports, fishing and watering grounds for game. More than 1,500 miles of streams cut through the forest. Skiing is big in the winter. Camping is permitted in 135 units at 30 locations.

SALMON NATIONAL FOREST

Office of the Forest Supervisor: Forest Service Building, Salmon, ID 83467 Some wild country is found in this forest, as is the Lewis and Clark trail; they discovered the same thing, as anyone who read the report will testify. Lakes and streams are numerous, with such eerie titles as River of No Return. Camping is permitted in 199 units at 17 locations.

ST. JOE NATIONAL FOREST

Office of the Forest Supervisor: St. Maries, ID 83861 Numerous trails cut through the forest. Many rivers and rugged country means great fishing and hunting. Camping is permitted in 93 units at 10 campsites.

SAWTOOTH NATIONAL FOREST

Office of the Forest Supervisor: 1525 Addison Avenue East, Twin Falls, ID 83301 Interesting rock formations highlight this forest, which also offers boating, fishing, scenic hikes, and hunting. Camping is permitted in 575 units at 43 locations. There are five winter sports areas, so dress warmly late in the fall.

TARGHEE NATIONAL FOREST

Office of the Forest Supervisor: 420 N. Bridge Street, St. Anthony, ID 83445 Another of the state's 1.5-million-plus acre forests, this offers boating, water sports, fishing, hunting and scenic routes as drawing points for the vacationer. Many rivers and streams present breath taking vistas for the hiker. Camping is permitted in 386 units at 25 locations.

ILLINOIS

SHAWNEE NATIONAL FOREST

Office of the Forest Supervisor: Harrisburg, IL 62946 Named after the famous Indian tribe that lived in the area, this forest has interesting prehistoric stone forts and Indian mounds for the geologically-minded camper. Many streams are great for the fisherman, and some of the best bird

Lamer Falls is often called the Grand Canyon of the Yellowstone National Park.

Left: The Rocky Mountains offer the backpacker a variety of terrain. From well travel marked trails to the more rugged rarely travel areas.

The Tuckerman Ravine Trail is one of the many access trails to Mount Washington and the Appalachian Trail. A backpacker's paradise.

hunting in the nation is prevalent here. Camping is permitted in 303 units at 13 locations.

INDIANA
HOOSIER NATIONAL FOREST
Office of the Forest Supervisor: Bedford, IN 47421 Migrating buffalo passed through this area for years, and the forest retains the atmosphere to this day. Water sports are big during the summer months in the lakes and streams. Many scenic routes pass areas of historical value, and the changing of the seasons is a sight unparalleled during the fall months. Hunting is a prime pastime in this area. Camping is permitted in 215 units at four sites.

KENTUCKY
DANIEL BOONE NATIONAL FOREST
Office of the Forest Supervisor: P. O. Building, Winchester, KY 40391 Located close to the town named after the famous American pioneer, Boonesboro, this forest generally is packed during the summer months. Many limestone caves await exploration by the hiker who takes time from his scenic cruising. The climate is temperate during

the summer, but expect some rain now and again. Camping is permitted in 169 units at 12 locations.

LOUISIANA
KISATCHE NATIONAL FOREST
Office of the Forest Supervisor: 250 Shreveport Highway, Pineville LA 71360 Located in the heart of the Bayou country, this forest houses the oldest city in the state, Natchitoches. Scenic routes pass by colonial homes that only the South could produce. Great fishing in the many lakes and streams, and some of the best bird hunting in the country is found here. Camping is permitted in 174 units at 11 locations. Get there early, and don't forget the bug juice.

MICHIGAN
HIAWATHA NATIONAL FOREST
Office of the Forest Supervisor: Escanaba, MI 49829 A fishing forest if ever there was one, this harbors part of Lakes Huron, Michigan and Superior, in addition to numerous smaller lakes and streams. Canoeing is a big sport here, as is hiking on forest trails, cycling down scenic

Shooting the rapids down the North Fork of the Feather River in the Plumas National Park is a pleasant diversion for the hiker.

routes or taking refreshing dips in the cool waters. Some great deer and bird hunting is found in the forest. Camping is permitted in 688 units at 23 locations. Get there early. Groups reservations are accepted.

HURON NATIONAL FOREST

Office of the Forest Supervisor: Cadillac, MI 49601 Named after the mighty warriors of the Huron tribe, this forest is easily reached from the southern portions of the state. It features water sports, scenic routes and historical monuments. Fishing and hunting are good, and winter sports like skiing are big during that period of the year. Camping is permitted in 203 units at 13 locations.

MANISTEE NATIONAL FOREST

Office of the Forest Supervisor: Cadillac, MI 49601 A beautiful site for the camper during the summer months, this area has many scenic routes in addition to the fishing

and hunting attractions. Camping is permitted in 395 units at 17 locations. It's popular during the summer months, so arrive early or be left out.

OTTAWA NATIONAL FOREST

Office of the Forest Supervisor: Ironwood, MI 49938 For those who have never seen a fish hatchery, this is the forest to visit. Camping climate is good, and water sports, fishing and hunting are prime reasons for its filling each summer. Heavy snows are endured in the winter months. Camping is permitted in 368 units at 23 locations.

MINNESOTA

CHIPPEWA NATIONAL FOREST

Office of the Forest Supervisor: Cass Lake, MN 56633 Named after and home of the Chippewa Indians, this forest has water sports, fishing and hunting as main attractors during the summer months, and winter sports during that

For spectacular scenery and quiet solitude, few places
can match the Rocky Mountains in the western states.

period. Camping is permitted in 513 units at 25 locations.
Come early.

SUPERIOR NATIONAL FOREST
Office of the Forest Supervisor: Duluth, MN 55801 This
mammoth forest comprises more than two million acres,
with over 5,000 lakes of varying size in it. There are more
than a million acres of virgin timber alone, which means
some seclusion. It also harbors the Boundary Waters Canoe
Area. Camping usually is pretty competitive, with 714 units
at 35 locations. Come early.

MISSISSIPPI

BIENVILLE NATIONAL FOREST
Office of the Forest Supervisor: Box 1291, Jackson, MS
39205 This state also has some fine fishing waters, and this
forest has numerous lakes in it. In addition, the relatively
level structure of the countryside promotes good hiking,
although a few steep grades await to challenge muscles.
Camping is permitted in 70 units at four locations. Expect
warm summer weather.

DELTA NATIONAL FOREST
Office of the Forest Supervisor: Box 1291, Jackson, MS
39205 Water sports are big during the summer months, but
fishing is on the upswing. Some great waterfowl hunting is
to be had at Greentree Reservoir. Expect rain during the
summer. Camping is permitted in four units at one location.

DESOTO NATIONAL FOREST
Office of the Forest Supervisor: Box 1291, Jackson, MS
39205 For those who like to watch gun dogs work, this is
the place to visit. It is the home of the South Mississippi
Gun and Dog Club field trails. There also are hunting and
fishing. Camping is permitted in 25 units at four locations.
Get there early.

HOLLY SPRINGS NATIONAL FOREST
Office of the Forest Supervisor: Box 1291, Jackson, MS
39205 A small forest of nearly 150,000 acres, it also
features dog trails, some hunting and fishing, in season.
Water sports draw some visitors, while others come to
examine the soil erosion projects currently underway.
Camping is permitted in 9 units at two locations.

HOMOCHITTO NATIONAL FOREST
Office of the Forest Supervisor: Box 1291, Jackson, MS
39205 There are numerous forest management projects

Dillion, MT 59725 Named after the Beaverhead River within its boundaries, this forest is comprised of some real rough area. Many historical locations like the Big Hole Battlefield Monument and Sacajawea Memorial Area make this site interesting out of the usual. Many roads and trails are suitable for the hiker. Camping in the two-million-plus acre forest is permitted in 194 units at 19 locations.

BITTERROOT NATIONAL FOREST
Office of the Forest Supervisor: 316 N. 3rd Street, Hamilton, MT 59840 Many scenic routes await the camper to this forest, and such historically-interesting scenes like Indian hieroglyphics and Fort Owen add to its attractiveness. Many lakes offer water sport opportunities. Hot springs bubble in varied locations. The Bitterroot Valley is wonderful scenery. Camping is permitted in 95 units at 15 different locations.

CUSTER NATIONAL FOREST
Office of the Forest Supervisor: 1015 Broadwater, Billings, MT 59103 This forest features many high peaks. There are numerous lakes and streams for the angler, and some fine hunting area for the hunter. Camping is permitted in 219 units at 15 sites.

DEERLODGE NATIONAL FOREST
Office of the Forest Supervisor: 107 E. Granite Street, Butte, MT 59701 Spectacular scenery awaits the visitor to this forest, which has much rugged terrain, including the Anaconda-Pintlar Wilderness. Alpine lakes and streams are great for fishing, and the habitat is superb for game. Camping is permitted in 201 units at 19 locations.

FLATHEAD NATIONAL FOREST
Office of the Forest Supervisor: North Main at Washington, Kalispell, MT 59901 Scenery includes varied geological formations, mountains and valleys. Boating and canoeing are attractive features, including fishing and hunting. Winter sports take over late in the year. Camping is permitted in 171 units at 8 locations. Arrive at the forest early.

GALLATIN NATIONAL FOREST
Office of the Forest Supervisor: P. O. Building, Bozeman, MT 59715 The climate is relatively cool throughout the year, with deep snow during winter. Many lakes and thousands of miles of streams are found in the forest, which do much to interest fishermen. Hunters climb the steep slopes and lush valleys in pursuit of their quarry. Camping is permitted in 323 units at 20 sites.

HELENA NATIONAL FOREST
Office of the Forest Supervisor: Steamboat Block, Helena, MT 59601 Ghost towns, lakes and streams, along with the Continental Divide, are drawing features of this forest. There are numerous boat trips throughout the summer season. Camping is permitted in 134 units at 10 sites.

KOOTENAI NATIONAL FOREST
Office of the Forest Supervisor: 418 Mineral Avenue, Libby, MT 59923 Many scenic trails are open to the hiker in this forest, which is located partly in Idaho. The numerous lakes and streams are prime for the fisherman, and the territory is favorable for the hunter. Camping is permitted in 164 units at 14 locations.

underway all the time at this forest, because it is one of the finest natural growing sites for timber in the States. Water sports are good, as is some fishing and hunting. Camping is permitted in 23 units at one location, although camping is also permitted at three picnic sites.

TOMBIGBEE NATIONAL FOREST
Office of the Forest Supervisor: Box 1291, Jackson, MS 39205 For the history-minded, there are numerous Indian mounds at this forest, which is relatively small — 65,000 acres. Water sports, fishing and limited hunting are drawing cards. Camping is permitted in 37 units at two locations.

MISSOURI
CLARK NATIONAL FOREST
Office of the Forest Supervisor: Rolla, MO 65401 A nice spot to witness the fall transformation of the trees in the Ozark Mountains, this forest has many trails that are suitable for hiking. Many streams and lakes are for the piscator, and there is some hunting of squirrels, raccoon and fox. There are 262 camping units at 16 locations, and they fill fast.

MARK TWAIN NATIONAL FOREST
Office of the Forest Supervisor: Springfield, MO 65806 Float trips on john-boats, as immortalized by author Twain, are offered to the visitor to this forest. Many caverns, mountains and streams break up the beautiful Ozark Mountains. Water sports are big, as are horseback riding, forest tours, trails and hunting. Camping is permitted in 151 units at 11 locations.

MONTANA
BEAVERHEAD NATIONAL FOREST
Office of the Forest Supervisor: Federal Building,

Jupiter Terrace Hot Springs in the Yellowstone National Park. A variety of outdoor activities are available.

LEWIS AND CLARK NATIONAL FOREST

Office of the Forest Supervisor: Federal Building, Great Falls, MT 59401 Named after the two great explorers and their expedition to the Pacific Ocean, this forest is filled with limestone canyons and rolling mountains. The hikers may sweat slightly, but the scenery is worth it. Fishing and hunting are big in this forest, which permits camping in 145 units at 13 spots.

LOLO NATIONAL FOREST

Office of the Forest Supervisor: P. O. Building, Missoula, MT 59801 This forest also extends into Idaho, and catches bits of the Selway-Bitterroot Wilderness. Clark Fork and Blackfoot Rivers are but two of the bodies of water found in the forest, which promises good fishing for anglers. Hunting for elk, deer and bear is popular. Camping is permitted in 151 units at 14 locations.

NEBRASKA
NEBRASKA NATIONAL FOREST and OGLALA NATIONAL GRASSLAND

Office of the Forest Supervisor: P. O. Building, Lincoln, NE 68508 This entire area is within a game refuge, home of such species as mule deer, antelope, great blue heron, grouse, prairie chicken, pheasant and wild turkey, so don't leave the camera at home. There are numerous forest plantations on sand hills. Swimming and fishing are the main types of water sports. No hunting is allowed. Camping is permitted in 44 units at 3 sites.

NEVADA
HUMBOLDT NATIONAL FOREST

Office of the Forest Supervisor: 976 Mountain City Highway, Elko, NV 89801 This two-million-plus acre forest is dotted with streams and lakes. Because Nevada has lots of desert, don't feel that the forest is nothing but the same — there is the Jarbridge Wilderness located within its boundaries. There are many old mining camps that the hiker can visit. Camping is permitted in 274 units at 23 locations.

TOIYABE NATIONAL FOREST

Office of the Forest Supervisor: P. O. Box 1331, Reno, NV 89504 The forest, which spills over into California, has great fishing and hunting, in addition to attractions like good trails for hiking. Winter sports are big in the area during that season, but the forest generally is warm during

Hiking along the Toxaway River
in the Pisgah National Forest.

the summer months. Camping is permitted in 704 units at 29 locations. Arrive early in the day during the summer.

NEW HAMPSHIRE
WHITE MOUNTAIN
Office of the Forest Supervisor: Laconia, NH 03246 Many miles of scenic trails with side diversions like fishing, hunting, swimming, hiking and rock climbing. There are numerous lakes and miles of streams to provide a lush setting for this forest, which is located partly in Maine. Camping is permitted in 741 units at 18 locations.

NEW MEXICO
CARSON NATIONAL FOREST
Office of the Forest Supervisor: Taos, NM 87571 The Rio Grande Valley, rimmed by the Sangre de Cristo Mountains, offers beautiful scenery. There are museums and archeological ruins prevalent in the forest, which encompasses nearly 1.5 million acres. Camping is permitted in 19 various campgrounds.

CIBOLA NATIONAL FOREST
Office of the Forest Supervisor: Albuquerque, NM 87103 Numerous prehistoric ruins and Pueblo Indian Villages are the primary drawing factors. There are numerous mountain ranges through the forest, which tend to make hiking somewhat difficult, although Sandia Crest at 10,700 feet is accessible by aerial tramway. Camping is permitted in 11 separate locations in the forest.

GILA NATIONAL FOREST
Office of the Forest Supervisor: Silver City, NM 88061 Terrain is exceptionally varied in this forest, from semi-desert to alpine peaks. Elevations range from about 4,500 feet to over 10,000. As much of the forest is undeveloped at this time, much of the real atmosphere of wildness remains for those who wish to tackle it on foot. Dress for hot weather during the summer, although the nights get chilly, even in the desert. Camping is permitted in 15 locations.

LINCOLN NATIONAL FOREST
Office of the Forest Supervisor: Alamogordo, NM 88310 Located near Capitan, the birthplace of Smokey the Bear, this forest is great for the backpacker. Many mountain roads exist, at the summit of one is the Mescalero Indian Reservation. Camping is permitted in 11 locations, which usually are full with fishermen and hunters.

SANTA FE NATIONAL FOREST
Office of the Forest Supervisor: Sante Fe, NM 87501 Many ancient ruins, Spanish missions, cliff dwellings and Indian Pueblos are of interest to many visitors. Hunting and fishing are big attractions, and the 27 campgrounds generally keep pretty full. Arrive early in the day, and don't forget the suntan lotion.

NORTH CAROLINA
CROATAN NATIONAL FOREST
Office of the Forest Supervisor: Box 731, Asheville, NC 28801 Much memorabilia of the Civil War remains behind, and attracts many visitors each year. There also is fine hunting, fishing and boating to be had on or near the large lakes inside its boundaries. Camping is permitted in 13 units at one location.

NANTAHALA NATIONAL FOREST
Office of the Forest Supervisor: Box 731, Asheville, NC 28802 An exceptionally beautiful area when the flowers are in bloom, this forest contains more than sixty miles of the Appalachian Trail, along with other scenic vistas. Many lakes and streams are located within the forest, which harbor fine examples of bass and trout. Camping is permitted in 311 units at 8 campsites and one picnic area.

PISGAH NATIONAL FOREST
Office of the Forest Supervisor: Box 731, Asheville, NC 28802 numerous scenic trails accessible on foot make this an interesting forest to visit. One area of the forest to avoid is that which contains Mt. Mitchell, the highest point east of the Mississippi River at 6,684 feet. Several wilderness areas and the Appalachian Trail are but a few of this forest's attractions. Camping is permitted in 288 units at 9 locations, and at two picnic sites.

OHIO
WAYNE NATIONAL FOREST
Office of the Forest Supervisor: Bedford, IN 47421 The area is particularly beautiful during the fall months, when the dense stands of hardwoods change from their greenish summer color to blazing oranges and red. If visiting at this time of year, dress warmly. Camping is permitted in 106 units at two locations.

OREGON
DESCHUTES NATIONAL FOREST
Office of the Forest Supervisor: P. O. Box 751, Bend, OR 97701 A truly beautiful forest of just over 1.5 million acres, it offers much to the backpacker. Nature trails, water sports, pack trips and the like are available, and if it's the right time of year, a few berries can be picked. Make sure, however, that you check what you have picked with a ranger to avoid eating a poisonous fruit. Camping is permitted in 1,756 units in 88 locations.

FREMONT NATIONAL FOREST
Office of the Forest Supervisor: P. O. Box 551, Lakeview, OR 97630 It's not unusual to see antelope roaming about, as they are protected in this forest. The forest also contains the second largest vertical fault in the world,

View from the Great Smoky Mountain National Park in North Carolina.

the Abert geological fault. Camping is permitted in 166 units at 22 locations.

MALHEUR NATIONAL FOREST

Office of the Forest Supervisor: 139 N.E. Dayton Street, John Day, OR 97845 Many fossil beds of prehistoric plants and the Strawberry Mountain Wilderness area are but two of the outstanding features of this forest. Hunting, fishing, horseback riding are main attractions. Camping is permitted in 205 units at 18 locations.

MOUNT HOOD NATIONAL FOREST

Office of the Forest Supervisor: P. O. Box 16040, Portland, OR 97266 Much of this forest's terrain is in two directions, either up or down. Hunting and fishing are big sports in this forest. Pick your own huckleberries. Camping is permitted in 1,181 units in 104 locations.

OCHOCO NATIONAL FOREST

Office of the Forest Supervisor: P. O. Box 490, Pineville, OR 97754 Many early range wars were fought in this territory, and a couple of frontier forts remain for the current visitor. Ponderosa stands are impressive, as is the

hunting and fishing potential. Camping is permitted in 144 units at 11 sites.

ROGUE RIVER NATIONAL FOREST

Office of the Forest Supervisor: P. O. Box 520, Medford, OR 97501 This forest receives it name from the mighty river that courses through it, down into California. Numerous scenic trails travel through beautiful areas where once vicious wars were fought between cavalry and Indian. Water sports are popular in this forest, as is hunting and fishing. Camping is permitted in 285 units at 27 different locations.

SISKIYOU NATIONAL FOREST

Office of the Forest Supervisor: P. O. Box 440, Grants Pass, OR 97526 Located along the Oregon coast part-way into California, this forest is home of numerous rare species of plants. It is exceptionally beautiful during the spring, when all manner of wildflowers bloom in profusion. Fishing is spectacular along several of the rivers and streams, along with hunting in the forest area. Camping is permitted in 190 units at 21 locations. A popular area, so arrive early in the summertime.

The Shenandoah National Park in Virginia is a panorama of smiling valleys and tree-covered mountains.

SIUSLAW NATIONAL FOREST

Office of the Forest Supervisor: P. O. Box 1148, Corvallis, OR 97330 Located along the Pacific Coast, this forest offers something unusual in many — clam digging. It also features miles of sand dunes, ocean, lake and stream fishing and many other attractions. Take care to pack warm clothes as the Pacific breeze sometimes gets chilly. Camping is permitted in 570 units at 30 locations.

UMATILLA NATIONAL FOREST

Office of the Forest Supervisor: 2517 S.W. Hailey Avenue, Pendleton, OR 97801 Numerous scenic routes offer spectacular vistas of canyons, mountain ranges and rivers. Water sports are popular, as is hunting for big game and upland game birds. Fishing is excellent in this forest, which extends across the Washington border. Camping is permitted in 326 units at 39 locations.

UMPQUA NATIONAL FOREST

Office of the Forest Supervisor: P. O. Box 1008, Roseburg, OR 97470 Filled with lakes and rivers, this forest offers beautiful scenery. Water sports are popular, as is berry picking in season. Again, check what you pick before eating it; belly aches on vacations are no fun. Camping is permitted in 661 units at 35 locations.

WALLOWA-WHITMAN NATIONAL FOREST

Office of the Forest Supervisor: P. O. Box 471, Baker, OR 97814 Located at a fairly high altitude — high enough to contain snowcapped peaks the year 'round and glaciers — this forest has exceptional scenery and wildlife rarely seen by man. Many lakes and streams appeal to the piscator, and the hunter can find plenty of room to stalk his quarry of elk, deer and bear, among some birds. Camping is permitted in 510 units at 46 sites.

Well marked trails crisscross the Willaby Creek Area in the Olympic National Forest.

WILLIAMETTE NATIONAL FOREST

Office of the Forest Supervisor: P. O. Box 1272, Eugene, OR 97401 This is the most heavily-timbered forest in the U.S., which means breath-taking scenery for back-packers. Other features include water sport possibilities, fishing and hunting, along with berry picking in season. Many lakes and waterfalls, wilderness areas and volcanic lavabeds await the curious. Camping is permitted in 949 units at 68 sites.

WINEMA NATIONAL FOREST

Office of the Forest Supervisor: P. O. Box 1390, Klamath Falls, OR 97601 Nearly half of this forest's 908,000-plus acres once belonged exclusively to the Klamath Indians, and some of their artifacts remain. Many lakes and streams present a beautiful picture to the viewer. Camping is permitted in 221 units at 9 locations.

PENNSYLVANIA
ALLEGHENY NATIONAL FOREST

Office of the Forest Supervisor: Warren, PA 16365 A couple of virgin stands of timber and numerous lakes highlight this forest of nearly 500,000 acres. Fishing and hunting, along with water sports, are prime attractions and the campgrounds fill fast during the summer season. Camping is permitted in 442 units at 16 locations.

SOUTH CAROLINA
FRANCIS MARION NATIONAL FOREST

Office of the Forest Supervisor: 1813 Main Street, Columbia, SC 29201 Water sports are the big attractions to the forest, along with fishing in many of the bays thought caused by meteoric falls. Ruins of early colonial settlements still exist. The climate generally is temperate during the summer months. Camping is permitted in 31 units at four locations.

SUMTER NATIONAL FOREST

Office of the Forest Supervisor: 1813 Main Street, Columbia SC 29201 Numerous scenic trails are open to the hiker, in view of the Piedmont and Blue Ridge Mountain ranges which generally have a profusion of flowering plants. Some fishing is prevalent in lakes and streams, and quail hunting is permissible during hunting season. Camping is permitted in 112 units at five sites.

SOUTH DAKOTA
BLACK HILLS NATIONAL FOREST

Office of the Forest Supervisor: Forest Service Office Building, P. O. Box 792, Custer, SD 57730 Many individuals famous in Western lore are buried in this area, including Wild Bill Hickok, Deadwood Dick, Calamity Jane and Preacher Smith. The scene of the historic gold rush, this forest has many scenic hiking trails. Mount Rushmore National Memorial alone draws many tourists and campers Camping is permitted in 629 units at 23 locations.

TENNESSEE
CHEROKEE NATIONAL FOREST

Office of the Forest Supervisor: Box 400, Cleveland, TN 37312 There is rugged mountain country present here, but one look at the Ducktown Copper Basin makes the rough hiking more than worth it. For Ducktown Copper Basin is one of the nation's worst examples of deforestation also contains the Boles Field Fox Hunt Area. Camping is permitted in 43 units at three locations.

TEXAS
ANGELINA NATIONAL FOREST

Office of the Forest Supervisor: Box 969, Lufkin, TX 75902 Some of the finest bass fishing in the country is to be found in Sam Rayburn Reservoir, within this forest. The predominately flat area is perfect for hiking, although it becomes quite warm during the summer months. Camping is permitted in 167 units at six locations.

DAVY CROCKETT NATIONAL FOREST

Office of the Forest Supervisor: Box 969, Lufkin, TX

An aerial view of the south slope of Mount Rainier. At its base there are numerous trails suitable for backpacking.

75902 A relatively small forest of only 161,556 acres, it houses hardwoods and pines that are enjoyable to hike through. There is some fishing and other types of water sports. Camping is permitted in 59 units at three locations.

SABINE NATIONAL FOREST

Office of the Forest Supervisor: Box 969, Lufkin, TX 75902 Toledo Bend Reservoir is regarded by many professional bass anglers to be the ultimate in fishing spots. There are stands of pine and hardwoods within the forest, which also contains the Boles Field Fox Hunt Area. Camping is permitted in 43 units at three locations.

SAM HOUSTON NATIONAL FOREST

Office of the Forest Supervisor: Box 969, Lufkin, TX 75902 Part of the Big Thicket area of Texas, this forest has some of the roughest country imaginable, However, some is located on flat or relatively level ground, which makes travel easy. Fishing and some hunting are about the only other attractions besides the water sports. Camping is permitted in 73 units at two locations.

UTAH
ASHLEY NATIONAL FOREST

Office of the Forest Supervisor: 437 E. Main Street, Vernal, UT 84078 Numerous scenic gorges and natural erosion formations are accessible to the camper in this forest, which totals over 1.25-million arces. Water sports, fishing and hunting are popular here, with with the variety of streams and lakes present. The elevation at some points is quite high, but it is doubtful the packer will reach such heights. Camping is permitted in 612 units at 37 locations.

CACHE NATIONAL FOREST

Office of the Forest Supervisor: 429 S. Main Street, P. O. Box 448, Logan, UT 84321 An exceptionally rough forest. The altitude is quite high, and numerous mountain ranges are present. There is a variety of water sports opportunities, along with hiking trails and the like. Camping is permitted in 370 units at 24 different locations. Dress warmly.

DIXIE NATIONAL FOREST

Office of the Forest Supervisor: 500 S. Main Street, Cedar City UT 84720 Cliffs of every color highlight a visit to this forest, which also contains a peak from which it is possible to see into the states of Colorado, Arizona, Nevada and Utah. Much of the forest is not accessible by road. Camping is permitted in 508 units at 19 locations.

FISHLAKE NATIONAL FOREST

Office of the Forest Supervisor: 170 N. Main, Richfield, UT 84701 Numerous scenic trails are open to the hiker in

Winter sports highlight the activities at the Mt. Hood National Park in Oregon.

this forest, which hosts some rough back country. A multitude of lakes and streams make the site popular for the angler and its remoteness in places is ideal for the big game hunter. Among the attractions which may interest the backpacker is the Petrified Wood Scenic Area. None of the existing material is removable, and stiff fines are levied for those who attempt such action. Camping is permitted in 166 units at 16 sites throughout the forest.

MANTI-LASAL NATIONAL FOREST

Office of the Forest Supervisor: 350 E. Main Street, Price, UT 84501 Located partially in Colorado, this forest features various Indian hieroglyphics and cliff dwellings, along with the world's largest Aspen trees. It is at quite a high altitude, but offers spectacular vistas from Skyline Road, which penetrates the high alpine meadows and forest groves. Camping is permitted in 231 units at 14 locations.

UNITA NATIONAL FOREST

Office of the Forest Supervisor: 290 N. University Avenue, P. O. Box 1428, Provo, UT 84601 High mountains rising from surrounding desert landscape make up this forest, which has numerous scenic routes throughout its borders. Stands of hardwoods make the fall transition memorable in the forest, located near Provo. For those wishing there is a six-mile hike to the top of 12,000-foot Mt. Timpanogos. Camping is permitted in 706 units at 32 locations.

WASATCH NATIONAL FOREST

Office of the Forest Supervisor: 4438 Federal Building, 125 S. State, Salt Lake City, UT 84111 Located right outside the hot summertime city of Salt Lake, this forest appeals to anglers, hunters, hikers, skiers, skaters and cyclists. There are numerous lakes and streams, and the snowfall during the winter months is great enough to support two recreational areas. Don't plan on arriving late in the day at this forest, because you'll never get a campsite. Camping is permitted in 1,220 units at 42 locations.

VERMONT

GREEN MOUNTAIN NATIONAL FOREST

Office of the Forest Supervisor: Rutland, VT 05702 This forest offers something for just about everyone. There are New England villages, beautiful valleys and rugged mountains, all with good roads save perhaps the latter. Many historic landmarks are present here, and many trails are open for the hiker. Water sports, in addition to hunting, fishing and winter sports, lure many to the forest yearly. Camping is permitted in 78 units at five locations. Don't come late.

VIRGINIA

GEORGE WASHINGTON NATIONAL FOREST

Office of the Forest Supervisor: Federal Building,

263

Overlooking Wonder Lake, Mount McKinley rises majestically in the background.

Harrisonburg, VA 22801 As would be expected, this forest is rich in historical landmarks and heritage. It includes the Blue Bridge, Shenandoah, Allegheny and Massanutten Ranges of mountains, along with many trails. Hunting is popular, as is fishing and exploring. Camping is permitted in 233 units at 10 sites.

JEFFERSON NATIONAL FOREST

Office of the Forest Supervisor: Carlton Terrace Building, 920 Jefferson Street S.W., Roanoke, VA 24001 The main transitional zone between northern and southern species of flora and fauna takes place in this forest, which also contains much Civil War memorabilia. Fishing, hiking, and hunting are activities that call many to the forest. Camping is permitted in 142 units at seven different spots.

WASHINGTON

COLVILLE NATIONAL FOREST

Office of the Forest Supervisor: Colville, WA 99114 This forest is popular with visitors during berry season, when they often fill buckets with sweet huckleberries. It also is noted for its edible mushrooms but take pains to check your collection with a ranger before eating them or you may suffer just that! Water sports are big, as is hunting and fishing. Camping is permitted in 126 units at 13 locations.

GIFFORD PINCHOT NATIONAL FOREST

Office of the Forest Supervisor: P. O. Box 449, Vancouver, WA 98660 Break out the berry buckets when visiting this forest in season, for this is the location of historic Indian Huckleberry fields. Other attractions include many lakes and streams. When berry picking, make plenty of noise: You may be sharing the harvest with a hungry bear or two. Camping is permitted in 1,186 units at 63 sites.

MOUNT BAKER NATIONAL FOREST

Office of the Forest Supervisor: P. O. Box 845, Bellingham, WA 98225 If visiting this forest, you no doubt will stand and crane your neck in awe at the 200-foot Douglas fir trees that grow here in heavy stands. The altitude is high, and the forest sports snowcapped peaks the year 'round. Some of the area is still wilderness and passable only by foot. Camping is permitted in 649 units at 50 locations. Hunting and fishing are popular, so arrive early.

OKANOGAN NATIONAL FOREST

Office of the Forest Supervisor: P. O. Box 950, Okanogan, WA 98840 Some primitive country exists in this 1.5-million-plus acre forest, which hosts several glaciers and snowcapped peaks. Water sports are popular and extensive hiking trails exist. Camping is permitted in 325 units at 53 locations. Pack the winter woolies.

OLYMPIC NATIONAL FOREST

Office of the Forest Supervisor: Federal Building, Olympia, WA 98501 Numerous lakes and streams are found in this rain forest-like spot, which means the camper had better not forget the rain gear. Fishing and hunting is outstanding, as is the scenery observed from the roadways. Camping is permitted in 309 units at 20 locations.

SNOQUALMIE NATIONAL FOREST
Office of the Forest Supervisor: 905 Second Avenue Building, Room 208, Seattle, WA 98104 All of the previously-mentioned activities found in other Washington forests are present here. Camping is permitted in 832 units at 57 locations.

WENATCHEE NATIONAL FOREST
Office of the Forest Supervisor: P. O. Box 811, Wenatchee, WA 98801 Water sports, fishing, hunting and sightseeing draw many visitors to the forest each year. As an added bonus, there is the Tumwater Botanical Garden with its array of rare flowers. The temperature drops rapidly in the fall months. Camping is permitted in 782 units at 88 sites.

WEST VIRGINIA
MONONGAHELA NATIONAL FOREST
Office of the Forest Supervisor: Elkins, WV 26241 A truely beautiful spot on the East Coast. Water sports, fishing and hunting are prime in this forest, which measures over 800,000 acres. Camping is permitted in 326 units at 15 sites. Group camping is possible.

WISCONSIN
CHEQUAMEGON NATIONAL FOREST
Office of the Forest Supervisor: Park Falls, WI 54552 Wisconsin is muskellunge country, and the fighting fish is found in numerous lakes and streams throughout the forest. It also is popular for hiking trails. Hunting is a big sport. Group campgrounds available by reservation. Camping otherwise is permitted in 351 units at 20 locations.

NICOLET NATIONAL FOREST
Office of the Forest Supervisor: Rhinelander, WI 54501 A rather wet forest what with all of the streams, lakes and swamps within its borders, this forest naturally is a haven for the angler. Camping is permitted in 539 units at 24 locations.

WYOMING
BIGHORN NATIONAL FOREST
Office of the Forest Supervisor: P. O. Box 914, Sheridan, WY 82801 Named for the Big Horn Mountains, presumably named for the Big Horn sheep, this forest is in some rugged country. Hundreds of lakes and streams criss-cross through the forest, which gets chilly in the evenings. Indian relics are a curiosity. Hunting for big game and fishing are popular. Camping is permitted in 335 units at 39 sites.

BRIDGER NATIONAL FOREST
Office of the Forest Supervisor: Forest Service Building, Kemmerer, WY 83101 Looking over this area makes one realize just how tough the early pioneers and mountain men must have been to survive in it. Rugged primitive areas still make up a big portion of the 1.7-million acre forest. Many trails are for the in-shape hiker. Camping is permitted in 314 units at 22 locations. This is prime hunting area, so plan on arriving before the hunters do — which is pretty early!

MEDICINE BOW NATIONAL FOREST
Office of the Forest Supervisor: Box 3355, University Station, Laramie, WY 82070 A site popular for its sporting capability, this forest draws many during hunting and fish-

ing season. Look for the beavers at work, or view their numerous colonial dwelling sites. Camping is permitted in 329 units at 16 locations.

SHOSHONE NATIONAL FOREST
Office of the Forest Supervisor: Blair Building No. 1, 1731 Sheridan Avenue, Cody, WY 82414 Some really rugged country prevails in this forest, including the largest glaciers in the Rocky Mountains. Much of the forest is wilderness area, cool and windy even during summer. Camping is permitted without reservation in this forest named after the famous tribe of Indians.

TETON NATIONAL FOREST
Office of the Forest Supervisor: Forest Service Building, Jackson, WY 83001 This forest comprises much of the same area as Grand Teton National Park. Many species of wildlife can be observed here, and camping is permitted in 143 units at 10 locations.

BACKPACKER'S GUIDE TO EQUIPMENT

With new firms entering the field of backpacking equipment almost daily, the catalog that follows can hardly be considered complete. However, it should afford the reader an opportunity to compare the various types and designs, selecting what he feels is best suited to his own needs.

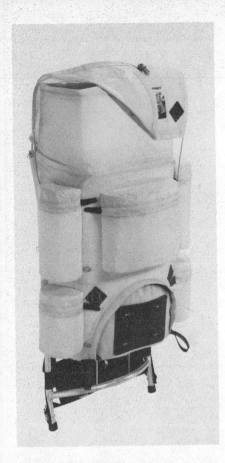

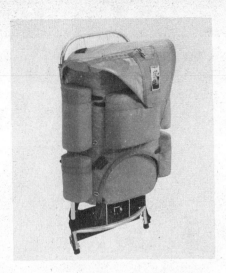

CONQUEST Model 263: Same as 264, except no extension collar, six leather accessory strap holders — two on bottom, three on flap, one on main bag. One ice axe loop on bottom of bag. Weight: 48 oz. Capacity: 3292 total cu. in.

CONQUEST Model 261: Large single-cavity bag of 420 Denier, 8-oz., waterproof, urethane-coated nylon pack cloth. Five outside pockets, weather covers over YKK number five self-repairing nylon coil zippers. Large zipper pulls, with leather assist pull tabs per pocket. Oversized pack cover flap with two map pockets and Velcro closure. Six accessory strap holders — two on bottom, two on bag, two on lid; ice axe loop on bottom of bag. All-nylon tie cords, brass grommets, aluminum pins and steel wire locking rings for attachment to frame. Aluminum hold-open bar for ease of loading. Weight: 32 oz. Capacity: 3414 total cu. in.

CONQUEST Model 264: Large divided compartment unit made from 420 Denier, 8-oz., waterproof, urethane-coated nylon' pack cloth. Upper compartment separated from lower by shelf set midway in bag. Hold-open bar for easy loading. Cutaway corners on shelf for tent poles, etc. Permanent 10" extendable collar for extra load space. Nylon drawstring closure through brass grommet. Lower compartment access through arc-zippered flap with zipper covers and twin zipper pulls. YKK number five self-repairing nylon coil zippers. Leather zipper assist pull tabs on five large outside pockets. Map pocket with Velcro closure on oversized cover flap. Eight leather accessory strap holders — four on lid, two on main bag, two on bottom of bag, with two ice axe loops on bottom of bag. All-nylon tie cords, brass grommets, aluminum pins and steel wire locking rings for attachment to frame. Approximate weight: 52 oz. Capacity: 4642 total cu. in.

CONQUEST Model 262: Same as 264, except two leather accessory strap holders — one on lid, one on main bag; one ice axe loop on bottom of bag. Weight: 36 oz. Capacity: 3449 total cu. in.

CONQUEST Model 260: Same as 261, except with three outside pockets. Weight: 30 oz. Capacity: 3097 total cu. in.

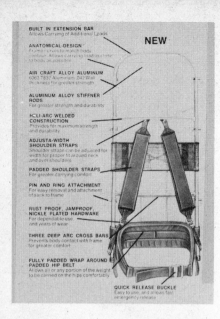

BUILT IN EXTENSION BAR
Allows Carrying of Additional Loads

NEW

ANATOMICAL DESIGN
Frame curves to match body contour. Allows carrying load as close to body as possible

AIR CRAFT ALLOY ALUMINUM
6063 T837 Aluminum .042 Wall thickness for greater strength

ALUMINUM ALLOY STIFFNER RODS
For greater strength and durability

HELI-ARC WELDED CONSTRUCTION
Provides for maximum strength and durability

ADJUSTA-WIDTH SHOULDER STRAPS
Shoulder straps can be adjusted for width for proper fit around neck and over shoulders

PADDED SHOULDER STRAPS
For greater carrying comfort

PIN AND RING ATTACHMENT
For easy removal and attachment of sack to frame

RUST PROOF, JAMPROOF, NICKLE PLATED HARDWARE
For dependable use and years of wear

THREE DEEP ARC CROSS BARS
Prevents body contact with frame for greater comfort

FULLY PADDED WRAP AROUND PADDED HIP BELT
Allows all or any portion of the weight to be carried on the hips comfortably

QUICK RELEASE BUCKLE
Easy to use, and allows fast emergency release

All packs for use with new Conquest Frame: Constructed of drawn seamless aluminum, .042 wall thickness heli-arc welded construction. Features as shown.

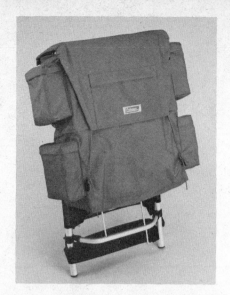

COLEMAN Backpack Frame And Sack: Urethane-coated, 8-oz. nylon pack. Sewn-on aluminum hold-open bar. Four side pockets and map pocket. Nylon-padded shoulder straps. Anodized aluminum frame. Sizes: small, medium, large and extra large.

HINE/SNOWBRIDGE Alpha: Features internal frame, two compartments. Lower compartment designed to hold winter down sleeping bag, with living necessities packed in upper section. Vertical divider in upper section and in-out snap clips on shoulder straps. Internal "X" Frame and modified yoke suspension system. Removable "X" stays for soft pack use. Four external pockets, crampon patches, ice axe loop and ski slots behind side pockets with tie-downs above and below. Two accessory patches under top flap for securing ropes, tent, etc. Alpha Special: Alpha equipped with additional map pocket on top flap, cross-chest strap and compression straps on bottom compartment. Mid-range and weight touring, backpacking and climbing. Weight: Alpha, 55 oz.; Alpha Special, 63 oz. Dimensions: 28x14x7½ in. Capacity: 3400 cu. in. Made of 8-oz. Cordura.

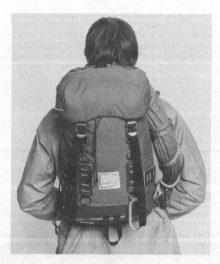

COLEMAN All-Around Day Pack: Big zippered pouch for easy storage of gear and provisions. Two side pockets. Utility flap to protect zipper, hold extra gear snugly, safely. Webbed nylon straps and waist belt to hold pack snug. Waterproof, nonshrinkable. Dimensions: 14x13x7 in. Weight: 12 oz.

HINE/SNOWBRIDGE Cirque I: Single-compartment soft pack for general day use. Features ½" foam backing pad in zippered envelope which doubles as map pocket if pad not in use. High-sided, full leather bottom, removable waist belt and thirteen accessory patches. Additional volume available with optional side pockets. Two sizes available. Rock or Alpine-style climbing, hiking or ski-touring pack. Weight: 34 oz. Dimensions: 20x5x11 in. Capacity: 1300 cu. in.

HINE/SNOWBRIDGE Chinquapin: Felt-padded leather, swing-mounted shoulder straps, removable aluminum stay bars, YKK coil zipper in large top flap pocket, drawstring closure on main compartment with Fixlock cord lock, canted leather bottom and removable waist belt. Weight: 31 oz. Dimensions: 16½x6x12 in. Capacity: 1425 cu. in.

HINE/SNOWBRIDGE Mountaineer: Felt-padded leather, swing-mounted shoulder straps, removable aluminum stay bars, YKK Delrin zippers, large leather bottoms. Three accessory strap holders on top flap, two extra large accessory strap holders on bottom. Top flap is extra packing compartment, has drawstring opener with Fixlock cord lock. Includes two permanently sewn-on side pockets, canted bottom to keep load close to the back, clip in-out shoulder straps for quick removal, and removable waist belt adjustable from either side. Used on long day hikes, climbs and ski tours; one-night bivouacs; cross-country hiking. Can be carry-on airline luggage. Weight: 43 oz. Dimensions: 18x6½x12 in. Ski Mountaineer: Same as Mountaineer, except has slots for skis behind side pockets. Side pocket dimensions: 9x3x5 in. Top pocket dimensions: 11x3x10 in.

HINE/SNOWBRIDGE Slant Line: Classic teardrop design with upper and lower compartments. Diagonal zippers with two sliders each allow access to both compartments at once. Swing-mounted shoulder straps of felt-padded leather, removable waist belt, ice axe carrier, hauling strap, two small accessory strap holders and canted nylon bottom. Weight: 18 oz. Dimensions: 17x6x11 in. Slant Line Deluxe: Same as Slant Line, except has leather bottom and larger accessory strap holders. Used on short hikes, ski tours, bicycle trips, climbs and around town general use. Weight: 28 oz. Dimensions: 17x6x11 in.

HINE/SNOWBRIDGE Day Pack: Rectangular shape, with 16" zipper all the way around the top front. Features front pocket for smaller items, swing-mounted shoulder straps, removable waist belt, hanging strap and covered zippers. Good for day hikes, ski tours, bike trips and as student's book pack. Weight: 16 oz. Dimensions: 16x5x12 in.

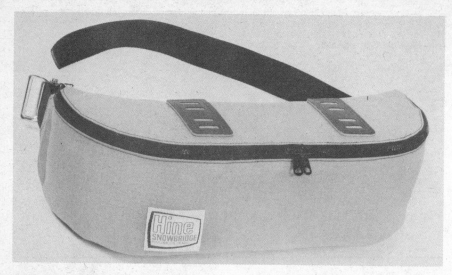

HINE/SNOWBRIDGE Powell Pack: Primarily designed for ski touring, but can be used as emergency pack. Large volume holds enough for daylong outing. Has two slides on top front zipper, two accessory strap holders on top, 2" wide waist belt. Contoured around wearer's back. Weight: 11 oz. Dimensions: 18x5½x5 in.

WENZEL Yucca Pack And Frame: Spring-bar frame of lightweight aluminum, with cargo shelf, backbands and foam-padded shoulder straps. Weight: 32 oz. Capacity: 1600 cu. in.

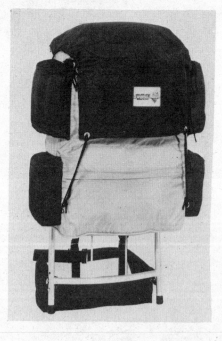

HINE/SNOWBRIDGE Basic: Used on short hikes, ski tours, bicycling and as a book pack. Drawstring closure with cord lock, top flap pocket, kangaroo pocket on front, nylon web shoulder straps, hang loop, double-sewn zipper, reinforced stitching at points of high stress, and D-rings for attachment of waist belt. Weight: 11 oz. Dimensions: 14x5½x10 in.

WENZEL Sierra: Offered in two sizes; 30x14½-in. frame with 2300 cu. in. capacity pack, and 34x14½-in. frame with 3000 cu. in. capacity pack. Anodized aluminum frames with ventilated nylon mesh backbands having double turnbuckle adjustment, padded shoulder straps and hip belt. Hold-open bar on pack top. Features two compartments, five exterior pockets with covered zippers and map pocket with Velcro closure.

HINE/SNOWBRIDGE Belt Pack: Used to sort items in larger pack. Weight: 2 oz. Dimensions: 7x2x4½ in.

WENZEL Sequoia Rucksack With Frame: Used with or without anodized aluminum A-frame. Has nylon backband, padded shoulder straps, detachable waist belt and two exterior pockets equipped with nylon covered zippers. Used for day hiking, ski touring and bicycling. Capacity: 1200 cu. in.

WENZEL Sun Valley Rucksack: Has one compartment, two exterior pockets and nylon shoulder strap. Capacity: 900 cu. in.

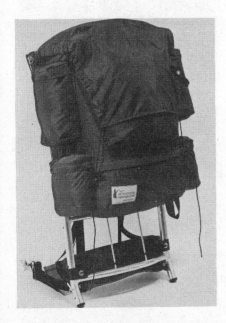

R.E.I. Super-Pak: Contoured frame made of high-strength aluminum alloy with tungsten-

arc welded joints. Hip-suspension system with foam-padded shoulder straps adjustable for length and shoulder width; 4½" wide, padded hip belt to eliminate floating; 5" wide backband. Available in medium (5'2" to 5'7"), large (5'8" to 5'11"), and extra large (6'0" and taller). Minor adjustments can be made for borderline heights and builds by moving frame backband and hip belt. Pack bag is 8-oz. coated nylon, mounted on frame with clevis pins and key wires, divided into upper and lower compartments. Has hold-open bar for top compartment, zippered flap access to lower compartment. Two covered zipper pockets on each side, one large back pocket, ice axe loop at bottom and two accessory tie-down patches on top flap. Frame extension optional. Weight: 4¼ lbs. Dimensions: Top compartment, 6½x14½x12½ in.; bottom compartment, 5x12x7½ in.; upper pockets, 3x4½x8½ in.; back pocket, 2½x8½x10 in.

R.E.I. Summit II Pack: Two-compartment, teardrop rucksack of coated nylon, with leather bottom, covered nylon coil zippers,

padded shoulder straps, waist strap, haul loop and ice axe holder. Weight: 1-1/8 lbs. Dimensions: Top compartment, 4x12x10 in.; bottom compartment, 6x13x8¼ in.

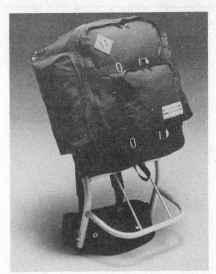

WILDERNESS EXPERIENCE Front Opening Bag: Entire front opens like a suitcase for easy packing and organizing. Compression bands on outside tighten up bag when hauling less than a full load, or can be used to strap on extra gear. Two large side pockets and back pocket open via zippered flaps. Hold-open bar attached to frame support items strapped to top of pack. Optional 8-oz. Cordura nylon or 8-oz. Parapack. Number ten YKK coil zipper used on main compartment closure. Ice axe loop at bottom. Accessory strap holders on top and back flap. Hip-suspension system, with padded belt.

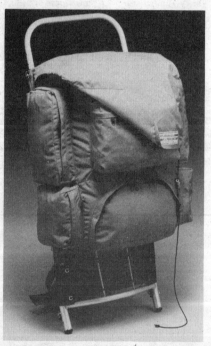

WILDERNESS EXPERIENCE Top Opening Bag: Two compartments with access to lower compartment by means of half-moon, double-zippered flap. Two pockets on each side and one on back. Accessory strap holders and map pocket on top flap. Hold-open bar for upper compartment attached to frame. Optional 8-oz. Parapack or 11½-oz. Cordura nylon. Frame is aluminum tubing.

WILDERNESS EXPERIENCE Kletter Sack: Single top-loading main compartment with top pocket in flap; additional side pockets available. Accessory strap patches on back, bottom and top flap. Upper pack of 8-oz. Cordura nylon; 11½-oz. Cordura used on lower portions. Optional leather bottom. Foam-padded shoulder straps, nylon web waist belt. Back pad of ½" foam. Weight: 24 oz. Capacity: 1600 cu. in.

WILDERNESS EXPERIENCE Backpacker: Internal frame pack with lower zippered compartment for sleeping bag; outside back, side and top flap pockets. Made of 11-oz. Cordura nylon with 8-oz. Parapack nylon back. Sizes: Small, medium and large. Weight: Small, 56 oz.; medium, 58 oz.; large, 60 oz. Capacity: Small, 2628 cu. in.; medium, 2784 cu. in.; large, 2940 cu. in.

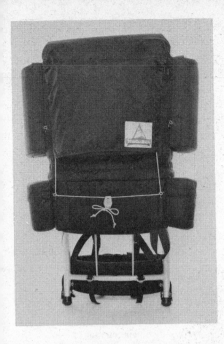

HOLUBAR Colorado Frame Pack: Frame constructed from aircraft aluminum with heli-arc welded joints. Zip-out divider separates main compartment into upper and lower sections, with access to lower via zippered opening around back. Padded shoulder straps and waist belt, 8-oz. nylon backband, hold-open bar for top compartment. Packsack attached to frame with clevis pins and steel wire pin retainer. Two pockets on each side, and outside back pocket. Sizes: Medium (up to 5'7"), large (5'7" to 6'0"), extra large (over 6'0"). Weight: Medium, 3 lbs. 14 oz.; large, 4 lbs. 3 oz.; extra large 4 lbs. 5 oz.

mounted to tubular aluminum frame, four-bar H-style heli-arc welded; multi-adjustable padded shoulder harness and padded nylon hip belt. Weight: 65 oz. Dimensions: 21x16x9 in. Optional Top Pocket Dimensions: 12x7x15 in.

CAMPWAYS Olympian Hip Hugger Combination: Two main compartments, five external pockets, fishing rod compartment, rear map pocket, five leather tie-down patches, axe loop and spreader bar. Mounted by pin and rod system. Same frame as Challenger. Weight: 79 oz. Dimensions: 21x16x8 in.

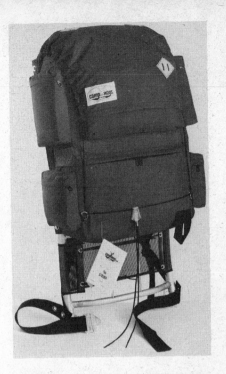

CAMPWAYS The Strider Combination: Same frame features as Challenger, except polypropylene waist belt, two 7" backbands where others in this line offer one 9" backband. Five external pockets, rear map pocket, five leather accessory strap patches, axe loop and spreader bar. Medium and large bags. Weight: Medium, 56 oz.; large, 58 oz. Dimensions: Medium, 17x15x7 in.; large, 19x16x7 in.

CAMPWAYS Challenger: Pack bag of urethane-coated Cordura, with three large side pockets, optional top pocket, upper and lower main compartments, rear map pocket; all are sealed with nylon zippers. Leather tie-down patches, ice axe loop, fishing rod compartment. Pin and rod-

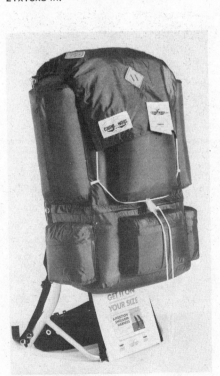

CAMPWAYS The Condor Combination: Two-compartment bag, six outside pockets, Delran zipper closures, five exterior leather accessory strap patches, axe loop, spreader bar, same frame features and attachment system as Challenger. Weight: 70 oz. Dimensions: 24x15x9 in.

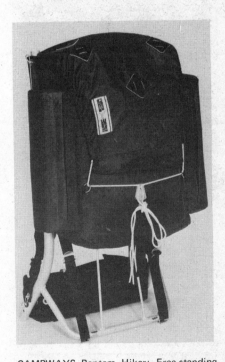

CAMPWAYS Bantam Hiker: Free-standing frame sized for women and youths. One main compartment, three external pockets with nylon zipper enclosures, rear map pocket, five leather tie-down patches, axe loop and spreader bar. Padded nylon hip pad, lashing strap. Weight: 36 oz. Dimensions: 17x13½x7 in.

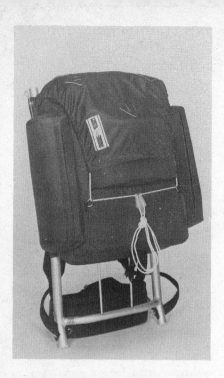

CAMPWAYS The Wolverine Frame: Same as Bantam pack, with H-style heli-arc welded frame of tubular aluminum. Padded backband, hip pad with quick-release buckle, lashing straps. Weight: 32 oz.

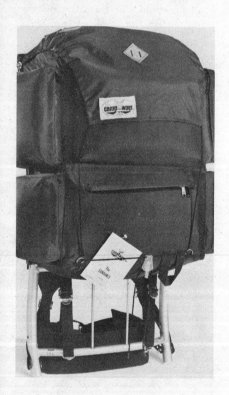

CAMPWAYS The Sundance Combination: Two main compartments, five external pockets, fishing rod compartment, rear map pocket, nylon zipper closures, five leather tie-down patches, axe loop and spreader bar. Eight-ounce coated nylon. Weight: Medium, 63 oz.; large, 65 oz. Dimensions: Medium, 21x15x7 in.; large 21x16x8 in. Medium frame: 43 oz., 30x15 in. Large frame: 45 oz., 31½x16 in.

CAMPWAYS The Rambler: Eight-ounce coated nylon, teardrop shape, arched zipper at top for easy access. Padded nylon shoulder pads and nylon waist belt. Leather bottom and three leather tie-down patches. Axe loop and two main compartments.

CAMPWAYS Snowmass Mountain Pack: Eight-ounce coated nylon, one main compartment, outside pocket on back and in top flap, accessory patches on top, axe loop and leather bottom. Padded shoulder straps. Detachable side pockets available.

CAMPWAYS Wilderness Hiker: Eight-ounce urethane-coated nylon with cotton back. Aluminum tubes inside pack to hold contour. Leather accessory strap patches on top and side. Axe loop and leather bottom.

Padded nylon-stitched shoulder straps and nylon waist belt. Pockets on back and top flap with nylon coil zippers. Detachable side pockets available. Weight: 32 oz. Dimensions: Top, 11½x6x20 in.; bottom, 17x6x20 in.

CAMPWAYS Eiger Mountain Pack: Eight-ounce coated nylon with thick split leather bottom, foam-padded wraparound hip belt and padded shoulder harness. Back of bag made of No. 10 duck. Large upper compartment further divided in half and roomy lower compartment, detachable side pockets available. Has accessory patches and axe loop. Weight: 32 oz. Capacity: 3200 cu. in.

CAMPWAYS Junior School Bag: Eight-ounce coated nylon, padded nylon-stitched shoulder straps, main compartment and outside zippered front pocket, drawstring closure, pencil holder inside main compartment, weatherproof tie-down cover. Weight: 10 oz. Capacity: 850 cu. in.

main compartment, two side pockets and storm flap. Frame is four-bar tubular aluminum, heli-arc welded, S-contoured, with wraparound hip belt, adjustable shoulder straps, turnbuckle backband. Camp Trails Spacer Kit adjusts frame through 4″ of torso length. Good for beginners, growing kids.

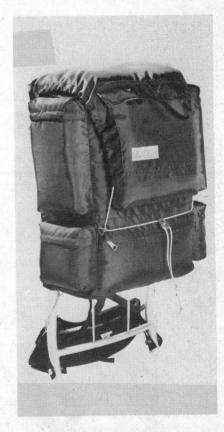

CAMPWAYS School Bag: Eight-ounce coated nylon bag, with leather bottom, tie-down patches, main compartment and outside pocket with nylon coil zipper closures. Padded nylon shoulder straps, nylon waist belt.

CAMP TRAILS Adjustable I: Urethane-coated nylon straight-through style bag with

CAMP TRAILS Adjustable II: Same frame features as Adjustable I, with two main compartments, five zippered pockets, map pocket in top flap, Fixlock and cord hooks, adjustable padded shoulder straps and wraparound hip belt. Weight: 3 lbs. 12½ oz.

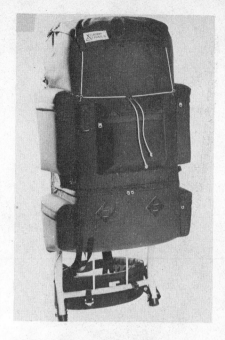

CAMP TRAILS Skyline: Two-compartment bag with four side pockets and top pocket, double zipper closures, toggle locks, laterally adjustable shoulder straps, two-position hip belt, backband which adjusts with turnbuckle. Cinch straps for stabilizing load or holding on extra gear. Weight: Medium, 3 lbs. 12 oz.; large, 3 lbs. 15 oz. Dimensions: Medium, 28 in. long; large, 31½ in. long.

CAMP TRAILS Astral: Truss-constructed, aircraft aluminum, heli-arc welded frame, with wraparound hip belt. Bag has two main compartments, five outside pockets, storm flap with map pocket, Fixlock and cord hooks, spreader bar, 8½" extendable top. Weight: Medium, 4 lbs. 5 oz.; large, 4 lbs. 7 oz.

CAMP TRAILS Centuri: Frame features aircraft aluminum, heli-arc welding, nonskid caps, self-aligning padded shoulder straps, tabler buckles, V-bar construction, double-contoured 8" mesh backband that adjusts up, down and sideways. Two-compartment bag has five tapered pockets plus map pocket, axe loop, two leather accessory strap patches, spreader bar, storm flap, Fixlock and cord hooks, top that extends 8". Made of weatherproof urethane-coated Cordura nylon. Weight: Medium, 4 lbs. 2 oz.; large, 4 lbs. 4 oz.

CAMP TRAILS Corona: Frame can be extended up to 4½" and features comfortable S-contour, lateral shoulder strap adjustment, wraparound hip belt, four-bar tubular aluminum construction, heli-arc welding. One compartment bag has three outside pockets, map pocket, 6" extendable top, slant bottom, Fixlock and cord hooks. Made of urethane-coated nylon. Weight: 2 lbs. 11 oz. Dimensions: Main bag, 14x12½x5½ in.

CAMP TRAILS Freighter Frame: Has special support shelf for extra-heavy or awkward loads, big game animals, outboards, generators, chain saws or packs of firewood. With support shelf removed, can be adapted for backpack use. V-bar truss design, heavy-gauge aluminum tubing, S-contour, padded wraparound hip belt and padded shoulder straps, heli-arc welding. Weight: (medium) 2 lbs. 15 oz., (large) 3 lbs.

CAMP TRAILS Trekker Soft Pack: Eight-ounce urethane-coated nylon with single main compartment, two side pockets and top pocket, six leather accessory patches, padded shoulder straps, extendable top for increased capacity.

CAMP TRAILS Scrambler: A-frame rucksack with removable frame for use as soft pack. Features padded hip belt, removable Ensolite foam back pad, leather reinforcing at high-wear areas. Made of heavy-duty Cordura nylon. Has extendable top, self-locking cord lock, single main compartment, two side pockets and top pocket, six leather accessory strap patches. Weight: 2 lbs. 5 oz.

CAMP TRAILS Cruiser Frame: Four-bar construction of lightweight aluminum with heli-arc welded joints, two 5″ nylon backbands and S-contour. Padded shoulder straps with two-position lateral adjustment and tabler buckles for adjustment in place. Weight: Medium, 1 lb. 15 oz.; large, 2 lbs.

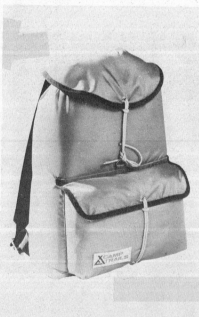

CAMP TRAILS Daypack: Made of weather-proof nylon. Has single main compartment, extra pocket on back, tie-down flaps and 2" nylon web shoulder straps. Weight: 10½ oz. Dimensions: 16x12x5 in.

CAMP TRAILS Dayhiker: Single main compartment with tie-down flap, outside pocket with zipper closure on back, padded shoulder straps with tabler buckles for easy adjustment. Weight: 11¾ oz. Dimensions: 16x12x5 in.

CAMP TRAILS Wanderlust: Teardrop design with haul loop, padded adjustable shoulder straps, ice axe loop, leather accessory patches, two compartments and leather bottom. Weight: 15 oz. Dimensions: 18x13x5 in.

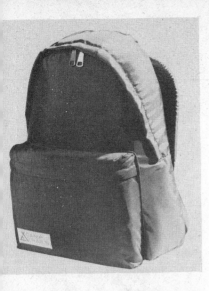

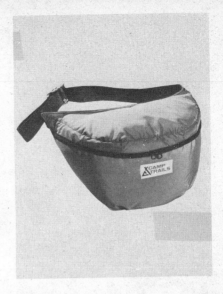

CAMP TRAILS Amigo: Single main compartment with outside pocket, zipper closures, padded adjustable shoulder straps with tabler buckles. Weight: 12 oz. Dimensions: 16x11½x5 in.

CAMP TRAILS Vag-Bags: Twin saddlebags with main compartments, elastic side pockets, semirigid foam panels, storm flap tabler buckles. Made of urethane-coated nylon. Weight: 1 lb. 2 oz. Dimensions: 13x5x9 in.

CAMP TRAILS Vagabond: Fanny pack with double zipper, elastic-lined pocket divider, nylon waist belt. Weight: 9 oz. Dimensions: 17x8x1½ in.

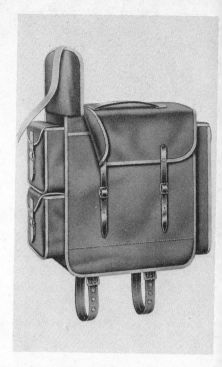

NESSMUCK Packsack: Made by Woods Bag and Canvas Company, Limited, of 12-oz. watertight canvas. Features main compartment and exterior pockets, bedroll straps at bottom, fabric shoulder strap. Dimensions: 16x18x5½ in.

JANSPORT Scout 1: Two main compartments, four exterior pockets, divided panel access, ice axe holder and permanent load control straps. Scout bag is adjustable on its frame. Weight: 3 lbs. 14 oz. Capacity: 41,732 cu. cm.

STAG BRAND 5+5: Three main compartments, four outside pockets and map pocket in top flap, pole pocket for tent or fishing pole and lashing patches for tying on extra gear. Capacity: 5724 cu. in.

STAG 4+5: Same as 5+5, but no lower compartment. Same vertical upper compartments and its lower compartment is the same as middle section of 5+5. Capacity: 4068 cu. in.

STAG Divider Pack Bag and Trail Frame: Two main compartments, hold-open bar on top compartment, four exterior pockets and map pocket in flap with Velcro closure. Triangle opening in one corner of the Divider provides a place for tent poles or fishing rod inside pack. Capacity: 3528 cu. in.

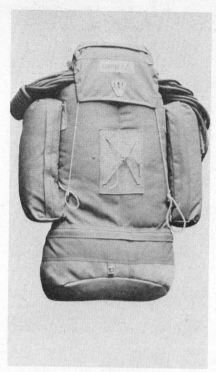

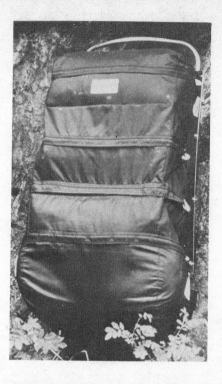

GERRY Makalu Pack: Frameless pack featuring wraparound, weight-bearing waist belt, lower compartment for sleeping bag, main compartment that may be divided, and top compartment. Back is padded with wool felt and D-rings allow pack to fold tightly even when not packed to capacity. Padded shoulder straps, ice axe loop, accessory strap patches and hauling loop. Optional side pockets. Handles loads up to 40 lbs. Weight: 3 lbs. 15 oz. Dimensions: 29x17x9 in.

GERRY Traveler: Has four horizontal zip-open compartments, accessory strap patches, YKK coil-type covered zippers. Lower compartment designed to fit sleeping bag. Weight: Regular 1 lb. 9 oz.; large, 1 lb. 11 oz. Dimensions: Regular, 27x15x9 in.; large, 30x16x9 in.

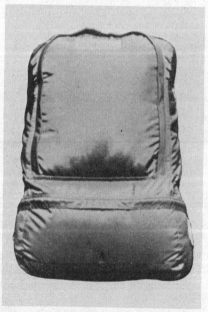

GERRY Nomad: Upper compartment with YKK ziplon zipper, lower compartment for sleeping bag, small outside pocket, built-in aluminum frame, waist strap and carrying handle. Weight: Regular, 2 lbs. 3 oz.; large, 2 lbs. 5 oz. Dimensions: Regular, 22x15x8 in.; large, 24x16x8 in.

GERRY Climbing Pack: Teardrop shape, waist strap, accessory strap patches, ice axe loop, two main compartments, foam-padded shoulder straps and heavy-duty leather bottom. Weight: 1 lb. 8 oz. Dimensions: 21x12x5 in.

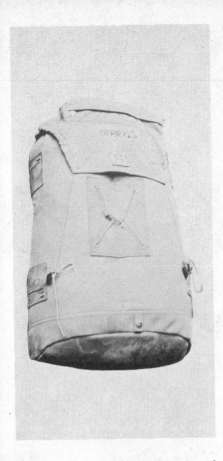

GERRY Assault Pack: Smaller version of Makalu. Has no sleeping bag compartment or weight-bearing belt. Features zipper-divided main compartment, wool felt, hauling loop, D-rings, etc. Optional side pockets available. Weight: 2 lbs. 15 oz. Dimensions: 25x15x9 in.

GERRY Continental II: External frame model with top compartment that can be divided into two at user's option, large bottom compartment, four exterior side pockets, map pocket under flap, exclusive drying pocket attached. Has heavy-duty hold-open bar. Weight: Regular, 1 lb. 9 oz.; large, 1 lb. 10 oz. Dimensions: Regular, 23x14x7½ in.; large, 23x15x7½ in.

GERRY Touring Pack: One main compartment, two side pockets and utility pocket in top flap. Features leather-reinforced sleeves for carrying skis, waist strap, accessory strap patches and padded, adjustable shoulder straps. Built-in aluminum stays provide extra support. Weight: 2 lbs. 4 oz. Dimensions: 18x12x6 in.

GERRY Vagabond: Internal frame pack with four zipper-closure compartments, padded shoulder straps and a waist strap. Weight: Regular, 2 lbs. 3 oz.; large, 2 lbs. 5 oz. Dimensions: Regular, 22x15x8 in.; large, 24x16x8 in.

GERRY Series 70 Frame: Constructed of 7001 aluminum alloy with epoxied joints. Features padded hip belt with sliding ring adjustment, adjustable neck opening between shoulder straps and mesh backbands. Weight: 2 lbs. 6 oz. Sizes: small, medium, large and extra large. Used with Gerry's Traveler and Continental II packs.

MANUFACTURERS & IMPORTERS

A-Brandt Company, Inc., P.O. Box 889, Midlothian, Tex. 76065; sleeping bags

Academy Broadway Corp., 5 Plant Ave., Smithtown, N.Y. 11787; camping, rainwear

Adventure 16, Incorporated, 656 Front St., El Cajon, Calif. 92020; packs, sleeping bags; tents.

Airlift, 2217 Roosevelt Ave., Berkley, Calif. 94703; sleeping pads

Allen Co., 803 N. Downing St., Piqua, Ohio 45356; underwear, parkas, pants

Don Alleson, (Div. Alleson of Rochester, Inc.), 165 N. Water St., Rochester, N.Y. 14604; jackets, hats

All American Products, Inc., 2200 W. Diversey, Chicago, Ill. 60647; camping inflatables, air mattresses

Almax Sportswear Corp., 752 Broadway, New York, N.Y. 10003; insulated garments

Alpine Designs, Inc., 6185 E. Araphoe, Boulder, Colo. 80303; packpacking clothing, packs, frames, tents, sleeping bags

American Footwear Corporation, One Oak Hill Road, Fitchburg, Mass. 01420; boots

American Import Co., 1167 Mission St., San Francisco, Calif; camping equipment

American Leisure, Inc., 111 Cheyenne Ave., Alliance, Neb. 69301; down insulated outerwear

American Recreation Group, 200 Fifth Avenue North, New York, N.Y. 10010

Anton Co., 320 E. 2nd St., Topeka, Kan. 66603; camping tents, tarpaulins

Arkansas Abrasives, Inc., P.O. Box 1298, Hot Springs, Ark. 71901; whetstones, oilstones

Baudinet International Corp., 104 W. 27th St., New York, N.Y. 10001; disposable flashlights

Bausch & Lomb, Inc., 635 St. Paul St., Rochester, N.Y. 14602; sunglasses, binoculars

Bear Archery, Rural Route 1, Grayling, Mich. 49738; bows, arrows, leather accessories

Blue Ribbon Gloves, 227 W. 1st St., Kewanee, Ill. 61443; hunting gloves, mittens

Broner Glove Co., 345 E. 9 Mile Road, Ferndale, Mich. 48075; gloves, mittens, caps, hats, goggles

Browning Arms Co., Route No. 1, Morgan, Utah 84050; boots, apparel, knives

Buccaneer Mfg. Co., Inc., 35 York St., Brooklyn, N.Y. 11201; outerwear

Buck Knives, 1717 N. Magnolia, P.O. Box 1267, El Cajon, Calif. 92022; knives, accessories

Buck Stop Lure Co., 3015 Grow Road, Stanton, Mich 48888; hunting, trapping scents, insect repellent

Bushnell Optical Corp., 2828 E. Foothill Blvd., Pasadena, Calif. 91107; binoculars, riflescopes, shooting glasses

Camel Mfg. Co., 329 S. Central St., Knoxville, Tenn. 37802; tents

Camillus Cutlery Co., Main St., Camillus, N.Y. 13031; pocket, hunting knives

Camp-Lite Products, Inc., (Div. Denver Tent Co.), 1408 W. Colfax, Denver, Colo. 80204; backpacking tents

Camp 7, Inc., 802 South Sherman, Longmont, Colo. 80501; tents, sleeping bags, down vests, jackets, camping gear

Camp & Trail Outfitters, 21 Park Circle, New York, N.Y. 10007; goose down sleeping bags

Camp Trails, 4111 W. Carendon Ave., Phoenix, Ariz. 85109; backpacking, hiking equipment

Camp-Ways, 415 Molino St., Los Angeles, Calif. 90013; backpacking, hiking, camping equipment

Cannondale Corporation, 35 Pulaski St., Stamford, Conn. 06902

Carnation Company, 5045 Wilshire Blvd., Los Angeles, Calif. 90036

W. R. Case & Sons Cutlery Co., 20 Russell Blvd. Bradford, Pa. 16701

Central Specialties Co., 6030 Northwest Hwy., Chicago, Ill. 60631; camping firearms accessories

Central Textile, Inc., 1410 Higgins Road, Park Ridge, Ill. 60068; thermal underwear, knit headwear

Cerf Bros. Bag Co., 2827 S. Brentwood, St. Louis, Mo. 63144; camping tents, tarps and nylon bags

Champion Industries, 35 East Popular St., Philadelphia, Pa. 19123; camping specialties

Chippewa Shoe Co., 28-36 W. River St., Chippewa Falls, Wis. 54729; boots and shoes

Clif-Tex Mfg. Co., (Div. of Walls Ind., Inc.), P.O. Box 98, Celeburne, Tex. 76031; apparel

Coghlan's, Ltd., 235 Garry St., Winnipeg, Canada, R3C 1H2

Cole National Corp., 5777 Grant Ave., Cleveland, Ohio 44105; Kabar, Monarch and Sabre knives

Coleman Company, Inc., 250 N. St. Francis St., Wichita, Kan. 67201; lanterns, coolers, jugs, catalytic heaters, sleeping bags, tents, campstoves

Comfy/Seattle Quilt, 310 First Ave. So., Seattle, Wash. 98104; sleeping bags, down garments

Compass Instruments & Optical Co., Inc., 104 E. 25th St., New York, N.Y. 10010; binoculars, riflescopes, knives, camping, hunting accessories

Converse Rubber Co., 2000 Mannheim Road, Melrose Park, Ill. 60160; outdoor equipment

Mark Cowan Co. Ltd., 307 Fifth Ave., New York, N.Y. 10016; hunting, camping, fishing

Cross Galesburg Co., 152 E. Ferris, Galesburg, Ill. 61401; insulated clothing

Cutter Laboratories, Inc., Fourth & Parker Sts., Berkeley, Calif. 94710; insect repellent, snake bite kits, first aid kits

Daco Safety Products Inc., 1712 E. Princess Dr., Tempe, Ariz. 85281; flashlights

Dana Home Products, Inc., P.O. Box 636, Port Ewen, N.Y. 12466; propane stoves, heaters, lanterns, accessories

Danto & Goldreyer Ltd. & GMS Sales, Inc., 1107 Broadway, New York, N.Y. 10010; camping goods, footwear, sleeping bags

Denali Co., Inc., 2402 Ventura Ave., Fresno, Calif. 93721; backpacks

Dexter Shoe Co., 31 St. James Ave., Boston, Mass. 02116; footwear

Dunham's, Vernon Drive, Box 813, Brattleboro, Vt. 05301; footwear

Duofold, Inc., P.O. Drawer A, Mohawk, N.Y. 13407; insulated underwear

Early Winters, Ltd., At the Alpine Guild, 300 Queen Anne Avenue North, Seattle, Wash. 98109; tents, climbing gear

Eastern Canvas Products, Inc., 17 Locust St., Haverhill, Mass. 01831; nylon and cotton buck backpacking equipment

Eiger Mountain Sports P.O. Box 150, San Fernando, Calif. 91341; backpacking, camping, mountain climbing equipment

Ero Industries, Inc., 714 W. Monroe St., Chicago, Ill. 60606; sleeping bags, tents, backpacking equipment

Eureka Tent, Inc., Subsidiary of Johnson Diversified, Inc., 625 Conklin Rd., Binghamton, N.Y. 13902; tents

Farwest Garments, Inc., 100 Poplar Place South, Seattle, Wash. 98144; backpacks, hiker's parkas, rainwear, downwear

Forrest Mountaineering, Ltd., 1517 Platte St., Denver, Colo. 80202; camping and climbing gear

Game Winner, Inc., 700 Wharton Dr. S.W., Atlanta, Ga. 30336; apparel

Garcia Corp., 329 Alfred Ave., Teaneck, N.J. 07666; camping equipment

General Recreation Industries, Fayette, Ala. 35555; sleeping bags

Gerber Legendary Blades, 14200 S.W. 72nd Ave., Portland, Ore. 97223; hunting, fishing knives

Gerry (Div. Outdoor Sports Industries, Inc.), 5450 N. Valley Hwy., Denver, Colo. 80216; lightweight camping, backpacking equipment

Gibraltar Industries, Inc., 254-36th St., Brooklyn, N.Y. 11232; outerwear

Gila River Products, 6608 N. 82nd Way, Scottsdale, Ariz. 85253; camping, specializing in pack tents

Gladding Corp., 1840 Lemoyne Ave., Syracuse, N.Y 13201; apparel, camping products

Gladding Corporation, P.O. Box 586, Back Bay Annex, Boston, Mass. 02117; camping equipment, inflatables

Gladding-Ranger, 1224 W. Genesse, Syracuse, N.Y. 13204; sleeping bags

Gun-Ho Sports Case & Equipment Mfrs., 110 E. 10th St., St. Paul, Minn. 55101; pistol boxes, gun cases, related products

Gutmann Cutlery Company, Inc., 900 South Columbus Ave., Mount Vernon, N.Y. 10550; knives, camping equipment

Halstead Imports, 704 Traction Ave., Los Angeles, Calif. 90012; backpacking items

Herter's, Inc., Mitchell, South Dakota 57301; tents, fishing gear, down garments, trail foods

High & Light, 139½ E. 16th St., Costa Mesa, Calif. 92627; sleeping bags, tents

Himalayan Backpacks, Pine Bluff, Ark.

Hine/Snowbridge, P.O. Box 1459, Boulder, Colo. 80302; stoves, tents, packs, camping gear

Hirsch Weis (Div. of White Stag), 5203 S.E. Johnson Creek Blvd., Portland, Ore. 97206; camp, backpack equipment, down clothing

Holubar Mountaineering, Ltd., 1975 30th St., P.O. Box 7, Boulder, Colo. 80302; climbing, camping equipment

Hunter Outdoor Products, 230 Fifth Ave., New York, N.Y. 10001, sleeping bags, tents

ILC Outdoor Co., 1200 Philadelphia Pike, Wilmington, Del. 19809; tents

Ideal Products, Inc., Sykesville, Pa. 15865; apparel, accessories

Imperial Knife, 1776 Broadway, New York, N.Y. 10019; pocket, hunting knives, camping caddy

Indian Head Shoe Co. Inc., 114 W. Central St., Manchester, N.H. 03101; footwear

International Supply-Standard Sales, 1509 S. Santa Fe Ave., Los Angeles, Calif. 90021; backpacking, camping equipment

Ithaca Gun Co., Terrace Hill, Ithaca, N.Y. 14850; firearms, apparel

Jana International Co., 17010 Aurora Ave. N., Seattle, Wash. 98133; backpacks

JanSport, Paine Field Industrial Park, Everett, Wash. 98204; tents, packs, sleeping bags

Jason/Empire, Inc., 2820 Warwick, Kansas City, Mo. 64108; binoculars, rifle scopes

Jet-Aer Corp., 100 Sixth Ave., Paterson, N.J. 07524; fabric and leather waterproofing, insect repellents

Kalmar Trading Corporation, 901 Minnesota St., San Francisco, Calif. 94107

Kel-Lite Industries, Inc., 1172 E. Edna Place, Covina, Calif. 91724; aluminum flashlights

Kelty Pack, Inc., P.O. Box 639, Sun Valley, Calif. 91352; pack bags, frames, soft packs, accessories

Kiffe Sales Co., 504 Broadway, New York, N.Y. 10012; camping equipment, backpacks, apparel

Knut & Knut, 487 Fullerton Ave., Elmhurst, Ill. 60126; socks, hunting, hiking, camping all wool sweaters and caps, mesh underwear

Thomas J. Lipton, Inc., 800 Sylvan Ave., Englewood Cliffs, N.Y.; convenience foods, beverages, soups

M.H. Manufacturing Corp., P.O. Box 338, Pelahatchie, Miss. 39145; sleeping bags, foam products

Mountain Equipment, Inc., 3208 E. Hamilton Ave., Fresno, Calif. 93702; tents, packs, sleeping bags

Mountain Products Corp., 123 S. Wenatchee, Wenatchee, Wash. 98801; down-filled sleeping bags, coats, packs, lightweight tents

Mountain Safety Research, 631 South 96th St., Seattle, Wash. 98108

National Canvas Products Corp., 901 Buckingham, Toledo, Ohio 43607; tents

National Outdoor Leadership School & Outdoor Leadership Supply, Lincoln & 2nd St., Lander, Wyo. 82520; backpacking, camping equipment

National Packaged Trail Foods, 632 E. 185th St., Cleveland, Ohio 44119; camping foods

Nelson Sales Co., 626 Broadway, Kansas City, Mo. 64105; camping, backpacking

Nicholl Bros., Inc., 1204 W. 27th St., Kansas City, Mo. 64108; flashlights, lanterns, battery-powered lights

Noni Corp., 1042 South Santa Fe Drive, Denver, Colo. 80204; compact stoves

Normark Corp., 1710 E. 78th St., Minneapolis, Minn. 55432; knives, boots

Nor-Pol Importer, 7331 Wayzata Blvd., Minneapolis, Minn.; footwear

North Face, 1234 Fifth St., Berkley, Calif. 94710; climbing equipment

Olsen Knife Co., Inc., 7-11 Joy St., Howard City, Mich. 49329; knives

Optimus, Inc., 652 E. Commonwealth Ave., Fullerton, Calif. 92634; camping stoves, packstoves, lanterns

Oregon Freeze Dry Foods, Inc., 770 W. 29th Ave., Albany, Ore. 97321; freeze-dried outdoor foods

Outdoor Supply Co., Inc., Industry Drive, Oxford, N.C. 27565; sleeping bags

Outdoorsman Co., 117 Brighton Ave., Boston, Mass. 02134; mountaineering, backpacking equipment

Pacific Tent, Box 2028, Fresno, Calif. 93718; down insulated sleeping bags, jackets, alpine gear

Pak Foam Products, 390 Pine St., Pawtucket, R.I. 02862; sleeping pads

Palco Products, 15 Hope Ave., Worcester, Mass. 01603; cooking utensils, propane stoves, lanterns, cook kits, canteens, mess kits

Paulin Products Co., 30520 Lakeland Blvd., Willowick, Ohio 44094; camping heaters, stoves, lanterns

Peter's Bag Corp., 350 Fifth Ave., Suite 1210, New York, N.Y. 10001; all-purpose sport bags, totes

Powers & Co., Inc., 31st and Jefferson Sts., Philadelphia, Pa. 19121; camping beds, cots, tables, packing and inflatable boats

Precise Imports Corp., 3 Chestnut St., Suffern, N.Y. 10901; camping, hunting equipment, inflatables

Primary Source, Inc., 1740 N. Wells, Chicago, Ill. 60614; footwear, down equipment, mountaineering supplies

Queen Cutlery Co., P.O. Box 500, Franklinville, N.Y. 14737; pocket, hunting knives

Raichle Molitor USA, Inc., 3 Erie Drive, Natick, Mass. 01760; hiking, climbing, mountaineering boots

Ranger Mfg. Co., 2808 Wilco Ave., Augusta, Ga. 30904; camouflage clothing

Recreational Equipment, Inc., P.O. Box 22088, Seattle, Wash. 98122; camping gear, backpacks

Redhead Brand Corp., 4100 Platinum Way, Dallas, Tex. 75237; hunting, camping, down clothing, sleeping bags, backpacking gear

Red Wing Shoes, Red Wing, Minn. 55066; climbing boots

Reynes Products, Inc., P.O. Box 914, Sonoma, Calif. 95476; frost, sun, wind, insect, toxic-guard outdoor creams

Rich-Moor Corp., 14801 Oxnard St., Van Nuys, Calif. 91401; lightweight freeze-dried foods

Rivendell Mountain Works, Box 198, Victor, Idaho 83455; climbing gear

Robert Shoe Co., Inc., Main St., Somersworth, N.H. 03878; cold weather footwear

Rome Industries, Inc., 1703 Detweiller Dr., Peoria, Ill. 61614

Rosco Industries, Inc., 222 N. Hydraulic, P.O. Box 11001, Wichita, Kan. 67202; camping tents

H. Rosenthal Co., 220 E. 5th St., St. Paul, Minn. 55101; camping goods, outerwear, rainwear, rubber footwear

M. Rubin & Sons, Inc., 10 W. 33rd, New York, N.Y. 10001; outerwear, sleeping bags

Safesport Mfg. Co., 1810 Stout St., Denver, Colo. 80202; hunter's safety garments, camping specialties

Samco Sportswear, Inc., 211 E. 4th St., St. Paul, Minn. 55101; thermal underwear

Scope Instrument Corp., 25-20 Brooklyn-Queens Expressway West, Woodside, N.Y. 11377; binoculars, rifle scopes

Seaway Importing Company, 7200 North Oak Park Ave., Niles, Ill. 60648

Buddy Shoellkopf Products, Inc., 4100 Platinum Way, Dallas, Tex. 75237; hunting, camping accessories

Sierra Designs, 4th & Addison Sts., Berkley, Calif. 94710; tents, camping gear

Harold J. Siesel Company, Inc., 845 Third Avenue, New York, N.Y. 10022

Silva, Inc., Highway 39 North, LaPorte, Ind. 46350; compasses

Skachet, 1104 Fernwood Ave., Camphill, Pa. 17011; all-purpose hunting, survival tool

Ski Hut, 1615 University Ave., Berkley, Calif. 94703

Slumberjack, Inc., 2103 Humboldt St., Los Angeles, Calif. 90031; sleeping bags

Southern Precision Instrument Co., 3419 E. Commerce St., San Antonio, Tex. 78297; binoculars, rifle scopes

Sportcaster Co., Inc., 322 Occidental South, Seattle, Wash. 98104; backpacking, camping equipment, apparel

Sportline, 3300 W. Franklin Blvd., Chicago, Ill. 60624; sleeping, slumber bags

Sportsmen's Laboratories, Inc., 12614 Round Lake Blvd., Anoka, Minn. 55303; lubricants, repellents, chemical specialties, waterproofers

Stag Brand, Division of Warnaco, Inc., 5203 S.E. Johnson Creek Blvd., Portland, Ore. 97206; tents, inflatables, backpacks, sleeping bags

Sterno, Inc., 105 Hudson St., Jersey City, N.J. 07302; canned heat fuel, folding stoves

Peter Storm Limited, Smith St., Norwalk, Conn. 06851; outdoor clothing

Tasco Sales, Inc., 1075 N.W. 71st St., Miami, Fla. 33138; rifle scopes, binoculars

10-X Mfg. Co., 100 S.W. Third St., Des Moines, Iowa 50309; hunting, shooting garments

Thermos, Thermos Ave., Norwich, Conn. 06360

Timberking Outerwear Corp., 27990 Valley Forge Drive, Southfield, Mich. 48076; insulated clothing jackets, underwear

Trailblazer by Winchester, 3100 W. Randolph St., Bellwood, Ill. 60104; camping, tents, lanterns, heaters, stoves, clothing

Trail Chef Foods, P.O. Box 60041, T.A., Los Angeles, Calif. 90060; outdoor, camping food

Trail Tech, 108-02 Otis Ave., Corona, N.Y. 11368; lightweight backpacking equipment

Underwood Rivert Co., Inc., 113 N. San Vicente Blvd., Beverly Hills, Calif. 90211; portable warmers

Universal Field Equipment Co., Inc., Mira Loma Space Center Blvd. 811-A, Mira Loma, Calif. 91752; backpacking, camping equipment

Utica Duxbak Corp., 815 Noyes St., Utica, N.Y. 13502; apparel

Vasque (Div. of Red Wing Shoe Co.), 419 Bush St., Red Wing, Minn. 55066; mountaineering, rock climbing, backpacking footwear

B.B. Walker Shoe Co., E. Dixie Drive, Asheboro, N.C. 27203; hiking footwear

Wallin, 1343 Camden Ln., Ventura, Calif. 93003

Weather-Rite Sportwear Co., Inc., 5802 Third Ave., Brooklyn N.Y. 11200; rainwear, footwear

Weinbrenner Shoe Corp., Merrill, Wis. 54452; hunting, camping, hiking footwear

Wenzel Co., 1280 Research Blvd., St. Louis, Mo. 63132; tents, sleeping bags, backpack equipment

Western National Products Corp., 10810 Cantara St., Sun Valley, Calif. 91352; portable warmer

J. Wiss & Sons Co., 400 W. Market St., Newark, N.J. 07107; pocket, hunting knives

Woods Bag & Canvas Co., Ltd., 90 River St., P.O. Box 118, Ogdensburg, N.Y. 13669; down sleeping bags, apparel

Woolrich Woolen Mills, Woolrich, Pa. 17779; apparel

BACKPACKER'S CHECKLIST

This list is provided for the convenience of assembling personal backpacking equipment. Some items may be dropped or added according to weight limits, weather conditions, or personal likes. Items listed are for beginning minimums. More expensive and exotic equipment may be selectively added with experience.

CLOTHING
Underwear
Wool Shirt
Light Shirt
Heavy Pants
Hiking Shorts
Sweater
Watch Cap
Sun Hat
Mittens
Wind Mitts
Boots (6" Max)
Extra Socks
Dark Glasses+
Poncho
Bandanna

TOILET KIT
Soap
Towel-small
Toothbrush & Paste
Comb

EATING
Sierra Cup
Spoon, large
Cleaning Pad
Water Bottle+

SHELTER
Tent
Nylon Cord+
Poles

SLEEPING
Sleeping Bag, Down or Dacron
Ground Sheet (Tube Tent)
Mattress

FIRST AID — PERSONAL ONLY+
(In addition to group equipment)
Band-Aids
Chapstick
Moleskin
Adhesive Tape 1"
Gauze Pad
Sun Cream
Bug Spray
Snake Bite Kit

EMERGENCY
Matches-in Waterproof Cases+
Flashlight+
Candles-Firestarters+
Pocket Knife-Boy Scout Type+
Toilet Paper+
Map+
Compass+
Emergency Blanket+

+ Items marked with plus are essentials and should be carried at all times when away from camp.

£35.99

Management
and the Arts